A Home Full of Furniture

79 More Furniture Projects for Every Room

A Home Full of Furniture

79 More Furniture Projects for Every Room

Percy W. Blandford

TAB BOOKS
Blue Ridge Summit, PA

FIRST EDITION
SECOND PRINTING

© 1990 by **TAB BOOKS**.
TAB BOOKS is a division of McGraw-Hill, Inc.

Library of Congress Cataloging-in-Publication Data

Blandford, Percy W.
    A home full of furniture : 79 more furniture projects for every
room / by Percy W. Blandford.
        p.   cm.
    Includes index.
    ISBN 0-8306-7500-0 (hard) : ISBN 0-8306-3500-9 (paper)
    1. Furniture making—Amateurs' manuals.   I. Title.
TT195.B5874   1990
684.1—dc20   90-11050
                                                         CIP

TAB BOOKS offers software for sale. For information and a catalog, please contact TAB Software Department, Blue Ridge Summit, PA 17294-0850.

Questions regarding the content of this book should be addressed to:

Reader Inquiry Branch
TAB BOOKS
Blue Ridge Summit, PA 17294-0850

Acquisitions Editor: Kimberly Tabor
Book Editor: Stephen Moro
Production: Katherine G. Brown
Book Design: Jaclyn J. Boone
Cover Design: Larry Selman, Waynesboro, PA

Contents

Introduction

Of course, making every piece of furniture for a home would be a massive undertaking. Although that may be possible, most of us would hesitate to attempt it. No book of this size can tell you how to make everything you need to fully furnish an empty house. You would need a library of books. Most of us want to fill the gaps in existing furnishings, make our home more comfortable to live in and put our own mark on it. That is what this book is about.

Here you will find instructions and drawings for 74 things to make. Some are major items of furniture. Others are the extra or occasional types of furniture the pieces that add to your comfort and convenience. They are the nonstandard items; the ones that personalize your home and give it your mark.

The instructions that follow are for many projects; there are things for woodworkers of all degrees of skill and for almost any range of equipment, from a few hand tools to an elaborately equipped shop. The materials needed range from a few scrap or salvaged pieces to fairly expensive choice hardwoods. Whatever the starting material, the finished product should be something that expresses your pride.

There is a tremendous satisfaction to be derived from saying, "I made that." If you select only a few projects from those offered, you will be able to stand in any room and see something you made. You will feel happier with the whole home, and you will take a pride in showing visitors the results of your endeavors.

In these days of mass-production, furniture made in that way may be cheaper than if it were individually made, but it means that large numbers of people have identical furniture. If you make your own, it is exclusive, and different from the normal run of store-bought pieces; in short, it expresses your individuality.

This book has been divided into chapters according to rooms, for convenient identification, but many projects could be used in more than one room. You are unlikely to move a bed from a bedroom or a dining table from the dining room, but some furniture has uses in more than one room. Check the whole book when looking for things to make, possibly for a different room from the first choice.

Most woodworkers have a preference for using natural wood. That is a fine thought and maintains tradition, but natural wood, particularly in large pieces, is costly, could be unobtainable and might not be the most suitable material today. We must move with the times. There are places for plywood, hardboard and particleboard, provided we are selective and use these materials with restraint in situations where they are obviously a better choice. Many suggestions are offered in the following instructions. Such materials are often used to excess in mass-produced furniture. Be careful not to fall into the trap of copying the products of a mass-production factory.

The designs in this book are original; some form different approaches to a problem. If you follow the step-by-step instructions you should get a lot of joy and satisfaction out of making something which has a function in your home. Something like it may be made by another reader, but it is different from anything your neighbors have! There are enough ideas in the following pages to keep you happy in your shop and your family happy with the results for a long time.

1
Furniture-Making
Techniques

Although this is not a book on tool handling, woodworking practices, workshop methods, or the choice of hand and power tools, there are a few special ideas that may help in the satisfactory building of the projects in this book. It is assumed that the reader has at least a basic knowledge of woodworking and the tools involved, and that he or she has enough tools and other facilities to make the chosen project. There are several projects described which could be made with just a very few hand tools. A few other projects call for a fairly high degree of skill and a more comprehensive range of tools. Power tools will lessen labor, make accuracy easier to obtain and make possible some things, such as moldings on curved edges, which would be very difficult for even the most skilled craftsman to do by hand.

Although power tools are very desirable and most of us will want all we can afford, you can do a surprising amount of good work with the much cheaper basic hand tools, especially if you can take a materials list to a lumber yard where you can be provided with all the wood finished to size. The power tool that can save you money and make production easier is a table saw; with it you can prepare wood to the correct section for most of the projects in this book. A few strokes of a hand plane will smooth it, ready for use. Use scrap lumber or salvaged wood; then even the parallel-cut waste pieces will go into stock for later work.

The next desirable tool is probably an electric drill. It need not be very elaborate or expensive, but there are many places where holes are needed often large numbers. With a drill of 3/8-inch chuck capacity and suitable bits, you can cope with the drilling needs of the furniture described in this book. You will have to decide if any of the accessories offered by some drill makers are worth buying. Some are effective, but others are not really serious power tools compared with the independent tools they are supposed to replace.

PREPARATIONS

Besides being able to use the tools you have, it is necessary to plan ahead, taking into account the stages of the work and how you will deal with it. Read the instructions through with references to the drawings, so you know exactly what has to be done and in what order. Do you have the necessary tools? Are there enough clamps? Is there bench or floor space to put together the sub-assemblies and then the whole thing?

Do you have the skill needed? Almost certainly, yes! If you are prepared to work a step at a time and know what will be the step after the next all through the job, you should be able to build a piece of furniture of which you will be proud. This is planning, which is much better than rushing into the first steps and then finding something is lacking or you have done something you should not have due to haste.

Part of the preparation is having the material ready. For each project there is a list of the wood needed. The first figure quoted is in the direction of the grain, and that usually allows a few inches extra. For strip material the widths and thicknesses given are the finished planed sizes. For sheet materials, the widths quoted may also be full. Be careful that you do not accept *nominal* sizes, particularly for small stock. It may not matter if wood bought as 2 inches × 3 inches is actually finished 1³/₄ inches × 2³/₄ inches, but in small sections such reduction by power planing will weaken the wood excessively.

Check over what other materials you need. There will always be a need for glue. In some cases use a waterproof type. You will need nails of several lengths and types. Similarly, screws will be needed with different lengths, possibly different heads and in several metals. The more nails and screws you buy at one time, the cheaper they are relatively. If you are thinking of tackling several projects, it will be worthwhile getting enough nails and screws at one time. Stocks of these things are always worth having, if only to avoid having to break off work to waste time for a visit to the hardware store for something overlooked. Hinges, catches, locks, handles and other hardware may be better bought as you need them, unless you anticipate a run of uses. Do not overlook such things as sheets of sandpaper, jigsaw blades and other consumable tools.

JOINTS

Inevitably, in making any piece of furniture you are joining pieces of wood together. The range of possible joints runs into many hundreds, but for most projects, such as those described in this book, the number of fitted joints needed are few.

Nailing and screwing make the simplest joints; then there are joints which use notches and others which go through. Some peculiarities in joining are described in particular projects, but here are ideas which will help you make up your mind about which joint to use when you have a choice.

Nails

Putting one piece of wood on top of another and nailing it seems simple, but there are variations. As a general guide, let the nail go into the lower piece a depth equal to about twice the thickness of the wood above (FIG. 1-1A). If the top piece is thin or you will be driving into end grain (where the grip is less), the nail should be longer. The hold will be better if alternate nails are angled different ways (FIG. 1-1B). If there is an open end, put the nails closer there (FIG. 1-1C). If you want to drive a nail near the edge, drill an undersize hole for it, to reduce the risk of splitting. Nails with normal heads have a good grip. If you use nails with reduced heads, possibly so you can set them below the surface and cover with wood filler, remember the hold is not as good and there should be more nails to compensate.

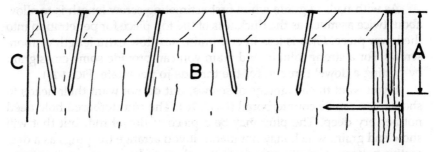

Fig. 1-1. *Nails should be long enough and may be driven at angles for extra strength.*

Screws

Screws have a better hold than nails. They will also pull parts together, so they are also effective as clamps. The range of gauges (thicknesses) and lengths are considerable and you have to learn to choose for particular circumstances. Thin screws have to be longer or used closer together than shorter thicker screws.

Holes for screws are essential. You cannot just drive even the smallest screw without a hole, as you would a nail. For a small screw it may be sufficient to make a hole with a spike or awl. For other screws provide a clearance hole in the upper piece and an undersize hole in the lower piece (FIG. 1-2A). In softwood, the lower hole may be smaller and not as deep as in hardwood. In particleboard the hole should go at least as far as the screw will penetrate, as it tends to burst the material if a shorter hole is drilled. For thin screws in wood you may make the lower hole with an awl. Other holes are made with twist drills of the type originally intended for use in metal. A screw grips by pulling with its head to press down the top piece of wood as the screw threads pull into the lower

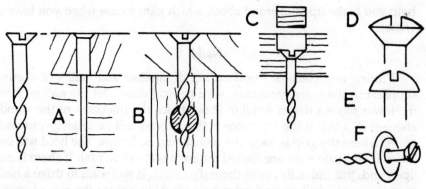

Fig. 1-2. *Drill for screws (A), strengthen end grain with dowels, (B) or counterbore and plug (C). Several heads are available.*

wood. There should not be any resistance in the top piece, so its hole should not be tight on the screw neck.

As with nails, a guide when first estimating screw length is to allow about twice as much as the thickness of the top piece for penetration into the lower piece. Grip is less in end grain, so allow extra length or more screws. For a strong joint in end grain you can provide some cross grain by putting a dowel through for the threads to penetrate (FIG. 1-2B).

If you want the advantage of screws, but do not want their heads to show, they can be counterbored (FIG. 1-2C). The counterbored hole need not be very deep. The plug may be a piece of dowel rod, but that will show end grain, which may not matter if you arrange the plugs as a decorative pattern. Usually, you want the plugs to be as inconspicuous as possible; that means they should be the same wood as they are going into, and the grain should be across the same way as the surrounding surface. Get a plug cutter, which is like a hollow drill, and use it to cut plugs from scraps of the same wood you intend to plug. The tool cuts a circle around the plug, which you break out with a narrow chisel. Glue the plugs in so they stand above the surface; then plane off level later.

Consider the available screw heads. The common flat head will serve for most purposes. Expect the head to pull into most woods, so do not countersink a hole too much if you want the head to finish level. If you are putting on a hinge or other metal fitting where the screw heads will show, oval (or raised) heads (FIG. 1-2D) look neater than flat heads. If what you are adding does not have countersunk holes, round heads look good (FIG. 1-2E).

For most furniture you will use ordinary slotted screw heads, but there are several special means of driving, intended originally for power driving in production work. A common example of these is the Phillips head, with a four-point recess. Use it, if those are the available screws, but for most purposes choose slotted heads.

A neat way of dealing with screw heads, particularly if you may have to disassemble a part later, is to have flat head screws through cup (or countersunk finishing) washers (FIG. 1-2F); this spreads the pressure while keeping the head away from the wood. An alternative is to use a round head screw through a flat washer.

When a table or other top has to be fastened down to a framework you do not usually want screws to show on top, so they have to be driven upwards. If the rails are shallow, you might have to counterbore enough to allow screws of reasonable length to be used (FIG. 1-3A). The holes will not normally show, so there is no need to plug them.

If the rails are deeper, you cannot use counterbored screws. Instead, the screws have to be driven diagonally from inside the rail. These are called *pocket screws* (FIG. 1-3B). Cut a notch with a gouge and chisel (FIG. 1-3C). Another quick way is to use a drill bit, preferably the Forstner type that does not make a deep hole with a center pin. Angle it enough to get the upper part of the hollow deep enough to clear the diameter of the screw head (FIG. 1-3D).

Pocket screws are satisfactory if the top material is not liable to expand and contract, such as plywood and particleboard. If the top is solid wood, it can be expected to get a little wider as it takes up moisture from the air and shrink when it dries out. This movement can be enough to matter and will result in cracks or breaks if you try to fix down firmly. The amount of movement varies between woods, but 1/4 inch in a 12-inch width is what you should anticipate. If the table top will be in a centrally heated atmosphere, it will help to store the wood in the same conditions for several months assuming you can spare that much time!

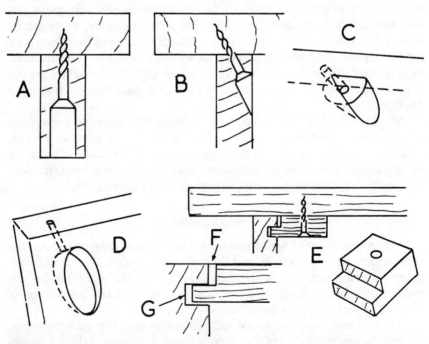

Fig. 1-3. *Tops are held with screws driven upwards in several ways.*

To allow for expansion and contraction, it is usual to hold a top down with buttons. Groove the inside edges of the rails. Make buttons to screw to the underside of the top and engage with the grooves (FIG. 1-3E). If the top moves, the button can slide along the groove. It is usual to fit buttons all round and not just in the crosswise parts. There must be a good clearance in the buttons so they can move in and out (FIG. 1-3F) as well as sideways, but they must be arranged to pull tight against the upper edge of a groove as the screw is fully driven (FIG. 1-3G). There are several applications of buttons in projects, but please note the refectory table (FIG. 5-25).

Notched Joints

The obvious application of a notched joint is where two pieces cross and have to be at the same level (FIG. 1-4A). This weakens both pieces, so cut the parts to make a tight fit and get the maximum mutual support. At a corner (FIG. 1-4B) or a T junction you should not rely on glue only, but you will need screws from both sides, if there is no plywood or other covering to reinforce the joint.

If the parts that cross are not the same section, you might put the thin one in a groove in the other without notching it (FIG. 1-4C). If the difference is not so much, do not take more than half the thickness out of the thin one (FIG. 1-4D).

The other common example of a notched joint is the dado supporting a shelf end (FIG. 1-4E). There might be other parts in the assembly which will hold this joint together, but end grain meets side grain and that does not make a good glued joint. For a stronger joint, there can be screws driven from outside (FIG. 1-4F) if the appearance of their heads on the surface are acceptable. If you do not want the heads to show outside, drive screws diagonally upwards from below (FIG. 1-4G). Make sure the angle is such that the threaded part of the screw goes into the middle of the upright part.

Shallow notches can be used for locating and stopping parts from sliding against each other. If you just nail a number of parts of a frame together you might not get all the positions exactly right and if there are sliding loads there could be movement later. Shallow notches (FIG. 1-4H) positively locate the pieces and prevent sideways movement.

Through Joints

When one piece of wood meets another squarely, or nearly so, the chosen joint usually takes its end through. At one time this would have always been a tenon, and in many cases this is still the best joint, but the modern alternative is the use of dowels, which takes advantage of the ease of making joints by drilling.

Mortise and tenon joints are still preferable in many circumstances. A correctly arranged joint of this type is normally stronger than a dowel-

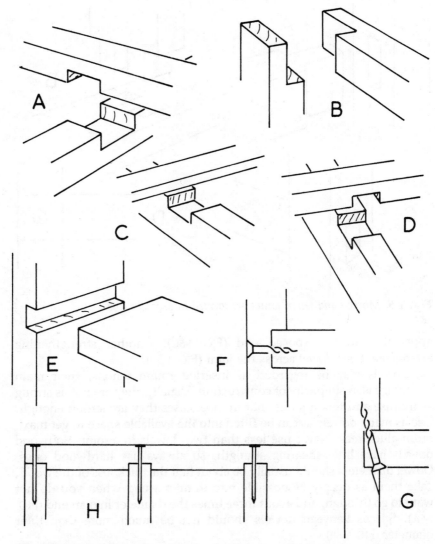

Fig. 1-4. *Notched joints are used at crossings or to support ends.*

led alternative. There are many examples included elsewhere in this book, but consider these points. A tenon should be about one-third of the thickness of the part being mortised (FIG. 1-5A). It should be arranged in the direction of the grain of the part being mortised. Cutting it across would be wrong, so there might have to be multiple tenons if the larger dimension is the other way (FIG. 1-5B). Tenons need not always go through, but allow ample length for good glue areas between side grain faces in a *stub* mortise and tenon joint.

With modern glues there should usually be no need for wedging, but wedges driven into saw cuts to expand a tenon end in the direction of the grain of the mortised piece is extra security and gives a traditional

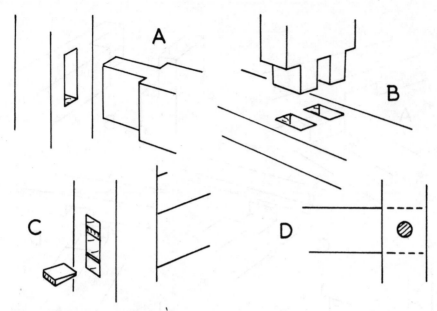

Fig. 1-5. Mortise and tenon joints are formed in several ways.

appearance to an exposed end (FIG. 1-5C). Another strengthening arrangement is a dowel across the joint (FIG. 1-5D).

Dowels may be regarded as inserted round tenons; their main advantage is in simplicity of construction. Usually, they are not as strong as mortise and tenon joints, but in most cases they are strong enough. Use as many dowels as can be fitted into the available space to get maximum glue areas. Never use less than two dowels in a joint. Softwood dowels have little shearing strength, so always use hardwood ones. Dowel diameters should usually be about half the thickness of the wood. Take them as deeply as possible into thinner wood when you do not want to go through, and about three times the diameter into an end (FIG. 1-6A). Spaces between dowels should not be much more than their diameter (FIG. 1-6B).

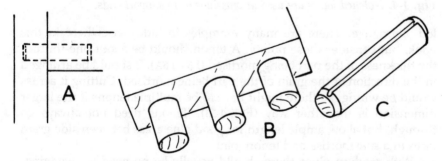

Fig. 1-6. Provide enough dowels long enough for strength. Grooving helps air escape.

Cut dowels shorter than the total depth of the intended holes. Remove raggedness from ends. It is helpful to cut a groove along a dowel with a saw (FIG. 1-6C); this lets air escape as the dowel goes into a hole like a piston. It is possible to buy prepared dowels with tapered ends and grooves, but these may not be exactly the size you want, and for most projects it is better to cut your own.

Remember that where the end grain of one piece comes against the side grain of another, there will be little strength from glue in this contact. All strength comes from glue on the dowels, so make sure the dowels are sufficient and long enough to give good glue areas. Tenons in mortises normally offer better glue surfaces.

Interlocked Corners

If you nail or screw a box corner together there is little to be gained by putting glue in the joint, as the end grain will not bond well enough with it. A simple way of increasing strength is to rabbet one piece; then, nails or screws may be driven both ways (FIG. 1-7A).

Nailed or screwed corners are not acceptable in good furniture and other ways have to be found to provide side-grain glued surfaces. This is done by grooving parts to interlock them.

One interlocking corner that is strong because of the large side grain glue area is a comb joint (FIG. 1-7B). This is particularly suitable with the precision which comes from machine cutting, but it could be made by

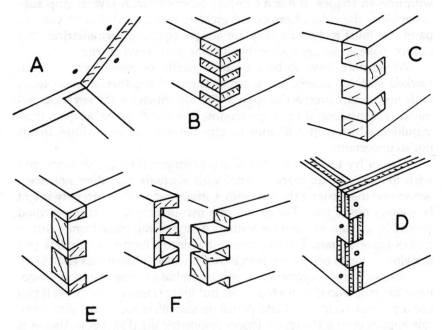

Fig. 1-7. *Interlocked corners have good glue area and may be comb, finger or dovetail.*

hand. For hand cutting the parts may be wider and it is then sometimes called a finger joint (FIG. 1-7C). If the corners are plywood, the material does not permit cutting combs or even narrow fingers, because the tendency to break in small sections. However, you can make wider fingers and secure them with nails or screws both ways (FIG. 1-7D).

A further step is to make the fingers wedge-shaped in one direction, which becomes a dovetail joint (FIG. 1-7E). The greatest value of this was in the days when the available glues could not be trusted and the dovetails gave mechanical strength in one direction. It is still an attractive joint and worth using, and is particularly good-looking when the corner is exposed.

The front of a drawer puts considerable strain on the corner joints, particularly when a stubborn loaded drawer is pulled. The stopped or half-blind dovetail is then the best corner joint to use (FIG. 1-7F), as it gives mechanical support to the glue and does not show when the drawer is closed.

SQUARING

It is important that any piece of furniture stands level and upright. If it does not, the fault is obvious to almost every observer. If it is framed with solid wood parts, which have been cut square, it is unlikely to assemble out of shape. But if it is a structure made of strips, with open places or plywood which may move in slots, it could be glued together with uneven shapes. If it is a complex assembly with several strip subassemblies, the risks of errors are greater; this means that as you cut parts you must make sure they are always square or symmetrical. You cannot make an accurate assembly if some part is out of true.

Where parts have to be the same length, or some have to reach marked parts on others, mark across them all together, if possible. A knife line is more precise than pencil. Decide which are the key measurements. For instance, if there are tenons, it is the distance between their shoulders which matter. If tenon lengths beyond that vary a little, that is not so important.

Always try to use a square which is longer than the distance you wish to mark. If you mark a panel with a square that does not reach across and then extend the line with a straightedge, the extremity might be slightly out of true. The corner of a manufactured sheet of plywood should be square; use that for testing. A large scrap piece from a corner makes a good square. Test its accuracy by placing it on a straight line and drawing along its edge; then turn it over and see if it matches (FIG. 1-8A).

Besides using a square when you assemble a frame, compare diagonals. You might do it with a tape rule, but there is less risk or errors if you use a piece of scrap wood and pencil on the reference points (FIG. 1-8B); this applies even if the shape tapers symmetrically (FIG. 1-8C). Also, it is necessary to see that there is no twist in the assembled frame. If it is put together on a known flat surface, it should be satisfactory if it lies flat.

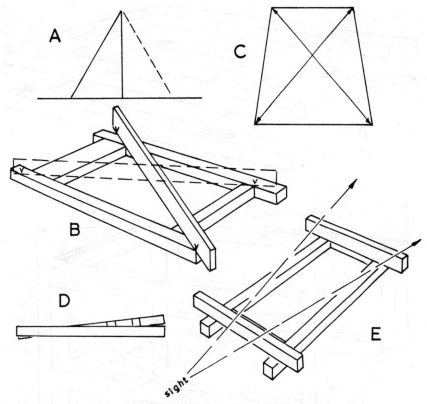

Fig. 1-8. *Checking squareness and lack of twist is important.*

Otherwise, sight across opposite sides, then you should be able to see any error (FIG. 1-8D). If the frame is not large you can exaggerate and see the probable twist by putting parallel strips over opposite sides; then sight over them (FIG. 1-8E). These are the traditional craftsman's *winding strips*.

You will usually have to assemble opposite sides first. When you have checked that one is true, it can be used to test the other, but if they are to make a pair, see that they face each other for testing (FIG. 1-9A). It might be best to let the glue set in the joints in these opposite sides before joining them with the crosswise parts. You will know then that they cannot distort during further work. Do it this way whenever possible during assemblies.

When you assemble the other way, check squareness at each side by comparing diagonals (FIG. 1-9B). Sight down a side to look for twists. Compare diagonals as viewed from above (FIG. 1-9C), at the top and lower down, if possible.

You can get all these squarings right and still have the whole assembly twisted. Put it on a flat surface—upside-down if that is the important way that should be true, especially if you think leg lengths may not be right. See that the assembly stands without wobbling. Get back and

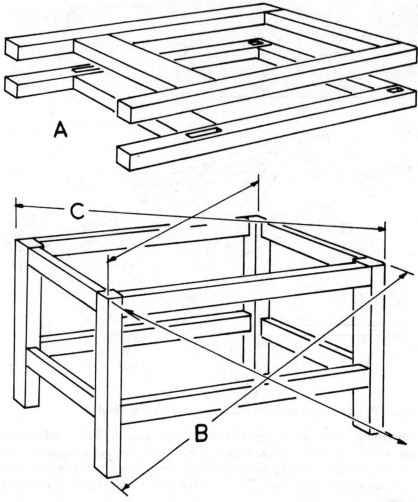

Fig. 1-9. *Parts should match and squareness should be tested in all directions.*

view it from all angles and check that it looks upright and opposite corners match; then leave it for the glue to set.

Of course, that is an extreme case, where the structure is all strips. If there are panels, shelves, diagonal braces and any other parts that secure framing in shape, you can be certain that those aspects of assembly can be assumed true. If you can put together a sub-assembly with parts in it that will hold it true and build other parts around it, you will be starting with a section of known accuracy. Therefore, there will be less trouble in getting added parts true.

Pay particular attention where doors and drawers have to be fitted. If either front is only slightly out of square, it will be obvious. Another problem with drawers is squareness of their guides front to back. A drawer may be made slightly narrower at the back for ease of sliding, but it should not be necessary to fit it askew because of faults in assembly of the carcass.

When all parts have been made, there is a great temptation to rush into assembling them to see what the piece of furniture looks like. Before doing that, check that every part has had all the work done to it that is necessary and possible. Prefabricate all you can. You may drill screw holes in some parts in advance of their need. You should certainly remove any pencil or other markings that are no longer needed. Now is the time to do any sanding of parts that may later be out of reach or difficult to sand full-length. It is always easier to do this sort of work while parts are separate on the bench. In overall timing of a project, doing all you can in early stages makes for quicker, more accurate and a better finished piece of furniture. Plan ahead all the way.

2
General-Purpose Furniture

There are some articles of furniture which cannot be identified with any particular room, but might be used almost anywhere about the home. Most of these things are small and portable, such as a stool. Usually they are simple and economical, so you might wish to make more than one to reduce the amount of moving about.

This furniture is mainly utilitarian, but it should be well-made and look attractive, even if it is primarily functional. If there is any general scheme for color or finish of other furniture, it should be made to match. If taken outside and left there, avoid unsuitable materials, such as plywood with a non-waterproof glue; apply a weatherproof finish.

THREE STOOLS

A stool has to perform two main functions. First, it can be used as a seat, or even a table, by a child. Secondly, it gives you something to stand on if you want to reach higher than you can when standing on the floor. These requirements have to be considered when deciding on sizes. You can vary sizes quite widely without affecting the method of construction. Sizes shown on drawings and in materials lists should suit many conditions. Stability is an important consideration. The area covered by the extremities of the stool feet should not be much less than the area of the top. If you allow much overhang, anyone stepping near an end could tip the stool, with unfortunate results. An overhang up to 1 inch would not matter.

Almost any wood can be used. A good furniture hardwood will be best, but much depends on the intended use. A good general-purpose stool may be softwood finished by painting, but a stool made from hardwood with a clear finish can take its place with your best furniture. For use by a child, choose a wood that does not splinter easily.

The three stools described here all fulfill similar functions; your choice of design depends on the appearance you prefer. The work involved in making them is about the same, and all are straightforward. If you are unsure of your ability to make more advanced furniture, building one or more of these stools will form a good introduction. The designs are simple enough to be quickly made, and you could soon produce a quantity for your friends or for sale.

First Stool

The first stool (FIG. 2-1) might be considered the basic nailed or screwed design. It is intended to be made of 1-inch softwood boards,

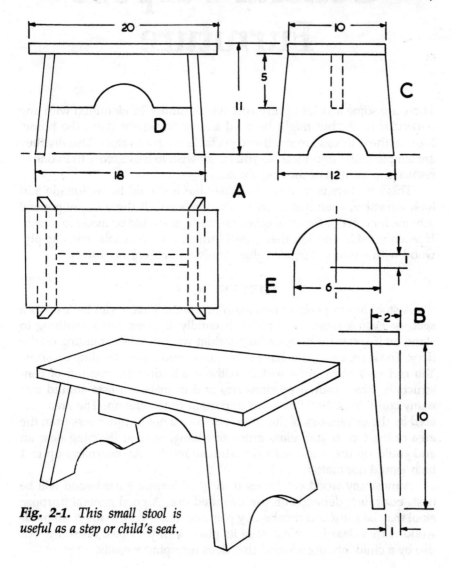

Fig. 2-1. This small stool is useful as a step or child's seat.

although you could use slightly thinner hardwood. The legs are splayed a little in the length and width, to improve appearance and provide stability. As shown (FIG. 2-1A), the stool is twice as long as it is wide.

Set out the leg slope (FIG. 2-1B). This gives you the angles to trim the tops and bottoms of the legs, and the length down the slope; although, you will probably not bother about the slight difference if you work to the vertical height.

Make the two legs with their grain vertical and tapering from 12 inches to 10 inches (FIG. 2-1C). The top is a simple rectangle. Mark on it where the legs will come. Round the corners.

The brace (FIG. 2-1D) has a top edge length to fit between the leg positions marked on the underside of the top. Take the angle for the ends from the leg setting out. The cutouts under the legs and the brace are the same. They are shown as parts of a circle (FIG. 2-1E). They form feet on the legs to help the stool stand level. The curve under the brace may be used as a hand grip, so round its edges.

Mark the brace positions on the legs; then drill for nails or screws and use glue as you join these parts together. Drill the top in a similar way and join it on, using the guidelines to see that the parts are assembled squarely.

Round all exposed edges. Check that the stool stands without rocking. If necessary, plane a little off a foot. Finish with paint or varnish.

Second Stool

The second stool is drawn using 3/4-inch wood, and it is smaller overall than the first (FIG. 2-2A), but you could make it any size. There is some decorative shaping, but the stool might be made with straight edges. Much early furniture had shaped edges, for the sake of appearance, but also to disguise errors in shaping the wood, which may have been rough and probably not fully seasoned. Errors in curves are not so obvious as in an edge which should be straight, but tore up or split under the plane.

Softwood with a painted finish would be suitable, but a clear finish on hardwood might be attractive.

Set out the slope of a leg (FIG. 2-2B). This will give you its length and the angles to cut the notches and ends (FIG. 2-3A). Make the two legs identical (FIG. 2-3B). Cut the notches to suit the actual thicknesses of the side braces (FIG. 2-3C). Alternatively, you could cut dado joints, as described for the third stool. However, for a small stool, glued and nailed or screwed joints should be adequate.

The braces (FIG. 2-3C) are parallel where they meet the legs, but otherwise the lower edges are shaped (FIG. 2-3D). Take sharpness off all curved edges of the legs and braces. Assemble the legs and braces, being careful to maintain squareness and avoidance of twist.

Make the top to match the lower parts. It is shown with a hand hole

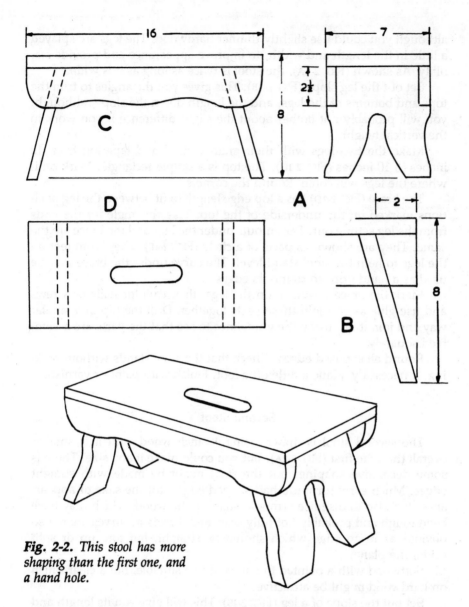

Fig. 2-2. *This stool has more shaping than the first one, and a hand hole.*

at the center (FIG. 2-2D) for carrying. This could be 1 inch × 5 inches, made by drilling its ends and sawing away the waste.

Round all exposed edges and corners. Correct any tendency to wobble by planing feet, if necessary, before applying your chosen finish.

Third Stool

The third stool (FIG. 2-4) is braced by three lengthwise pieces of comparatively reduced depth, so the effect is a rather lighter appearance, but with no reduction in strength. In some ways the stool is similar to early

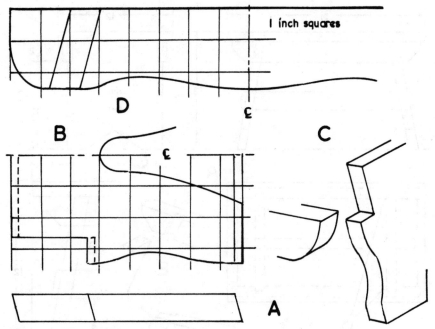

Fig. 2-3. *The shaped parts of the stool.*

tables. The suggested sizes (FIG. 2-4A) are for a stool made of 1-inch softwood boards, but oak with a waxed finish would give a contemporary appearance with some tables; although, a hardwood stool might be rather heavy if it is intended to be moved frequently.

The top overlaps the other parts by ¹/₂ inch. The legs fit into dado grooves in the top braces. The lower brace has tenons through the legs, and they may extend with rounded ends. The method of construction provides more strength in itself than in the other stools, but the parts should be glued and nailed or screwed.

Set out an end (FIG. 2-4B) to get the angles and lengths of the legs and braces. Make the two legs. The bottom cutout is shown as a simple V (FIG. 2-4C), but you could curve it. Mark the positions of the mortises, but do not cut them until you prepare the brace tenons. The legs will fit into dados in the top braces, without themselves being notched (FIG. 2-4D).

Make the top braces and cut the dados to match the thickness of the legs (FIG. 2-4E). Length is 1-inch shorter than the top. Bevel the ends.

Use your end setting out to get the length between the shoulders of the bottom brace. Mark tenons ¹/₂-inch thick and long enough to go through the legs and project ¹/₂ inch. Cut the tenons and round the projections (FIG. 2-4F); then make mortises in the legs to match.

Glue the parts and clamp them tightly while nails or screws are driven. Check squareness and freedom from twist. Cut the top to overlap ¹/₂-inch all round. This allows you to well round the edges and corners. The edges of the lower brace could also be rounded as it might

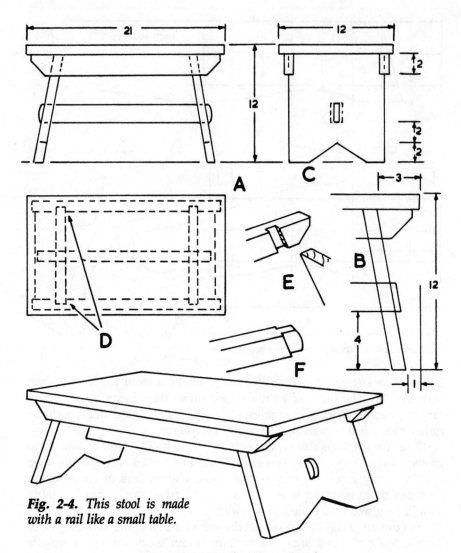

Fig. 2-4. *This stool is made with a rail like a small table.*

Materials List for Three Stools

First stool

1 top	1	×	10	×	21
2 legs	1	×	12	×	12
1 brace	1	×	5	×	18

Second stool

1 top	3/4	×	7	×	17
2 legs	3/4	×	7	×	9
2 braces	3/4	×	2 1/2	×	17

Third stool

1 top	1	×	12	×	22
2 legs	1	×	10	×	12
3 braces	1	×	2	×	21

be used as a handle for carrying the stool upside-down. Finish the wood with paint, varnish or wax.

PORTABLE SIDE STAND

At first glance this might be a bookcase (FIG. 2-5). It could be, but it may have many other uses. It is wider than it need be for most books. It could be used as a side stand to hold odds and ends in a den or office. It could also find a place beside an easy chair for magazines, knitting and refreshments. In a dining room it might hold food, crockery and cutlery. For all these and other uses, it has the advantage of being portable. It will carry food from the kitchen or take back dishes and crockery to be washed. If you want to move your center of interest to another chair, you can carry the stand and its contents there easily.

Fig. 2-5. The side stand has several shelves and hand holes for lifting.

The sizes (FIG. 2-6) show a stand which is broad enough to be stable under most loads, yet light enough to be carried. The shaped top provides decoration. The overall height is about level with a table or bench, and allows easy lifting from a standing position.

Construction may be with solid wood 3/4-inch finished thickness, or you could use veneered particleboard. However, top edges would have to be straight, as iron-on edge veneer cannot be secured to a pronounced curve. There are strips across at the back of each shelf, which look better than an overall plywood back, which would be satisfactory against a wall, but would not look good in positions where both sides of the stand are visible.

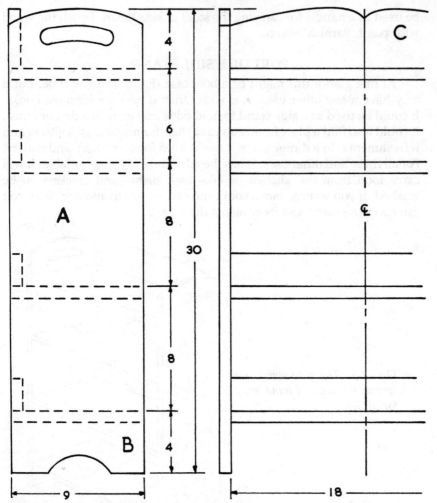

Fig. 2-6. *Suggested sizes for the portable side stand.*

Mark out the pair of sides (FIG. 2-6A) with the positions of the shelves and rear strips.

Cut away the bottom to leave feet 2-inches wide (FIG. 2-6B). At the top, mark the hand holes and the curve of the edge (FIG. 2-7A). Cut the hole by first drilling its ends and cutting away the waste. Round and smooth the edges of the hand holes and the top edges to provide comfortable grips.

Mark all the crosswise pieces together to get the lengths the same. Carefully square the ends, as slight variations may affect the accuracy of the assembly.

Shape the top edge of the back (FIGS. 2-6C and 7B). Check that the shaped ends of the back and sides will meet level. Round the edges of the back.

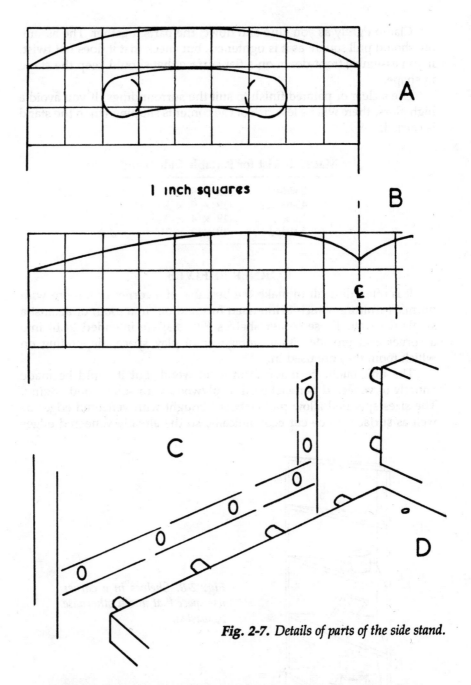

I inch squares

Fig. 2-7. *Details of parts of the side stand.*

Mark out for dowels, which may be 5/16 inch or 3/8 inch in diameter, with four in each shelf and two in each narrow part (FIG. 2-7C).

The shelves can be screwed upwards into the rear strips (FIG. 2-7D).

Drill all dowel holes and cut dowels to length at the same time. Drill as deeply as possible into the sides to give good glue areas.

Clamp tightly as you glue and dowel the parts together. The assembly should pull square as it is tightened, but check that it does not twist. If you assemble front-down on a flat surface that should keep the stand in shape.

Use a clear or painted finish to suit the surroundings. If you avoid a high gloss, there will be less risk of the contents slipping when the stand is carried.

Materials List for Portable Side Stand

2 sides	31 × 9 × 3/4
4 shelves	19 × 9 × 3/4
1 back	19 × 4 × 3/4
3 strips	19 × 2 × 3/4

CORNER SHELVES

It is often difficult to make the best use of a corner of a room with normal furniture, which is intended to stand out in a room or against a single flat wall. These corner shelves (FIG. 2-8) are intended to fit into a corner and provide either storage or display space, depending on which room they are used in.

The unit might be made from solid wood, but it could be made entirely of veneered particleboard or plywood with solid wood edging. The sizes specified allow particleboard bought with veneered edges as well as surfaces to be cut economically, so the already-veneered edges

Fig. 2-8. Shelves in a corner use space that might otherwise be wasted.

might be used almost everywhere exposed. In short, the minimum amount of iron-on veneer strip will be needed. If plywood is used, the exposed edges should be covered with solid wood strips.

The unit is about 52-inches high, depending on how much clearance has to be allowed for the room baseboard, and it extends 16-inches along each wall. Shelf spacings are graduated to give the most effective appearance, as well as convenient storage or display spaces (FIG. 2-9).

Check the angle of the corner of the room where the shelves are to be placed. It should be 90 degrees, but many corners are a few degrees out.

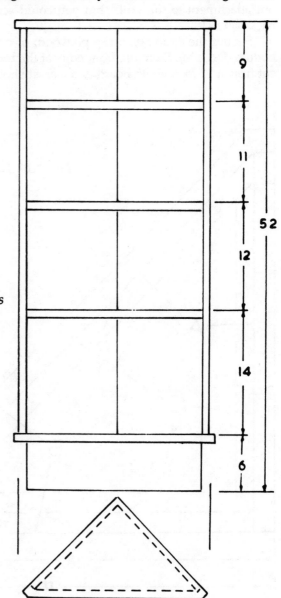

Fig. 2-9. Suggested sizes for corner shelves.

If the corners is more than 90 degrees, and you make the unit 90 degrees there will be gaps showing. If the corner is less than 90 degrees a squared unit will not be so obviously different as any gaps will be towards the back. However, if the corner is not square, it would be advisable to use the actual angle instead of 90 degrees when setting out.

The main unit is intended to go against the wall above the room baseboard. The plinth, or unit base, is made as high as the baseboard and arranged to support the unit while fitting inside, so the whole piece of furniture makes a close fit with both walls. It should stand safely without attachment to the walls, but you could screw through each of the back panels.

Set out the corner on scrap plywood, or on what will be the top or bottom (FIG. 2-10). From the front edge of the top to the corner should be cut from a 12-inch width board and a shelf should be cut from a 10-inch

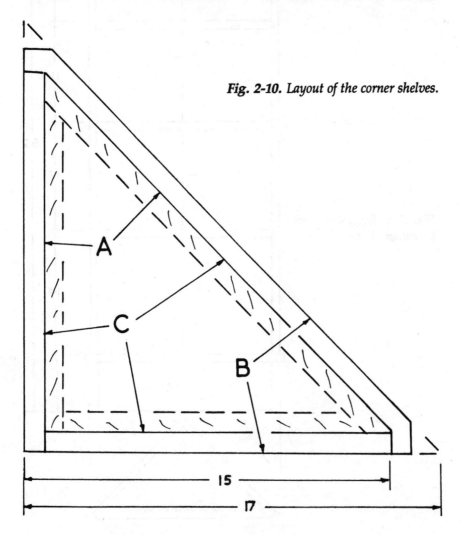

Fig. 2-10. Layout of the corner shelves.

width. By working from alternate sides, you should be able to cut economically and use the already-faced edges.

This setting out will give you the widths of the two backs. One is 15 inches and the other is cut back to allow for the overlap. Cut these boards and mark on them where the shelves will come.

Since the backs will be against the wall and their rear surfaces will not show, screws can be used for most of the assembly without any need for hiding screwheads. Drill for the overlap and for screws into the shelves #8 × 1½ inches or 1¾-inch screws should be suitable in most positions. Screws about 6-inches apart may be sufficient at the corner back joint. At the shelves, a 4-inch spacing may be adequate.

Make the three shelves (FIG. 2-10A) to reach or come a short distance in from the outer edges of the back.

Assemble the two backs together and to the shelves, using glue.

Make the top and bottom the same (FIG. 2-10B) with the corners beveled square to the walls. Check that angles match those of the assembled backs.

Glue and screw on. Screwheads through the bottom will not show. Counterbore for the screws through the top; then plug after screwing.

The angles in room corners are often not sharp. If necessary, round or bevel the back corner so you can push the unit tight against both walls.

Check the height of the baseboard. Allow a little clearance and that is the height to make the base.

The base is a triangle to fit inside the room baseboard (FIG. 2-10C). As only the front shows, it does not matter if the two side pieces do not actually meet in the corner. Screw these pieces under the bottom of the unit.

Your corner shelf unit is now complete. Check that it stands close to the wall. If it tends to tilt forward, plane a little off the rear of the base sides. It is better for the unit to be kept upright by the front edge of the base and by pressure against the walls at the top.

Finish will depend on the materials and the need to match any other furniture.

Materials List for Corner Shelves

2 backs	46	×	15	×	¾
1 top	24	×	12	×	¾
1 bottom	24	×	12	×	¾
3 shelves	24	×	10	×	¾
1 base	24	×	5¼	×	¾
2 bases	14	×	5¼	×	¾

ROOM DIVIDER

Quite often it is convenient to use one large room for two different purposes. Building a complete partition may seem too drastic a way of making the division, particularly if you may still want communication between the users of both parts of the room. However, a positive division may be required, and a room divider that is not a permanent barrier, nor as plain as a wall or partition, can be an attractive piece of furniture, enhancing the amenities in both directions.

A room divider can take many forms, make yours to suit your needs and the size of the room. It is usually best to have the divider close against one wall, but leave space to move through at the other side. The height will depend on requirements, but a fairly solid division between people sitting is usually desirable, while a see-through upper part may be acceptable.

This divider (FIG. 2-11) is 6-feet high and 7-feet wide and made of boards 12-inches wide. The lower section is arranged as cupboards with sliding doors on both sides. The two sections above this have divisions off-center, so there is space for books on one side and shelf for

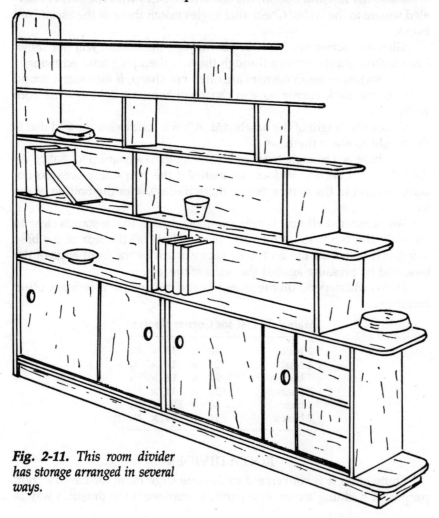

Fig. 2-11. *This room divider has storage arranged in several ways.*

ornaments or smaller items on the other side, arranged alternately. The top sections, at eye level, are open through. The shelves are reduced in length towards the top, and there is space at the ends for vases of flowers or other decorations.

Hardwood is advisable for a quality furniture finish, but you may use softwood and either paint or stain and varnish it. It would be possible to join the parts with mortise and tenon joints or have dados in some places, but 3/8 inch or 1/2-inch dowels are suggested, with four in each wide joint and comparable spacing in other parts.

All main parts are the same section, so prepare enough straight stock, and select to suit the various lengths needed. Offcuts will make the dividing upright pieces.

Mark the back (FIG. 2-12A) with the positions of the shelves.

Make the bottom shelf (FIG. 2-12B) and the one above it (FIG. 2-12C). Mark the positions of the two uprights between them. Cut and round the outer ends of these and all other shelves. You might find it worthwhile to make a template, so you get these curves all the same (FIG. 2-13A).

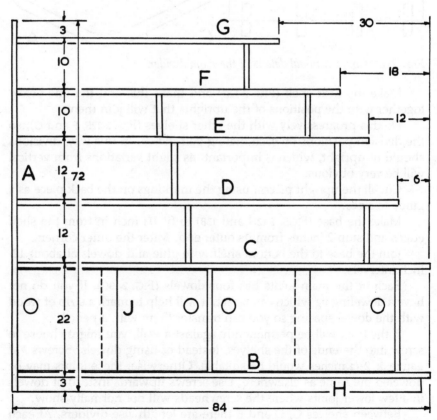

Fig. 2-12. *Main sizes of the room divider.*

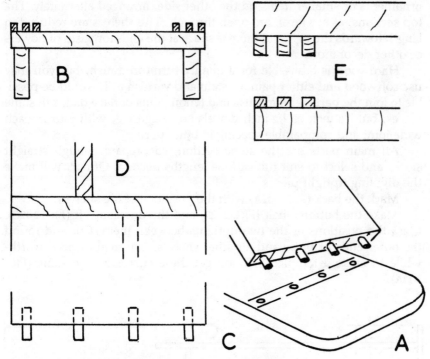

Fig. 2-13. *Constructional details of the room divider.*

Make the next shelf (FIG. 2-12D) and mark this and the one below together with the positions of the uprights that will join them.

Do this progressively with the other shelves (FIG. 2-12E, F and G), so the division positions on each mating pair match. In this way, divisions should fit upright, which is important, as slight variations from vertical will be very obvious.

Cut all the upright pieces, using the markings on the back piece as a guide to sizes.

Make the base (FIGS. 2-12H and 13B) to fit 1/4 inch in from the shelf edges and stop 2 inches from its outer end. Miter the outer corners.

Join the base to the bottom shelf with glue and dowels at about 12-inch intervals.

Each of the main joints has four dowels (FIG. 2-13C). If you do not have a doweling jig which can be set, it will help to mark a strip of wood with the dowel spacing so you can transfer them with a pencil.

If the back will be permanently against a wall, you might choose to screw into the ends of the shelves, instead of using dowels. Screws #12 gauge × 2 1/2 inches would be suitable. Otherwise, these joints may be doweled the same as elsewhere. Use screws upwards instead of dowels in a few lower joints where the screwheads will not normally show.

Between shelves C, D and E there are lengthwise dividers. At each level they are staggered so there is a space wide enough for books in alternate bays (FIG. 2-13D) with a narrower shelf on the other side. Make these dividers, allowing for just a few dowels in each to locate them.

Prepare all joints for dowels. Work from the bottom of the divider upwards, with the bottom shelf and its base attached to the back first. Check squareness, but when you fit the lengthwise dividers they will hold the assembly true.

The sliding doors (FIG. 2-12J) are best made of hardwood plywood 1/4 inch or 3/8-inch thick. They run between guides which are 3/8-inch wide × 1/4-inch deep on the bottom shelf, and 3/8 inch-wide × 1/2-inch deep under the upper shelf (FIG. 2-13E). The doors are cut so they only go 1/4 inch into the top grooves; this allows you to lift a door clear of the bottom guides for putting in or taking out.

Use straight-grained hardwood for the guide strips. Glue and pin them to the shelves, so the gaps are an easy fit on the sliding plywood doors.

Make the doors to overlap each other by 3 inches (FIG. 2-12J).

Near the outer edges of each door drill a 1 1/4-inch hole to serve as a finger grip for sliding. Round edges of these holes and all outer edges of the doors. During initial assembly, wax in the lower guides will help the doors to slide.

Put one or more shelves inside each cupboard. This is most easily done by letting a shelf rest, without screwing, on cleats on the uprights. Change shelf arrangements later if you wish.

Finish to suit the wood and surroundings. You might secure the room divider with a few screws through the back into the wall. Cloth, glued below the base, will limit accidental slipping or marking floor covering.

Materials List for Room Divider

2 shelves	84	×	12	×	1	
1 shelf	78	×	12	×	1	
1 shelf	72	×	12	×	1	
1 shelf	66	×	12	×	1	
1 shelf	54	×	12	×	1	
1 back	74	×	12	×	1	
2 uprights	22	×	12	×	1	
4 uprights	12	×	12	×	1	
4 uprights	10	×	12	×	1	
2 bases	84	×	3	×	1	
1 base	12	×	3	×	1	
2 inner shelves	40	×	8	×	1	
6 door guides	40	×	3/8	×	1/4	
6 door guides	40	×	1/2	×	3/8	
4 dividers	35	×	11	×	1	
8 doors	21	×	21	×	1/4 or 3/8 plywood	

CHEST

In pioneer days, a chest was an important piece of furniture. It held and protected linen and things of value, particularly when moving. It served as a seat or table and might have been the only connection with the old life. One or more chests still have their uses. In a suitable size, the box becomes a blanket chest in a bedroom. Another chest will store children's toys. It will keep a variety of things together and clean in a storeroom. A chest is the traditional container for tools.

Early settlers did not have the benefit of plywood, so their chests were mostly made of thick solid boards. Moving a loaded chest was work for at least two men. More desirable today is a lighter container, which can conform to the traditional pattern. This chest (FIG. 2-14) is made of plywood with light solid wood reinforcing strips. Sizes are suggested (FIG. 2-15A), but the method of construction can be used for a chest of any reasonable size. For a chest to be located among other indoor furniture, the plywood might be hardwood and the strips solid hardwood to match, but for a painted and lighter chest use softwood plywood and softwood strips. For a chest of the suggested size, use 1/2-inch plywood and 1/2-inch × 1 1/2-inch strips, but for a much larger chest the strip section should be increased a little.

Corners might be simple screwed overlaps, but finger joints are suggested with glue and screws both ways. When cut neatly and sanded, this has an attractive visual effect under a clear finish. Whether varnished or painted, this is a very strong joint.

Cut the back, front and end panels to size.

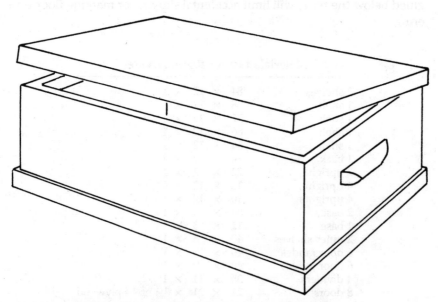

Fig. 2-14. *A chest provides portable storage for many things.*

Mark and cut the finger joints (FIG. 2-15B). Fingers 1½-inches wide will be satisfactory. Allow a little excess length on the fingers for leveling after assembly.

Drill the fingers for fine screws. Heads will probably pull in flush in softwood plywood, but you might have to countersink hardwood. Alternatively, prepare for driving screws.

Join the panels together. Delay leveling projecting fingers until after the bottom has been fitted and is steadying the assembly.

Cut the bottom plywood to make a close fit inside (FIG. 2-15C). Edge it with solid wood underneath. For this and other strip reinforcing, use glue and ¾-inch pins or fine nails driven from the plywood into the solid wood.

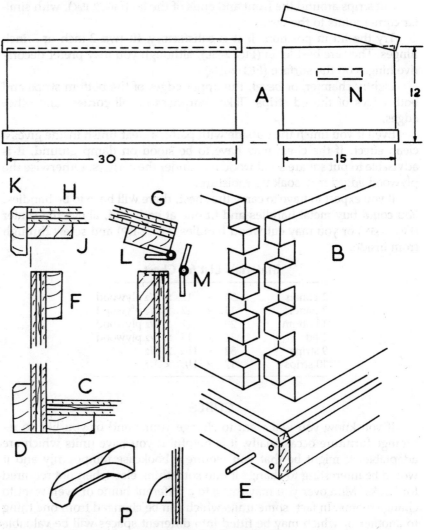

Fig. 2-15. *Sizes and constructional details of the chest.*

Fit the bottom inside, using glue and nails or screws driven from outside. Level all projections and edges.

Fit a base around the lower edges (FIG. 2-15D). This could be mitered at the corners, but a strong alternative is to overlap and put 1/4-inch dowels through (FIG. 2-15E).

Put strips around the inside edge of the top of the box (FIG. 2-15F). Level these edges to take the lid.

The lid must be level at the back (FIG. 2-15G) and overlap at the front and ends (FIG. 2-15H).

Cut the top plywood to size, allowing sufficient clearance over the box.

Frame around the underside of the plywood with strips (FIG. 2-15J).

Put strips around the front and ends of the lid (FIG. 2-15K), with similar corner joints to the box.

Try the lid in position. If it is satisfactory, fit two 2-inch or 3-inch hinges. They are best let in (FIG. 2-15L), although you may prefer decorative hinges on the surface (FIG. 2-15M).

Lightly chamfer, or bevel, the upper edges of the bottom strips and both edges of the lid strips. Take sharpness off all corners and other edges.

Even if you finish the outside with paint, a clear finish inside gives a clean effect. If the chest may have to be stood on damp ground, it is advisable to put square solid wood feet under the corners. Otherwise the plywood edges may soak up moisture.

If you expect to have to carry the chest, there will have to be handles. You could buy metal handles and fit one at each end, above the center (FIG. 2-15N) or you may cut wood handles (FIG. 2-15P) and screw through from inside.

Materials List for Chest

2 panels	30	×	12	×	1/2	plywood
2 panels	15	×	12	×	1/2	plywood
1 bottom	29	×	11	×	1/2	plywood
1 lid	31	×	13	×	1/2	plywood
9 strips	32	×	1 1/2	×	1/2	
10 strips	17	×	1 1/2	×	1/2	

CUBES

If you know you will want to change your mind or you like to rearrange furniture occasionally, it is helpful if you have units which are adaptable. It might be that you require a bookcase temporarily and it would be interesting to change it into something else when not required for books. Moreover you may move to a different home or even want to change rooms. In fact, some units which can be changed from one thing to another or which may be fitted into different spaces will be valuable and avoid the need for discarding some furniture and obtaining others.

A collection of cubes might be fitted together in various forms. Those suggested here are true cubes and others equal to two cubes (FIG. 2-16). With a basic dimension of 8 inches, there is depth for most books and ornaments and you can assemble many racks, cases and similar things. With a few matching boards you can make tables, desks and display stands. If made in a good hardwood and given a clear finish, a cube assembly is suitable for any room. You could use softwood with a painted finish for a greenhouse or displaying plants or flowers on a patio or deck. If you prefer a different basic size, the cubes may be made in the same way.

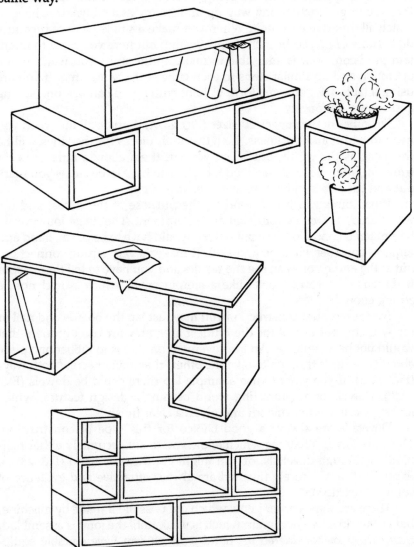

Fig. 2-16. *With single and double cube units you can build various types of furniture and change them when you wish.*

Solid wood $^5/_8$ inch or $^3/_4$-inch thick is suggested. For painted cubes, you might use $^1/_2$ inch or thicker plywood. It would be possible to use veneered particleboard, but that and plywood are limited in the choice of joints. The four sides may be joined in several ways. The back is the same thickness wood and fits inside, where it can be located during assembly with a few dowels. If you put two dowels along two opposite edges and one dowel centrally on the other edges, that should be sufficient, as the dowels only have to locate the back during assembly.

Although a cube is really a box it is not as deceptively simple to make as it might appear. If you are going to make a reasonable number and they are to go together any way up and in any assembly, sizes have to match all round in each unit. When you make a single piece of furniture differences of maybe $^1/_8$ inch do not matter, but here you need to maintain precision, so it is advisable to make all the units you want in one operation and do similar steps to each cube at the same time. If you are using a table saw, or some form of joint cutter, you can use one setting and ensure uniformity.

For cubes of the suggested sizes (FIG. 2-17A) prepare all the wood you need to width and thickness. Lengths of all pieces for the sides will be the same as the width, but when you cut them allow a little extra for trimming after the joints are made. Backs will have to be cut as you mark out and cut outside joints, so as to get sizes right.

What joints you use depend on the purpose of the cubes, and the wood used, as well as your skill and equipment. The finest joint would be a mitered concealed dovetail, which would have to be cut by hand and requires considerable time and skill. It makes a very strong connection, but at the end no one can see the results and you have to tell them about it, because the corner looks like a simple miter, which would not be strong enough.

For the simplest construction you may just lap the boards and nail or screw them, but except for the crudest assembly for use outdoors that would not be acceptable. An improvement on that is to rabbet one piece about two-thirds through to take the other; then nail or screw both ways (FIG. 2-17B). If you want to use a simple lap there could be dowels (FIG. 2-17C). Dowels of a contrasting wood become a design feature, which looks good if sanded smooth and given a clear finish.

Dovetails are always a good choice for this type of construction. There are jigs and fixtures which allow you to cut accurately either half-blind or through dovetails, or you might cut them by hand (FIG. 2-17D). Exposed dovetails nicely finished are always attractive and evidence of sound construction.

There are some corner joints which are possible if made by machine, but as they involve short grain which is weak until the joint is assembled, they cannot be considered for hand work. If you have suitable equipment you might try a dado and rabbet joint (FIG. 2-17E) or a dado, tongue

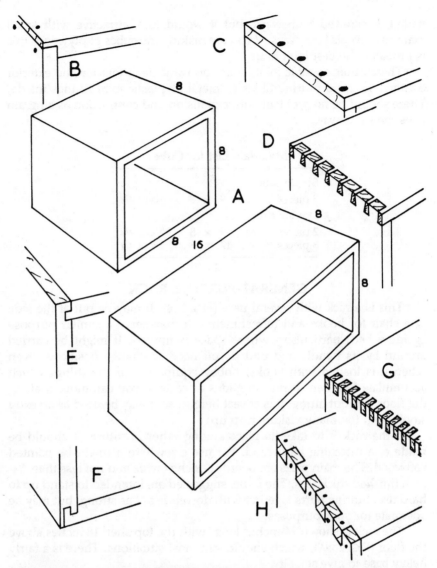

Fig. 2-17. *Sizes and several possible methods of construction of the cube units.*

and rabbet (FIG. 2-17F). In both cases, leave some excess wood when cutting the dados; then trim to length.

Another joint which is appropriate for these cubes is a comb (FIG. 2-17G). This can be cut accurately, neatly and quickly with a suitable tool, but the procedure is tedious and difficult by hand. However, it makes an exceptionally strong glued joint as there is considerable side grain area for the glue to grip.

If you do not have the facilities for making a comb joint you can cut the similar, but wider, finger joint (FIG. 2-17H) by hand. This could be nailed or screwed both ways, but it would look attractive with small diameter dowels both ways. If you are making the cubes of plywood, this is probably the best joint to use.

There other possible joints, but you want clean interior and exterior corners, so avoid putting fillets or metal or plastic joint fittings inside. There should be no problem with expansion and contraction as all grain goes the same way.

Materials List for Cubes

Single cube

5 pieces	9 × 8 ×	5/8 or 3/4

Double cube

2 pieces	9 × 8 ×	5/8 or 3/4
3 pieces	17 × 8 ×	5/8 or 3/4

GENERAL-PURPOSE RACK

This is a rack with several uses (FIG. 2-18). It may be put at the side of a chair for books and refreshments. It may serve a similar purpose beside a bed, particularly where space is limited. It might be carried around by its handle and end if you need to change positions, even when it is loaded with books, hobby equipment or the things which accumulate in a den. If put on glides or casters, you can move it along the floor without lifting. It is at seat height, so it may be used as an extra stool when too many visitors turn up.

If the rack is to take its place among other furniture, it should be made of a matching hardwood. For use elsewhere it might be painted softwood. The main parts are boards 8-inches wide and not less than 3/4-inch finished thickness. The joints suggested are intended to stand up to hard use. Butting parts together with dowels is not as strong, but may be adequate for your purposes.

The rack is shown 24-inches long, with the top shelf 18 inches above the floor (FIG. 2-19A), which should suit most situations. There is a fairly heavy base to give stability.

Make the back piece first (FIGS. 2-19B and 20A). Mark on it the positions of the shelves, and cut dado grooves 1/4-inch deep to fit the ends of the shelves.

Shape the top and cut the hand hole (FIG. 2-19C). Round the edges of the hole and the top down as far as the first shelf.

Make the three shelves (FIGS. 2-19D and 20B) the same overall sizes, but they will differ where they meet the two uprights. Round the outer corners.

At the inner ends of all shelves prepare for 3/8-inch dowels (FIG. 2-20C). Drill inside the dados to match. The dowels may go right through the back, or you can stop them short if you do not want them to show

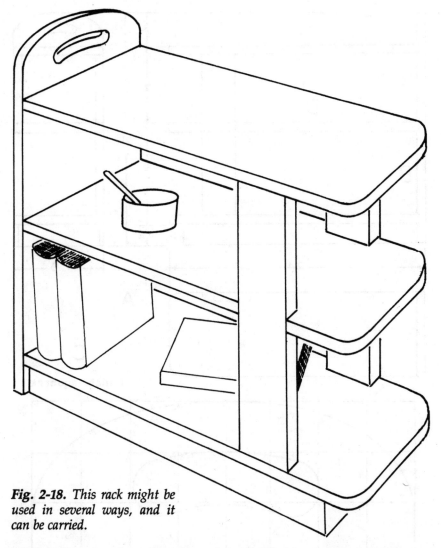

Fig. 2-18. *This rack might be used in several ways, and it can be carried.*

behind. Dowels taken through and sanded level may be regarded as a design feature.

The pair of uprights are 3 inches from the shelf ends. There is a choice of methods of joining to the top and bottom shelves. Use dowels (FIG. 2-20D) at top and bottom, or barefaced tenons with mortises in the shelves (FIG. 2-20E).

Cut half out of each piece at the middle joints (FIG. 2-20F). The notches here and at the back positively locate parts and prevent them slipping against each other under load.

Prepare the material for the base (FIG. 2-20G). This is wide, so as to provide good fixing for glides or casters if they are fitted. Cut the bottom of the back, so it extends to the underside of the base.

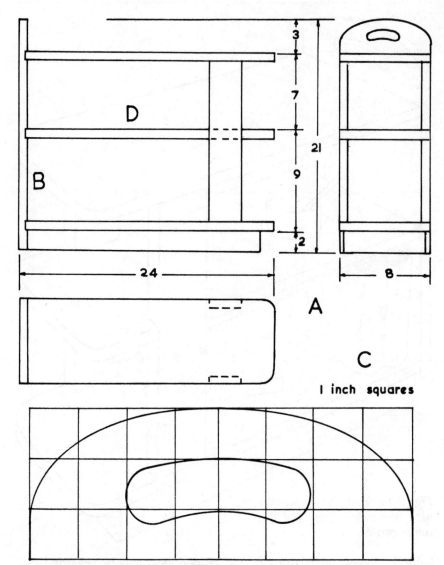

Fig. 2-19. *Sizes of the general-purpose rack.*

Assemble the shelves to the back and uprights squarely.

Miter the front corners of the base 2-inches back from the shelf end. At the sides, set the base in 1/4 inch from the shelf edges. The base can be joined on with glue, but counterbore some screw holes, so you can drive a few screws upwards into the bottom shelf. There can be screws or dowels through the back into the ends of the base.

If you have used an attractive hardwood, it may be given a clear finish, but staining the base darker will improve the appearance. A painted finish might be arranged in a similar way in two tones.

40   *General-Purpose Furniture*

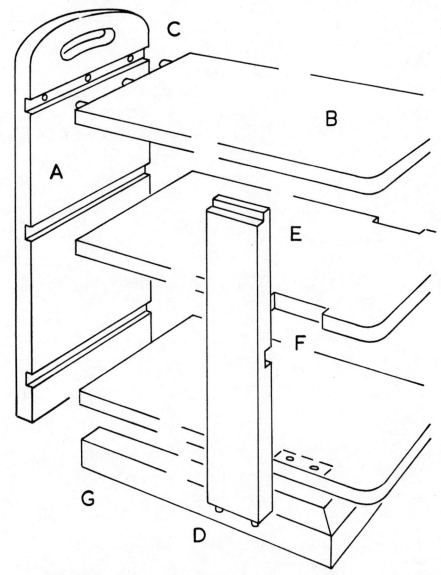

Fig. 2-20. *How the parts of the general-purpose rack fit together.*

Materials List for General-Purpose Rack

1 back	23 × 8 × 3/4
3 shelves	25 × 8 × 3/4
2 uprights	20 × 3 × 3/4
2 bases	24 × 2 × 2
1 base	9 × 2 × 2

3
Entrance and Exit

There is not usually much space inside exterior doors, but there is usually some sort of vestibule, enclosed porch or passageway where you can change from outdoor to indoor clothes and leave articles that are only needed outside. By building your own furniture for this area you can make the maximum use of the limited space in a way that may not be possible with bought stock items.

It is also the first area that visitors will see, even if you do not invite them inside the door, so what you make for use there can display your craftsmanship.

UMBRELLA STAND

Somewhere to put such things as walking canes, umbrellas, golf clubs, fishing poles and anything else long and thin will be welcome inside any outer door. The contents are readily available when you go out, and there is somewhere to put them when you come in, a particular advantage to the house-proud if you bring them in wet or dirty.

This stand (FIG. 3-1) is made of framed plywood and intended to have a painted finish. The suggested sizes (FIG. 3-2) should suit most needs, but you might wish to measure the intended contents before marking out the wood. Also, you might wish to measure the available space. Making larger or smaller is simple at the planning stage.

The main parts could be $1/2$-inch plywood, but thinner plywood would be satisfactory. Hardwood plywood $1/4$-inch thick would be just as suitable as $1/2$-inch softwood plywood. The framing strips are $3/4$-inch square section, and may be hard or soft wood. Assemble with glue and fine nails. Instead of the usual way of making two opposite frame sides

Fig. 3-1. *A tall tapered box makes a stand for umbrellas and canes.*

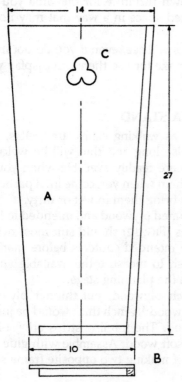

Fig. 3-2. *Sizes of a panel of the umbrella stand.*

and joining them with two plywood sides, this stand is put together with four identical sides, with framing attached so each fits into the next.

Mark out and cut four panels (FIG. 3-2A), working each side of a centerline to get the shape symmetrical.

Attach a strip along one long edge and another piece along the bottom edge; cut back enough to clear the plywood thickness and the next side strip (FIG. 3-2B). Allow enough for planing the overlapping edge after assembly.

Decorate the panels in any way you wish, but the example is shown with three overlapping 1-inch holes, to give a clover leaf effect (FIG. 3-2C).

Bring the parts together to overlap at each corner (FIG. 3-3A) and join with glue and nails. The assembly should bring itself symmetrical, but check squareness at the top and bottom before the glue has set.

Make the plywood bottom to glue and nail on (FIG. 3-3B). Plane units edges level.

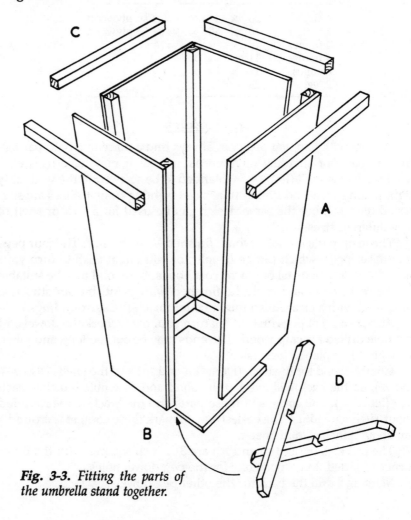

C

A

D

B

Fig. 3-3. *Fitting the parts of the umbrella stand together.*

Fit strips around the top edge (FIG. 3-3C). The corners could be mitered, but for covering with a painted finish they could be overlapped.

Put similar strips round the lower edges (not shown), to give a matching appearance, but for stability, you should add feet. The edging is not essential.

The feet (FIG. 3-3D) are two strips halved together. Their spread should be a little more than the diagonal of the top. If you expect some of the contents to be top-heavy, make the feet longer than that. Bevel the outer ends of the feet. If the floor is uneven, put thin pads under the ends of the feet or use metal or plastic glides. Join the feet with screws downwards through the bottom of the box.

Well round all outer corners and the edges of the top before painting thoroughly.

Materials List for Umbrella Stand

4 sides	28	×	14	×	1/4 or 1/2 plywood
1 bottom	10	×	10	×	1/4 or 1/2 plywood
4 frames	28	×	3/4	×	3/4
4 frames	11	×	3/4	×	3/4
4 edges	17	×	3/4	×	3/4
2 feet	28	×	2	×	1

HALL SHELF

A shelf with hanging pegs can always find a place in a hall, particularly if space for standing furniture is limited. It may have uses elsewhere, but this shelf (FIG. 3-4) is intended to be screwed to the wall fairly high, so long coats and similar things can be hung from it. Sizes are suggested (FIG. 3-5), but the same design can be used for a rack or shelf of very different sizes.

The main parts are solid wood, finished 5/8-inch thick. The four pegs are Shaker pegs, which can be bought, or you might wish to turn your own (FIG. 3-6). Use metal or plastic coat hooks. Softwood may be suitable for the main parts and could be finished with paint, but an attractive hardwood with a clear finish might better match the surroundings.

Prepare a set of pegs first. If you turn your own, check the dowel end in a hole drilled in scrap wood. The ends may be cut too long and taken through, to be planed level later.

Cut the wood for the back (FIGS. 3-5A and 7A) and the shelf (FIGS. 3-5B and 7B), so the back will overlap the shelf and assemble 5 inches each way (FIG. 3-5C). The corners of these parts and the brackets are rounded about 1 1/2-inch radius. The easiest way to mark these corners is around a can about 3 inches in diameter.

The brackets (FIGS. 3-5D and 7C) are 3 1/2-inch squares with the outer corner rounded. Mark positions for the peg dowel holes.

Mark and drill the back for the other peg dowels.

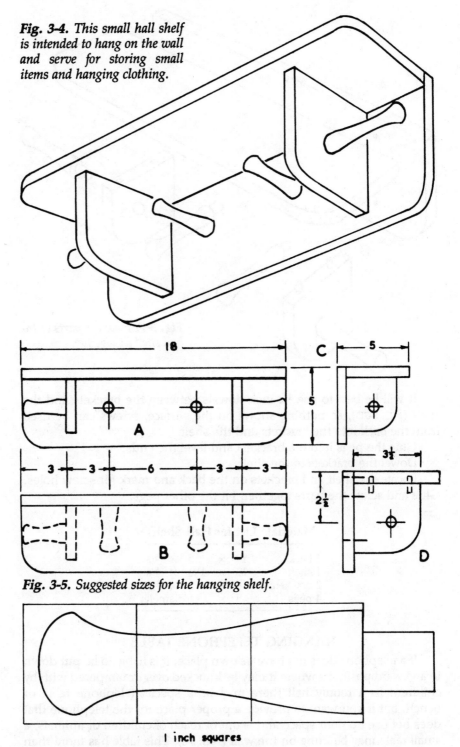

Fig. 3-4. This small hall shelf is intended to hang on the wall and serve for storing small items and hanging clothing.

Fig. 3-5. Suggested sizes for the hanging shelf.

1 inch squares

Fig. 3-6. The shape of pegs for the hall shelf.

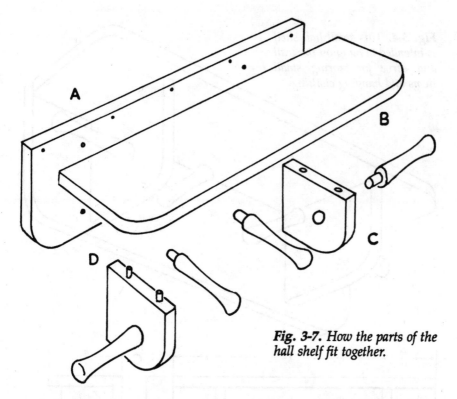

Fig. 3-7. *How the parts of the hall shelf fit together.*

It will be best to use ¼-inch dowels between the brackets and the shelf (FIG. 3-7D), so nothing shows on the surface, screws can be used from the back into the brackets and the shelf.

Glue the pegs into the brackets and level the **ends.**

Dowel the brackets to the shelf.

Locate the shelf and brackets on the back and mark for screw holes. Glue and screw the parts together. Fit the other pegs.

Materials List for Hall Shelf

1 back	19	×	5	×	5/8
1 shelf	19	×	4³/8	×	5/8
2 brackets	6	×	5	×	5/8
4 pegs	5	×	1 diameter		

HANGING TELEPHONE TABLE

If a telephone does not have its own place, it is liable to be put down in awkward positions where it may be knocked over or tampered with by children. In a roomy hall there may be a special telephone table or bench, but if you want to provide a proper place for the telephone that does not use up floor space and is out of reach of children or animals, a small table may be hung on the wall (FIG. 3-8). This table has more than

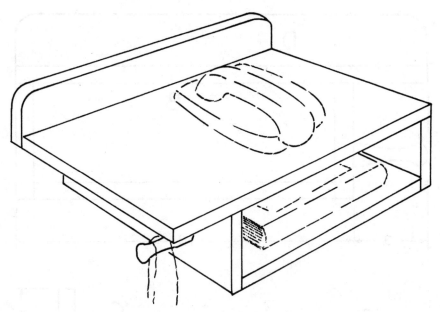

Fig. 3-8. *This wall-mounting telephone shelf has space for directories and a peg for keys or clothing.*

enough area for the instrument, so there is space to write notes and the rack beneath is large enough for more than one directory, plus your own telephone book and maybe a few magazines.

The suggested sizes (FIG. 3-9) should suit most equipment and directories, but measure what you have and modify, if necessary. All of the parts might be solid wood about 5/8-inch finished thickness or use veneered particleboard, with iron-on matching edging where it is cut.

Join with dowels, but counterbored screws with plugs over make a strong construction (FIG. 3-9A). If you have a plug cutter to use in a drill press, the plugs can be cut cross-grained from scrap of the same wood, so they will not be very obvious. Alternatively, you may choose a different wood, so the pattern of plugged screws may be regarded as a design feature.

Cut the table top (FIGS. 3-9B and 10A) to size, allowing for the back to overlap it (FIG. 3-9C).

Make the back (FIGS. 3-9D and 10B) to fit behind it.

Screw the back to the top. In these and other joints you may use #8 × 1 inch or 1¹/₄-inch screws.

Make the two sides (FIGS. 3-9E and 10C) and the bottom (FIGS. 3-9F and 10D) to fit between them.

The top is shown projecting to one side. It could be either way. Drill for one or two Shaker pegs. If you turn your own, make them to project 3 inches with a maximum diameter of ³/₄ inch and a ¹/₂ inch in diameter dowel end.

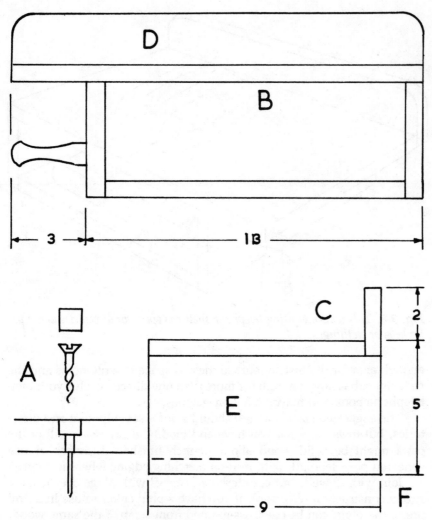

Fig. 3-9. *Sizes of the hanging telephone table.*

Mark out the screw holes carefully, so as to get a symmetrical and regular pattern. A spacing of 3 inches should be satisfactory.

Do all drilling and counterboring at the same time, using a counterbore drill to suit the plugs your cutter produces. It does not matter if the plug diameter is slightly more than that of the screw head.

Assemble all parts with glue and screws. Glue plugs over the screw heads, with grain direction matching. When the glue has set, plane the plugs level and sand all over the hanging table.

If you have used an attractive hardwood, a clear finish may be best, but softwood can be painted. If you use particleboard with a plastic veneer, it will not need treatment, but if it has wood veneer, finish it in the same way as solid wood.

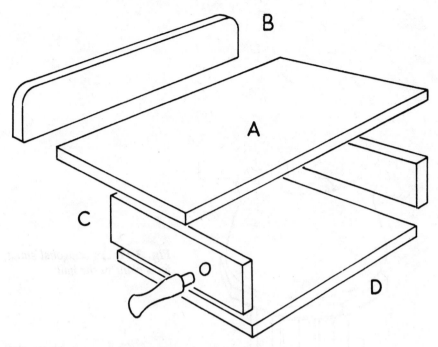

Fig. 3-10. *Parts of the hanging telephone table.*

In most situations two screws through the back may be all you need to hang the table. Check that it is level.

**Materials List for
Hanging Telephone Table**

1 top	17	×	8¹/₄	×	⁵/₈
1 back	17	×	2	×	⁵/₈
2 ends	10	×	4¹/₄	×	⁵/₈
1 bottom	13	×	9	×	⁵/₈

PLANT STAND

A fairly large plant in a pot makes an attractive scene as you open the door onto a hall. For the best effect, the pot should not be too high off the floor a downward view seems to provide a better welcome than having to look upwards. This means the pot should be stood on a stand that gets it into the best position, probably about 12 inches off the floor.

This stand (FIG. 3-11) is octagonal and 12-inches high, suitable for a pot with a base about 10 inches in diameter. If the pot is the same height, foliage will reach about 36 inches from the floor. If you would prefer a different height, this adjustment is easily arranged by altering the length of the pillars. As a bonus, the gap between the pillars will take a folded newspaper or mail waiting to be collected!

Fig. 3-11. *An octagonal stand for a plant in the hall.*

Construction is suggested with ¾-inch plywood and 1-inch dowel rods, all finished with paint. The stand is the same both ways, although you could put feet underneath if that would be better on the hall floor surface.

The only problem is laying out the octagons with the positions of the eight pillars. You might prefer to do this on paper or a scrap piece of plywood; then use that as a template for marking the actual stand ends.

For the size stand suggested (FIG. 3-12), draw squares 11 inches and 8 inches across and mark diagonals (FIG. 3-13A).

Mark half a diagonal length from each corner along each edge of the squares. Join these points, and check that you now have eight equal sides (FIG. 3-13B) in each place.

Draw a 3-inch radius circle, and mark lines across it from the corners of the smaller octagon (FIG. 3-13C); these crossings are the centers for the pillar holes.

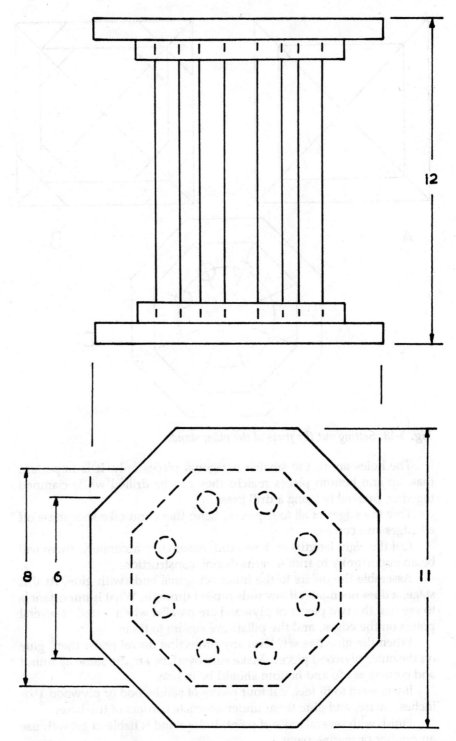

Fig. 3-12. *Sizes of the plant stand.*

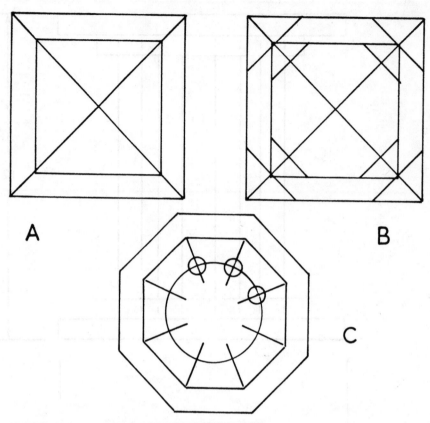

Fig. 3-13. *Setting out the parts of the plant stand.*

The holes are in the smaller octagonal pieces only. It is important that top and bottom pieces match; they can be drilled while clamped together, preferably using a drill press.

True the edges of all four pieces. Sand them and take sharpness off all edges and corners.

Cut the eight lengths of dowel rod, reasonably accurately; there will be an opportunity to trim lengths during construction.

Assemble the pillars to the inner octagonal ends with glue. At this stage, it does not matter if any rods project through. What is important is to see that the two pieces of plywood are parallel when tested at several points on the edges, and the pillars are square to them.

When the glue has set, level any projecting dowel ends; then, glue on the outer plywood pieces. Make sure overlaps are the same all round and corners at top and bottom should be in line.

If you want to fit feet, cut four pieces of solid wood or plywood 1½-inches square, and glue them under alternate corners of the base.

Finish with several coats of paint. If the stand is liable to get wet, use an exterior or marine paint.

2 pieces	11	×	11	×	3/4 plywood
2 pieces	8	×	8	×	3/4 plywood
8 pillars	11	×	1	diameter	

FOLDING HALL TABLE

Many entrance halls are small and there is little room for furniture, yet there is often a need for a table. Even a small rigid table may take up too much room when it is out of use. The answer may be a table which folds back to the wall when out of use. The size will have to be adjusted to suit your requirements and the available space, but this one (FIG. 3-14) is 24-inches long and projects 15 inches from the wall when in use, but drops to only 3-inch thickness (FIG. 3-15A).

If you use this design to make a table of a different size, it should be about twice as long as the top of the supporting bracket, if that is to be

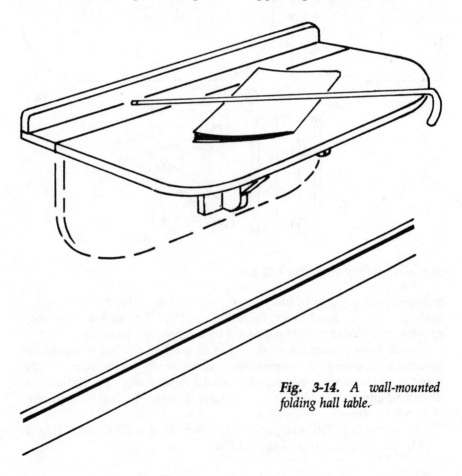

Fig. 3-14. A wall-mounted folding hall table.

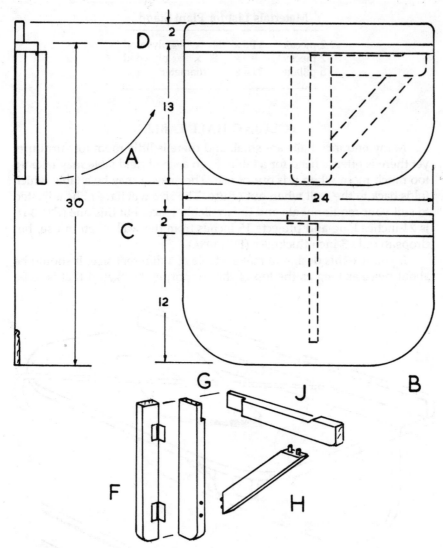

Fig. 3-15. *Sizes of the folding hall table.*

arranged centrally and hidden when folded. If the table has to be relatively shorter, the bracket will be just as effective if mounted off-center, so when it is folded it will be covered by the hanging table top.

It will be best to make all the parts of solid wood, but it would be possible to use veneered particleboard or plywood for the flap, except these would have to be edged. The usual adhesive edging is difficult to fit around curves; therefore, you may have to make the flap with square or beveled corners.

Make the flap (FIG. 3-15B) and the strip behind it (FIG. 3-15C). Edges may be left square, rounded or molded.

The backboard (FIG. 3-15D) could have a similarly molded edge, but it is shown with rounded corners and square edges. Join it to the horizontal strip with glue and screws driven upwards.

The bracket assembly has a strip to attach to the wall (FIG. 3-15F) and the bracket itself, which hinges to it so it can be turned flat to the wall or brought out square to it to support the flap.

The bracket parts could be joined in several ways, but they are shown with a halved joint at the corner (FIG. 3-15G) and dowels on the diagonal (FIG. 3-15H).

Use screws as well as glue in the halved joint. Round outer corners and all exposed edges. Check that the assembled bracket is square, as a sagging table top will be very obvious.

Join the bracket to its upright with two, 2-inch hinges, arranged so when the bracket closes to the wall there is only a minimal space between the wood edges.

It should be satisfactory to use three, 2-inch hinges to join the flap to its strip, but arrange clearance for the bracket to swing back.

Notch the top of the bracket enough to clear the hinge knuckles (FIG. 3-15J). The hinge away from the folded bracket can be 3 inches in from the end. The one the other way should be inside the folded bracket end, and the other as near the center as the swinging bracket allows. When the hinges on the undersurfaces are opened so the flap is up, the edges should meet closely for a good appearance.

Mount the table on the wall so the top surface is 30 inches above the floor. Three screws through the backboard should be enough to hold it, and two screws through the bracket support will be adequate. The bracket does not have to be exactly central, if you can get a better wall attachment to one side of the middle.

No stop for the bracket is shown under the flap. You might find it satisfactory to merely swing the bracket to about a square position, but if you feel there is a need, a small block can be screwed under the flap to limit the movement of the bracket.

The finish should be appropriate to the wood and might match other furniture.

**Materials List for
Folding Hall Table**

1 flap	25	×	12	×	1
2 strips	25	×	2	×	1
4 brackets	13	×	2	×	1

COMBINATION HALL STAND

A hall unit that combines several functions is of value in a small entrance hall. This compact combination unit has a small table top, a rack for canes and umbrellas, a drawer for small items, a shelf and a cupboard. It is raised on a base and occupies a floor space of 12 inches × 18 inches and is 24-inches high. Vary the size to suit your needs or space.

The rather angular shape (FIG. 3-16) suits construction with veneered particleboard, which cannot be satisfactorily veneered in the shop on curved edges. Also, this applies to veneered plywood, but if you make the stand of solid wood you might do some curving of the top and uprights (FIG. 3-17A). The sizes (FIG. 3-17B) are for the angular form, but they are easily adapted.

If you use veneered particleboard, most of the joints could be screwed or doweled. Where screw heads come on visible surfaces they

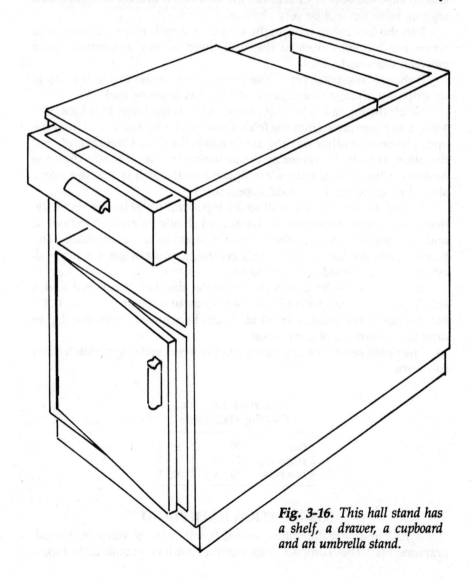

Fig. 3-16. This hall stand has a shelf, a drawer, a cupboard and an umbrella stand.

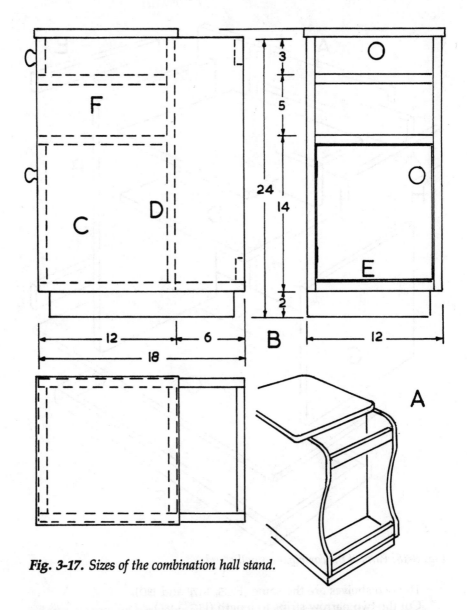

Fig. 3-17. *Sizes of the combination hall stand.*

might be counterbored and the heads covered with plastic plugs. In 3/4-inch particleboard the dowels may be 3/8 inch at about 3-inch intervals on long joints. Do not have fewer than two dowels in short joints.

Start with the pair of sides (FIGS. 3-17C and 18A). Mark on them the positions of other parts.

Make the division (FIGS. 3-17D and 18B). Use this and the sides to control the sizes you cut the other parts.

The bottom (FIGS. 3-17E and 18C) extends the full length of the sides and is the same width as the division.

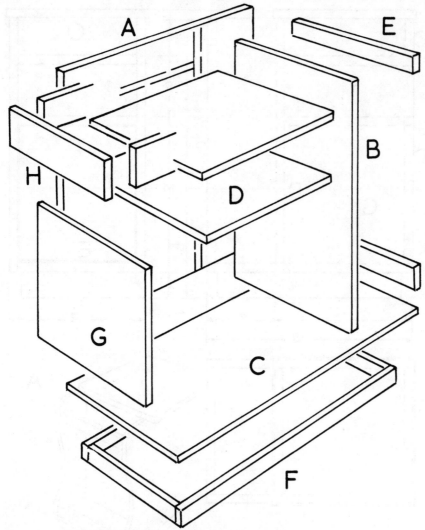

Fig. 3-18. *Parts of the combination hall stand.*

The two shelves are the same (FIGS. 3-17F and 18D).
Cut the two narrow strips to length (FIG. 3-18E).
Veneer all cut edges that will be exposed.
Mark all joints for screws or dowels and drill to suit.
Assemble by joining all the crosswise parts to one side, starting with the division and the bottom, which will steady the assembly; then, add the second side, with all joints pulled together as tightly as possible while the glue sets.
The base (FIG. 3-18F) could be strips of particleboard or solid wood. It would look attractive if made in a contrasting darker color. Make it like an open box standing 1 inch in from the front and ends of the framework. Join it on with pocket screws or screwed blocks inside.

Make the door as a piece to fit inside the opening (FIG. 3-18G). Hinge it at the back and provide a spring or magnetic catch. A knob or handle should come fairly high, so it is easy to reach.

The top should overhang up to 1/4 inch all round. This avoids the need for extreme precision if you try to fit exactly to size.

Make the drawer as a doweled box. Dowel the sides into the front (FIG. 3-18H), but have the back and bottom between the sides.

If the veneer is plastic, it will not need special finishing, but for other surfaces apply a clear finish.

Materials List for Combination Hall Stand

2 sides	24	×	18	×	3/4
1 division	24	×	10¹/2	×	3/4
1 bottom	18	×	10¹/2	×	3/4
2 shelves	12	×	10¹/2	×	3/4
2 strips	11	×	2	×	3/4
1 door	13	×	10¹/2	×	3/4
1 top	12¹/2	×	12¹/2	×	3/4
1 drawer front	11	×	3	×	3/4
2 drawer sides	12	×	3	×	3/4
1 drawer bottom	12	×	9	×	3/4
1 drawer back	11	×	2¹/4	×	3/4

4
Living Room

What constitutes a living room depends on the size and layout of the home. All rooms are intended for living in. For the purpose of this book, a living room is a general-purpose room where the family may congregate. It is used for resting and lounging; also, it may occasionally double as a dining room or den.

Many of the items of furniture described here might also have uses in other rooms. Much depends on your style of living and how much space you have.

MAGAZINE RACK/TABLE

A rack for magazines and newspapers keeps these things tidy and is often positioned beside a chair, where it would also be useful to have a small table for books and refreshments. This unit combines the two functions (FIG. 4-1). In the lower two compartments there is space for a reasonable number of newspapers and magazines. Above this is a top 12 inches × 24 inches.

The suggested construction is plywood for all the lower parts and solid wood for the top. Attractive hardwood with a clear finish for the top might be set off by all the other parts painted. The sizes shown should suit most needs, but if you check such things as armchair height and sizes of the usual papers that come into your home, you can modify the measurements to match. The compartment divisions and the bottom fit through the ends with tenons and these provide rigidity. A scroll saw would be the ideal tool for cutting the shaped parts, but you could also use a band saw or jigsaw.

The two ends (FIGS. 4-2A and 3A) are the key parts which will settle several sizes of other parts. Mark them about centerlines to get them

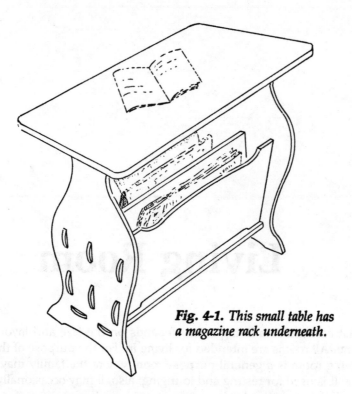

Fig. 4-1. *This small table has a magazine rack underneath.*

symmetrical. Although 3/4-inch plywood is suggested, you might be able to use 1/2-inch plywood if it is stiff.

Cut the outlines; smooth and round the shaped edges. Leave cutting the mortises until you can match them to the tenons.

The three divisions (FIGS. 4-2B and 3B) are basically the same, but only the outer ones need shaped edges. The cutouts in the lower edges allow easy cleaning out of dust or paper scraps.

Make the divisions the same length, and match their tenons with the mortises on the ends; then cut the joints.

Make the bottom (FIGS. 4-2C and 3C) to the same length, with straight rounded edges.

Well round the exposed ends of the tenons.

Put strips across for attaching the top (FIGS. 4-2D and 3D).

Round exposed edges of all parts and sand the surfaces; then glue the parts together. Clamp the joints tightly and see that there is no twist.

The top (FIG. 4-3E) may be one piece of solid wood or several pieces glued to make up the width. It would be possible to use framed plywood (as described for some other projects) or veneered particleboard with suitable edging. A hardwood top could have its edges molded or rounded.

Attach the top with screws up through the end strips. Work with the assembly upside-down and check that the parts are correctly centered.

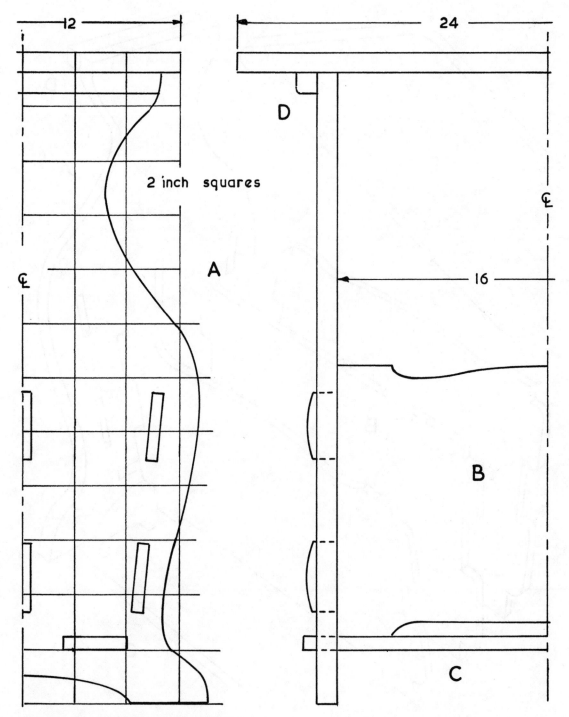

12

2 inch squares

A

24

D

16

B

C

Fig. 4-2. *Sizes of the magazine rack/table.*

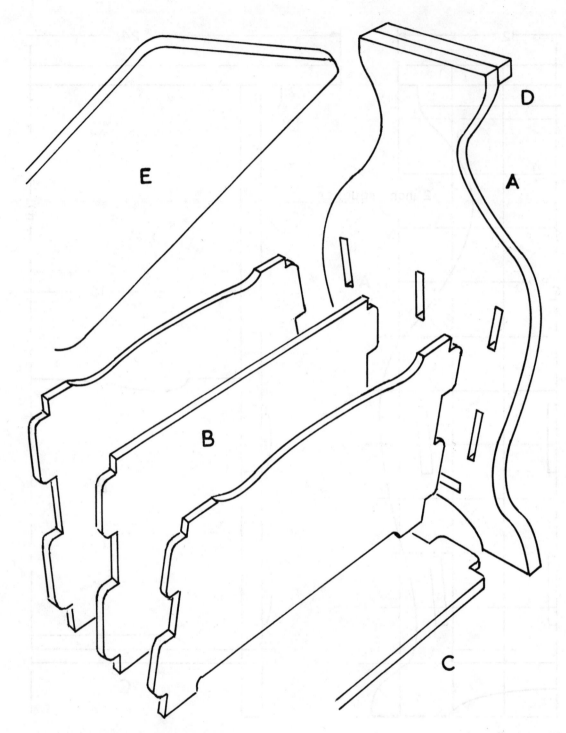

Fig. 4-3. *Parts of the magazine rack/table.*

Complete the project with a clear finish appropriate to the wood on the top and several coats of paint on the lower parts. You could have a lighter color inside the compartments.

Materials List for Magazine Rack/Table

2 ends	26	×	14	×	3/4	plywood
3 divisions	20	×	10	×	1/2	plywood
1 bottom	20	×	10	×	1/2	plywood
2 strips	12	×	3/4	×	3/4	
1 top	25	×	12	×	3/4	

DISPLAY RACK

Some racks intended to display your treasures and collectibles are so enclosed and heavy in appearance that attention is drawn to the stand rather than to what it contains. It is better to have the rack as light and open as is possible, providing there is sufficient strength. This rack (FIG. 4-4) is lightly framed so the items put on it are in view in any direction. Besides display, it could have uses for storing pots and pans in the kitchen. Also, it would take care of books and papers in a den or office, or take folded linen and blankets in a bedroom. In short, you could find a use for it in any room.

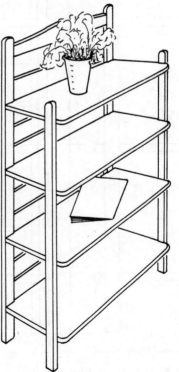

Fig. 4-4. This display rack provides shelves for books, plants and many other items in a living room.

The sizes are for a rack with four shelves (FIG. 4-5) which could be solid wood. They might be plywood with solid wood edging, or you could use veneered particleboard. The rest of the rack should be straight-grained hardwood. For these parts of light section avoid twisting grain, which might lead to warping. The dowel rods across the back should also be hardwood.

The key parts are the shelves (FIGS. 4-5A and 6A), which should be identical.

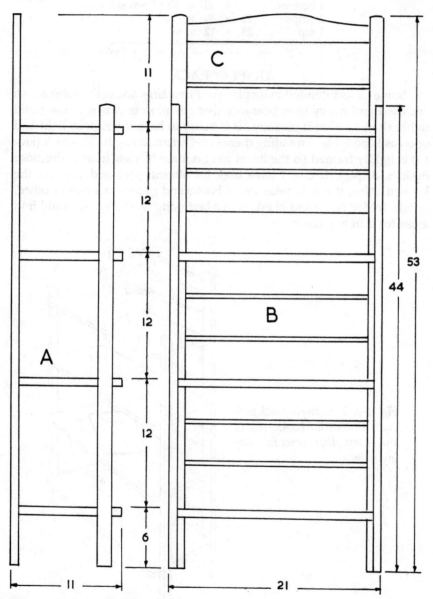

Fig. 4-5. *Sizes of the display rack.*

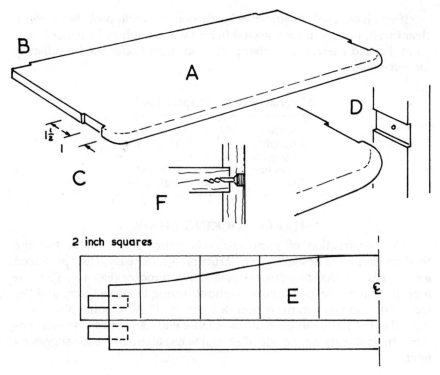

Fig. 4-6. *Details of parts of the display rack.*

To ensure accuracy in locating the uprights, cut notches 1/8-inch deep (FIG. 4-6B) at the rear corners, and 1-inch back from the front edge (FIG. 4-6C).

Round the front corners and round the edges as far back as the notches. Leave the edges square at the ends.

Mark the shelf positions on the uprights together, to avoid slight errors. At each shelf position, cut notches 1/8-inch deep to engage with the shelf notches (FIG. 4-6D).

Mark and drill for dowel rods (FIG. 4-5B) in the rear legs. Space them at 4-inch intervals between the shelves.

Cut the front legs to length and round their tops.

The crossbar at the top of the back (FIG. 4-5C) has a shaped edge (FIG. 4-6E) and the ends are joined to the uprights with dowels.

The crossbar and the shelves set the spacing of the rear uprights. Be careful that the dowel rods are not cut too long, so they prevent the uprights being brought into position. They do not have to reach the bottoms of their holes.

Join the uprights to the shelves with counterbored and plugged screws (FIG. 4-6F). These could be #8 gauge by 1$^{1}/_{4}$-inch screws. The plugs may be cross-grained matching wood, or you might prefer wood of a contrasting color as a design feature.

If you have used an attractive hardwood, you will probably prefer a clear finish, but if you have used different woods, it may be better to use paint. Painted shelves and other parts clear might offer the best display for some items.

Materials List for Display Rack

4 shelves	22 ×	11 ×	3/4
2 uprights	45 ×	1 1/2 ×	3/4
2 uprights	54 ×	1 1/2 ×	3/4
1 crossbar	21 ×	3 ×	3/4
7 rails	22 ×	3/8 diameter	

SHAKER ROCKING CHAIR

The construction of some chairs is rather complicated, but the Shakers simplified designs, so construction is fairly easy. They produced a range of chair designs; this example shows a rocker (FIG. 4-7). The rear legs slope in use to give comfort without having to curve them, and the legs all fit over comparatively narrow runners. There is some plain turning; all of the parts can be made on a lathe with 30 inches between centers. Original seats were made in several ways; alternatives are suggested later.

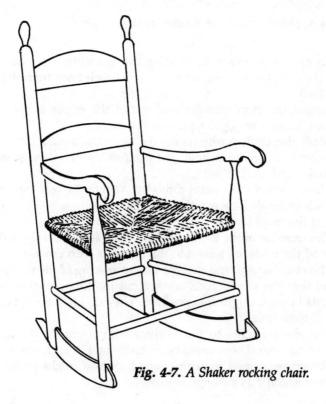

Fig. 4-7. A Shaker rocking chair.

The sizes suggested (FIG. 4-8A) are for a chair suitable for use in a living room or on a porch. All parts need not be made of the same hardwood, but if you mix the woods, there might have to be a painted finish to give an even appearance. Choose a wood with a compact grain that will grip strongly at the joints, where rails have to go into rather shallow holes.

Make the legs first. From 2-inch stock, turn as large a diameter as possible—at least 1³/₄ inches. The Shakers lightly scribed lines round at the hole positions while the wood was in the lathe, so you can do this, too. Aim to leave just the lightest cut showing after sanding.

The rear legs are shown 30-inches long (FIG. 4-8B) to come within the capacity of most lathes, but if your lathe has a long bed, add a further 6 inches so you can have three slats at the back, which will be closer to the

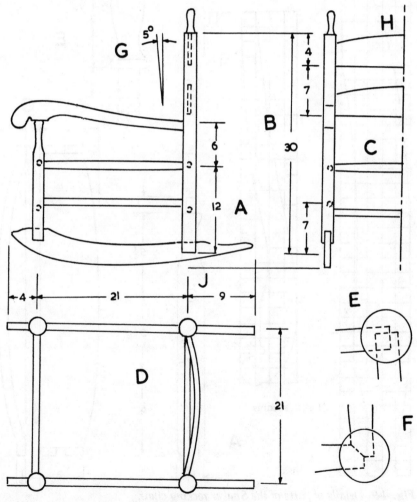

Fig. 4-8. *Main sizes of the Shaker rocking chair.*

original design. All other sizes and arrangements remain the same. Note that the lower rail holes are staggered enough for the holes one way to *just miss* those the other way. At the seat they have to be at the same level both ways.

Turn the front legs (FIG. 4-9A) in a similar way. Do not cut the notches for the runners yet, but round the ends slightly in readiness. Reduce to a slender curve above the seat level, with a ³/₄-inch dowel to join the arm.

The lower rails are parallel ³/₄ inch in diameter. Turn them from wood to match the other parts, or use hardwood dowel rod. The seat rails need to be thicker or they will tend to bend inwards and downwards eventually. Turn them a full 1 inch in diameter for most of their length, but taper towards the ends to fit into ³/₄-inch holes (FIG. 4-8C).

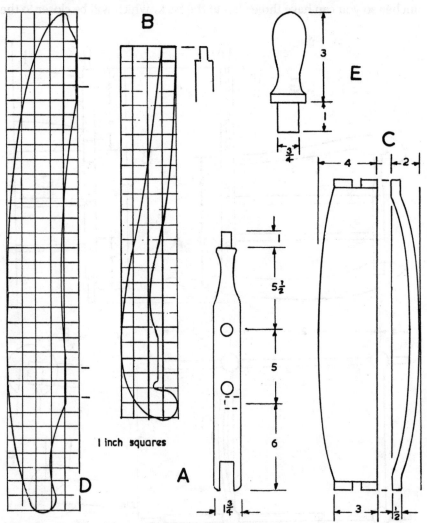

Fig. 4-9. *Details of parts of the Shaker rocking chair.*

The chair is shown with a square seat (FIG. 4-8D), but at this stage you can check what sizes you need and alter width or depth to suit. You could make the back narrower than the front, but in a rocker this adjustment was never as much as might be allowed in an ordinary chair.

Check rail hole sizes by drilling scrap wood first and trying the rails. Strength will depend on a good fit. At lower rail level drill so the holes overlap (FIG. 4-8E), but get all depths the same. At seat level, drill so the rails meet and can be mitered (FIG. 4-8F). Although the chair is intended to settle at an angle of about 5 degrees when unoccupied (FIG. 4-8G), all parts are square to each other. Use a drill press or a guide to ensure that holes are drilled squarely.

The arms (FIG. 4-9B) are prominent in the finished chair, so they must match and be well finished if they are to look right. Perform steps to make both at the same time. Allow for flat surfaces that will be drilled for the dowels on the front legs, and cut tenons to fit into the rear legs.

After cutting the profiles, well-round the shaped surfaces, particularly at the front. Delay drilling for the dowels on the front legs until the rails have been joined to the legs, to allow for slight variations during assembly.

The back slats (FIG. 4-8H) should match the lengths of the back rails. They have to be given a curve for comfort (FIG. 4-9C). It would be possible to bend thin wood round a former, but that method is more suited to quantity production. In this case it may be better to cut from solid wood. Allow for tenons at the ends. Smooth all surfaces and round edges. Cut matching mortises in the legs.

Turn finials, or decorative tips, for the tops of the rear legs (FIG. 4-9E). Drill the legs for the finial dowels and glue them in.

Do not make the runners (FIG. 4-8J) less than 1-inch thick, as they have to spread the load on the floor covering. Cut the outline (FIG. 4-9D), leaving flat surfaces where the legs have to fit. Take the sharpness off corners, but do not round the edges much. Cut slots in the legs to fit over the runners.

You have two options: put together the two side assemblies first and then join them, or assemble the back and front before completing the chair frame. It is probably easier to make up the two sides first. Check for squareness and see that legs are parallel. Match one side over the other as you assemble them. When the rails and arms have been fitted, join in the runners. Besides gluing them in place, drill for 3/8-inch dowels across the joints.

As you assemble the other way, besides checking squareness and parallel legs, stand away and look from front to back to ensure there is no twist in the chair. Front and rear legs should be in line with each other when viewed from a distance.

The chair frame could be finished with paint, that may be your best choice if you have used woods of different colors. Alternatively, the chair would look lighter and show your skill better, as well as probably be a more suitable match for other furniture, if given a clear polish or varnish finish.

Rush Pattern Seat

Original rush seats were made from natural rushes, used damp and twisted into rope as the seating progressed. This requires practice, and it can be rather messy. Suitable rushes might be difficult to find. Fortunately, there are satisfactory alternatives, with several cord-like materials, both natural and synthetic. One of these is seagrass, in the form of a rope under 1/4 inch in diameter which, in its undyed form, looks very much like rush. As this is in long lengths and can be used dry, weaving a rush pattern seat becomes a fairly simple task.

Prepare a few shuttles to wind the seagrass on (FIG. 4-10A); cut them from plywood or thin solid wood. Towards the end of forming a seat you need a wood needle (FIG. 4-10B) to pull the line through. Make this of hardwood, as you might have to lever with it.

The finished chair seat shows a pattern, above and below, with lines of seagrass pointing inwards to a mitered joint (FIG. 4-7); how this is obtained appears a mystery. However, the actual technique of making the pattern is simple.

With a shuttle full of line, knot an end and tack it inside one rail. Take the line over the adjoining rail, back around the leg to go over the first rail, so the shuttle is brought under in the direction of the next corner (FIG. 4-10C). That is the entire action, to be repeated at the next leg (FIG. 4-10D) and so on. When you get round to the first corner again, put the new turns inside the first. Continue round-and-round the chair until the seat is filled.

Maintain a good tension all the time. If you have a helper, work at opposite sides, with one person holding the tension gained while the other works the line around the next corner. You will see the pattern build up at the corners, while the lines between corners will become hidden. When you join in new line, have the knots here, where they will not show. Press the turns close together on the rails and see that the pattern, as it builds up, is square to the rails.

If the seat is square, the pattern should build up equally both ways. If you have made the frame wider at the front than the back, go round the front legs twice occasionally as you progress, until the remaining bare wood at the front is the same as at the back; then continue normally.

If the seat is wider than it is deep, you will fill the side rails before the other rails. This may also happen in one direction with a tapered seat. When you have as many turns as you can put on covering the side rails, fill back and front rails by a figure-eight action (FIG. 4-10E) until the rails are tightly covered.

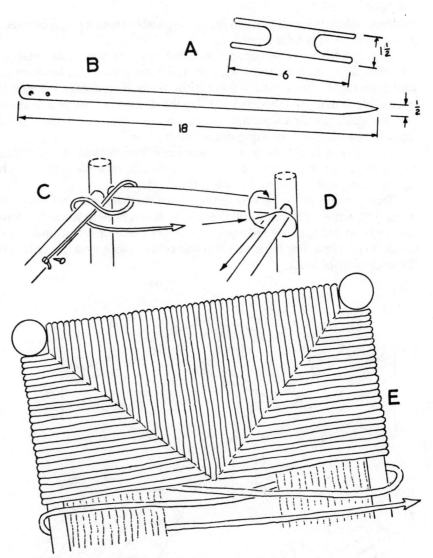

Fig. 4-10. *How to weave a rush-pattern seat.*

As you progress you will reach a stage where you will not be able to pass a shuttle through the center. Use a loose end as far as possible; then for the final turns, put the line in the holes in the needle. Use its point to lever a gap. When you have packed in as many turns as possible, tack the line under a rail and hide the end inside the pattern below.

Checker Tape Seat

Some Shaker chairs had seats formed of cloth tape, woven in a checker pattern. They wove the tape themselves as a fairly coarse material about 1-inch wide. If you can get a comparable tape, it could be used. It should have very little stretch.

The tape has to be wrapped over the frame one way; then wrap in the other direction over-and-under, to make the pattern underneath as well as on top. To get a good tension without reaching a stage where it is impossible to make the final tucks, judge the degree of slackness to allow in the wraps in the first direction. This procedure depends on the type of tape, its stretch and your experience with it.

The only special tool is a pointed stick longer than the distance across the chair. You might use a seagrass needle or a piece of 1/2-inch square wood with rounded corners (FIG. 4-11A).

Tack the end of the tape securely under the back rail and wrap on turns (FIG. 4-11B) sufficient to fill the width. It might help to get the tension right to put the pointed stick or a larger piece of wood under the turns. To join in a new tape, tack the end of one piece over the other on the underside of a rail.

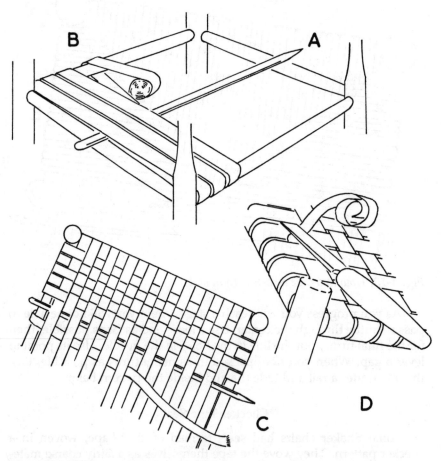

Fig. 4-11. *Making an interwoven tape seat.*

In the other direction you cannot use the tape in a roll, but you will have to use a convenient length; then join in another by tacking under a rail. Use the pointed stick to lift alternate turns, so you can tuck the tape across (FIG. 4-11C). Do the same on the return underneath. After each set of tucks, pull tight and press the tape along the rails as close as possible to the previous turn. Towards the end you will not be able to use the pointed stick across, but will have to lever the turns one at a time. A broad screwdriver or a blunt chisel will do this (FIG. 4-11D). Tack the final end underneath.

In an original seat of this type, the space between might have been filled with cloth as padding. In a modern version it would be better to use a slab of plastic foam, if you wish to add padding; it could be held in place with adhesive tape while the tape seat pattern is worked over it.

Materials List for Shaker Rocking Chair

2 legs	2	×	2	×	32
2 legs	2	×	2	×	19
4 rails	23	×	1 diameter		
4 rails	23	×	3/4 diameter		
2 slats	2	×	4	×	23
2 arms	1¹/₄	×	4	×	28
2 runners	1	×	5	×	36
2 finials	1¹/₄	×	1¹/₄	×	7

OCTAGONAL COFFEE TABLE

This little table (FIG. 4-12) shows a Victorian influence, with legs simplified from the popular cabriole type. The height (FIG. 4-13A) is suitable for chairside use, or it could serve as a base for drinks among a group of chairs.

It should be made of solid wood, although you could use plywood or particleboard for the top, preferably with a solid wood edging. To be authentic, construction should be with one of the common furniture hardwoods. A solid wood top will have to be made by gluing several boards together. As much as possible, have the grain of the top surface of the boards in the same direction, so they can be planed and sanded without the risk of tearing up.

Glue sufficient boards to make the top. Trim to an 18-inch square. There are two ways of marking this as a regular octagon. Firstly, draw a circle to touch the edges of the square; then draw lines at 45 degrees to touch this at each corner. Secondly, draw diagonals to the square; measure half a diagonal from each corner in both directions along the edges. Join these points. In both cases, measure the eight sides to see that all are the same. The diagonal lines you mark should be the same length as the spaces left along the original sides.

Cut the top to shape. Leave the edges square, but the table will look better if you mold them. A partially curved section (FIG. 4-14A) looks bet-

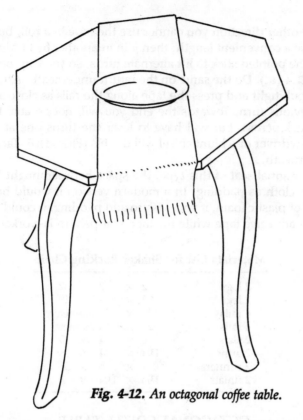

Fig. 4-12. *An octagonal coffee table.*

ter than a full semicircle. Two other possible moldings are shown (FIG. 4-14B and C). Much depends on your available molding cutters.

Make the four legs (FIG. 4-14D). It will help to get them all the same if you make a hardboard template first and use that to mark the wood. Shape the curved parts of the legs into a slightly rounded section (FIG. 4-14E).

Make the two crossbars (FIGS. 4-13B and 14F) the same, except for the cuts for the halving joint at the center (FIG. 4-13G). It is important that this joint is cut squarely and the meeting surfaces with the legs are also square.

Join the crossbars to their legs with dowels (FIG. 4-14H). Check that both assemblies match and are without twists; then, drill for dowels on the top edges and join the assemblies together, preferably with the top surfaces downwards on a flat surface, so they are kept flat and square.

Locate the inverted leg assembly on the underside of the top and mark for dowel holes.

Do all final sanding before joining the top to the rails and legs. To obtain the best resistance to warping, arrange the grain direction of the top as shown (FIG. 4-13C).

Stain, if you wish, and apply a clear finish.

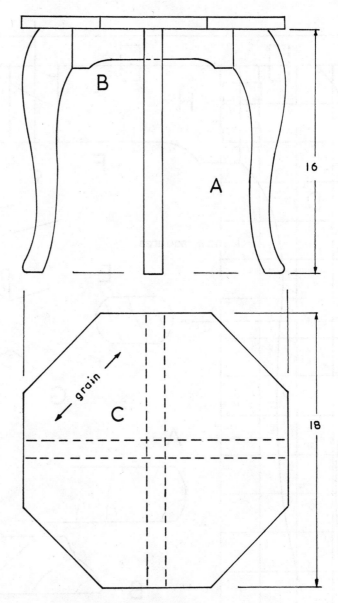

Fig. 4-13. Sizes of the octagonal coffee table.

Materials List for Octagonal Coffee Table

1 top	18 ×	18 ×	3/4
4 legs	16 ×	3½ ×	1¼
2 rails	12 ×	2½ ×	1¼

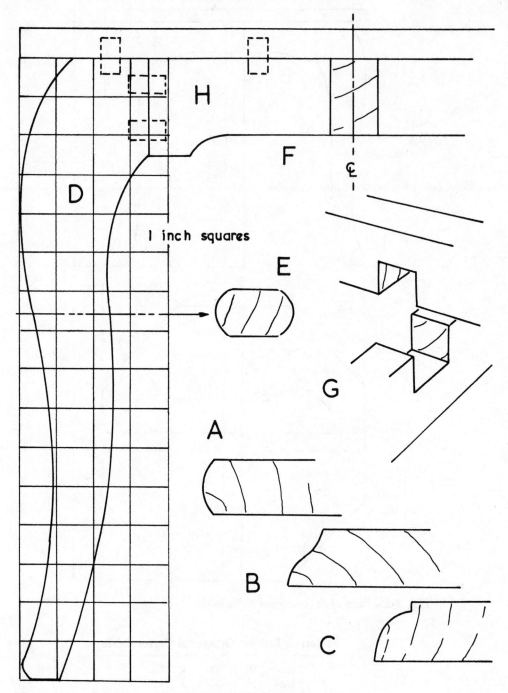

Fig. 4-14. *Details of parts of the octagonal coffee table.*

1 inch squares

UNDER-WINDOW SHELVES

The space under a window, which is often wasted, is a good position to have a block of shelves. These shelves may be used as a bookcase or somewhere to display items. If the height is suitable, the top of the block of shelves may be used as a seat, with or without cushions. Sizes may be arranged to make the best use of available space, but for a low block of shelves (FIG. 4-15) some possible sizes are suggested (FIG. 4-16). These give roomy storage space and a top which is not too high for sitting on, if it is not to be used for display.

Fig. 4-15. *These shelves are intended to be used under a window.*

Solid wood construction is suggested, although you could use plywood with solid wood edging at the front, or veneered particleboard with iron-on edging. It would be possible to use dado joints in several places, if you wish, but the instructions are for the use of dowels throughout. With 3/4-inch wood, use 3/8-inch dowels, with not less than two in each joint and about 2-inch spacing in wider boards.

Mark out the pair of ends first (FIGS. 4-16A and 17A), with the positions of the shelves and back strips. Shape the bottoms.

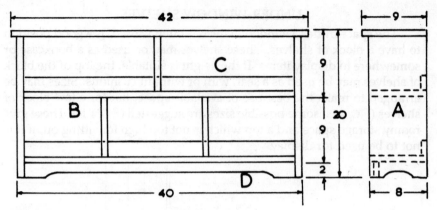

Fig. 4-16. *Sizes of the under-window shelves.*

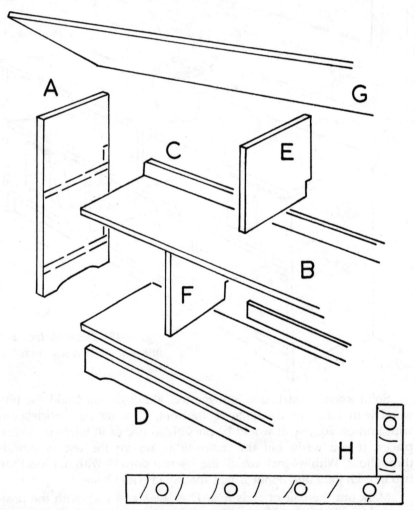

Fig. 4-17. *How the parts of the under-window shelves fit together.*

Cut the two shelves with squared ends to fit between the case ends (FIGS. 4-16B and 17B).

Cut the back strips to the same length (FIGS. 4-16C and 17C).

Join the strips to their shelves, either with glue and dowels or by screwing from below. A 6-inch spacing will serve for either method.

Make the base (FIGS. 4-16D and 17D); cut away to match the ends. Join it to the bottom shelf with dowels.

Use the setting out on an end to get the sizes of the divisions (FIGS. 4-17E and F), with notches to fit over the rear strips.

Make the top to fit level with the case ends at the back, but to overhang about 1 inch at the front and ends (FIG. 4-17G).

Mark and drill dowel holes for all the joints (FIG. 4-17H).

Assemble the shelves to the ends, and pull the joints tight; then add the top. The assembly should pull itself square, but check that it stands level without twist.

Round projecting corners and take sharpness off edges before applying your chosen finish.

Materials List for Under-window Shelves

2 ends	20	×	8	×	3/4
2 shelves	42	×	8	×	3/4
1 top	44	×	9	×	3/4
1 base	42	×	2	×	3/4
3 divisions	9	×	8	×	3/4

TELEVISION STAND WITH MAGAZINE RACK

With television there is usually a video recorder and a large number of tapes, all needing storage. You will also have newspapers and magazines that would benefit from a neat storage. This unit functions (FIG. 4-18) as a stand for the television set, and storage below for video equipment, with racks at each end for magazines and newspapers. The unit may be on casters or glides, so it can be moved about or turned to give the best angle of viewing.

Arrange the sizes to suit your own equipment, but some sizes are suggested as a guide (FIG. 4-19). If you alter sizes very much, keep the proportions so the unit will be stable—have a fairly broad base in relation to the height.

As described, construction is almost completely of veneered particleboard, which may already have a satisfactory finish, or you might treat it as wood, with a clear finish. In any case, cut and exposed edges must be covered with iron-on veneer strips. It would be possible to use plywood of the same thickness; either edge it with solid wood, or give it a painted finish. Solid wood is possible, but it could be expensive. Also, you would have to glue pieces to make up the width.

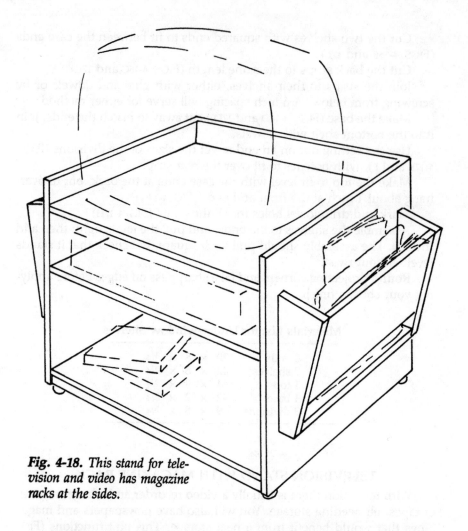

Fig. 4-18. *This stand for television and video has magazine racks at the sides.*

All of the joints may be doweled, except in some places where their heads will not show; then, you can use screws. If you choose to use screws elsewhere in place of dowels, their heads must be counterbored and covered with wood or plastic plugs, which may be regarded as a decorative feature. Use 3/8-inch dowels and space them about 3 inches apart on most joints. For narrow parts, do not have fewer than two dowels.

Cut the pair of ends (FIGS. 4-19A and 20A). Mark on them the positions of the other parts. The shelves come level at the front, but at the back edge they are covered with upright strips. The base is set back 1/4 inch.

The three shelves are the same (FIGS. 4-19B and 20B). Allow for the covering pieces at the back.

Make the base strip (FIG. 4-20C) the same length as the shelves.

Make the top back piece (FIGS. 4-19C and 20D) to cover the back of the shelf and come level with the top of the sides. The one behind the middle shelf (FIGS. 4-19D and 20E) may be the same, unless you would prefer it deeper to retain something larger on the shelf.

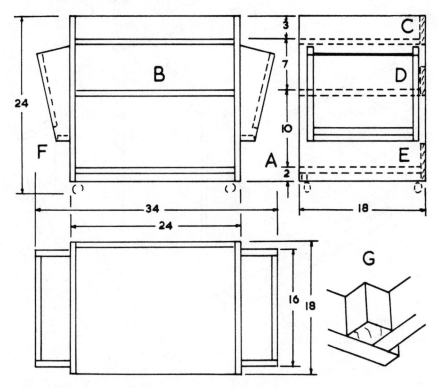

Fig. 4-19. *Sizes of the television stand with magazine racks.*

The piece behind the bottom shelf (FIGS. 4-19E and 20F) should stand high enough above the shelf and reach to the lower edges of the sides.

Mark and drill all these parts for dowels. A few widely-spaced parts may go between the base and its shelf. Do not assemble these parts yet, as the magazine racks are more easily fitted to the sides before the main parts are assembled.

Mark out and cut the sides of the magazine racks (FIGS. 4-19F and 21A). These sizes should be adequate, but if you want to accommodate special papers or books there is room for larger racks. The top outer corner is shown at 90 degrees.

The piece across the front of each rack (FIG. 4-21B) does not reach the bottom (FIG. 4-21C), so there is space for cleaning out.

Join these parts with dowels, while the back edges are on a flat surface, to prevent twisting.

Mark the positions of the magazine racks on the outside of the sides and drill through for screws from the inside. Glue and screw on the racks.

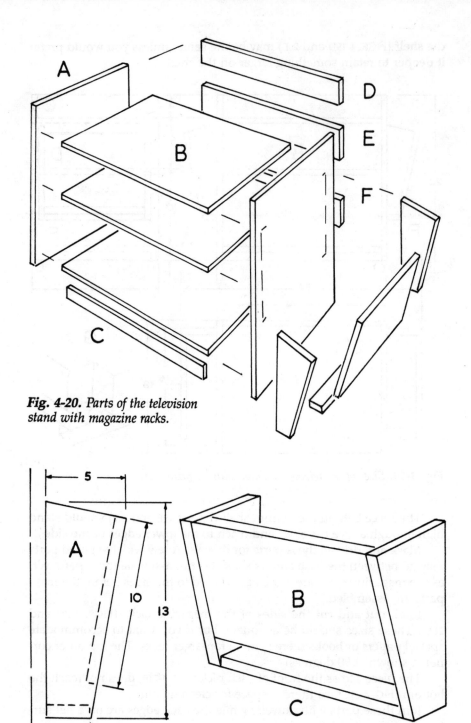

Fig. 4-20. *Parts of the television stand with magazine racks.*

Fig. 4-21. *Details of a magazine rack.*

Prepare sufficient dowels for all the joints. Join the back strips to their shelves and the base to the bottom shelf. Allow the glue to set in these joints before joining to the ends. Position the assembly on a flat surface when you join on the sides. Clamp tightly; the parts should pull themselves square without twist.

The arrangements for fitting casters or glides will depend on their design, but for most types it should be satisfactory to increase the corner areas below the bottom shelf with blocks screwed in the corners (FIG. 4-19G). Make their sizes to suit the casters.

Remove any excess glue and apply your chosen finish.

Materials List for Television Stand with Magazine Rack
(All 3/4-inch veneered particleboard)

2 sides	24	×	18
3 shelves	24	×	18
3 backs	25	×	5
1 base	24	×	1 1/4
4 rack sides	14	×	6
2 rack fronts	16	×	10
2 rack bottoms	16	×	2

GALLERIED DISPLAY RACK

If you bring home souvenirs of the places you visit or have collections of similar small items to display, shelves on the wall will not only show your collection, but also serve as a decorative feature. Items with flat bases, such as cups and vases, may stand without much risk of falling off, but plates will look best if stood on edge; this means that you have to provide a stop at the front to hold them in place. It is an advantage if the rack itself is decorative, and in this case (FIG. 4-22), the fronts of the shelves have galleries with small turned spindles.

You can turn the spindles on the smallest lathe, but if you buy them, it would be advisable to get them first, so rack sizes can be modified to match the suggested sizes (FIGS. 4-23A and 24A). Other parts of the rack are made from wood mostly 1/2-inch thick, which may be hardwood or softwood. Avoid cutting joints into this thin wood by using a combination of screws and pins with glue, where parts meet. Loads on the assembly should not be great.

Prepare the wood to a uniform 1/2-inch thickness. If you are using softwood, a few moderate knots in the broad pieces may be acceptable, but the narrower parts should be free from knots and straight-grained.

Mark the wood for the sides with shelf positions. Draw and cut the outlines (FIG. 4-24B). Remove saw marks and lightly round the shaped edges. The notch at the top (FIG. 4-24C) should fit the piece of wood used for the back (FIGS. 4-23B and 24D).

Make the two shelves the same. Glue a strip 3/4 inch × 1 inch to the front edge and cleats under the ends (FIG. 4-24E). The front strips should

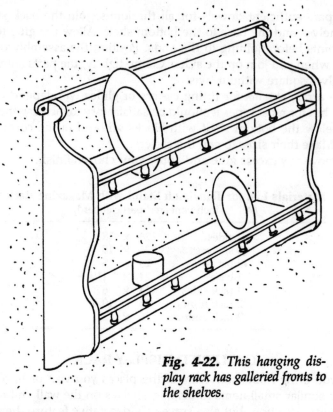

Fig. 4-22. *This hanging display rack has galleried fronts to the shelves.*

match the depth of the end cleats. There should be no need for pins or screws in these joints.

Drill the cleats for fine screws (FIG. 4-24F) that will be driven from inside into the rack ends.

Make the rails that come above the spindles (FIG. 4-23C). They are 1/2-inch × 3/4-inch sections with the top surface rounded, but it will be easier to drill for the spindle holes while the top is flat.

Mark and drill the holes for the spindle dowel ends in the shelves and rails altogether, so the spindles will be uniformly spaced and upright.

Glue the spindles in place; then glue and screw from inside the shelf cleats to the ends. Although glue does not hold very well on end grain, the spindles provide stiffness for the rails. Glue alone on their ends should be sufficient, but if you are doubtful about them being secure, drive pins through the ends; then, set them below the surface and cover with stopping.

Make the back strip (FIG. 4-23B). Round its extending ends and drill for the screws which will hang the rack on the wall (FIG. 4-24G).

Screw the back to the sides to complete the assembly.

Stain and apply whatever finish you prefer.

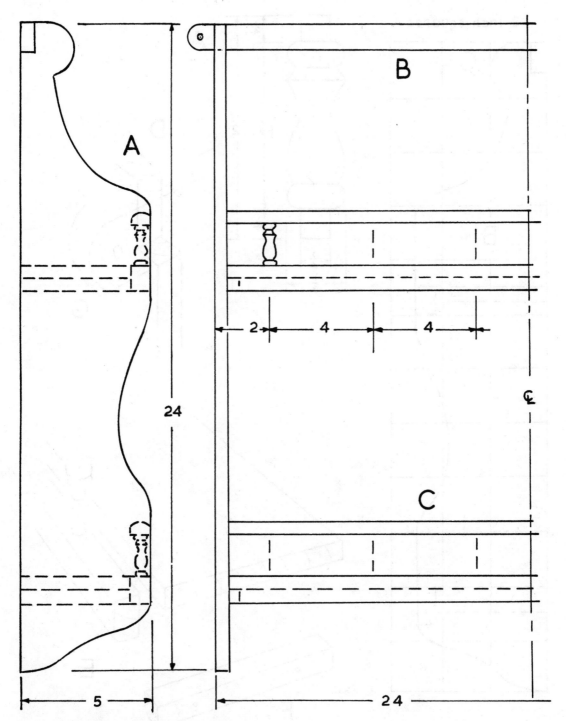

Fig. 4-23. Sizes of the galleried display rack.

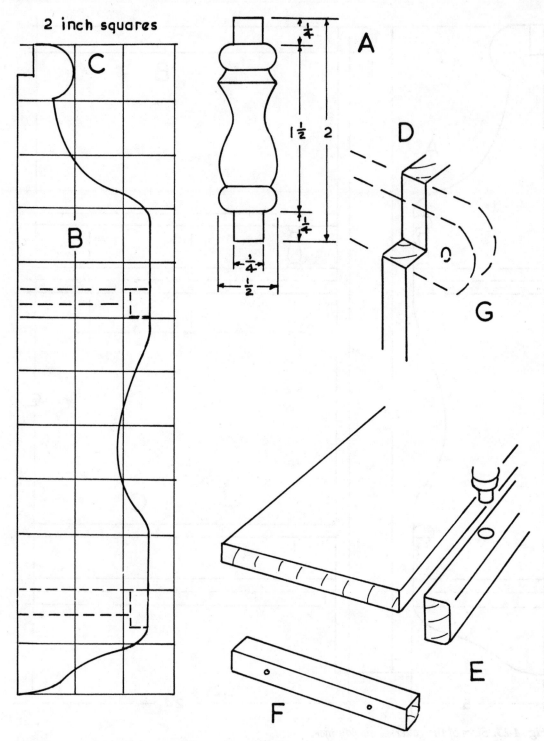

Fig. 4-24. *Sizes of parts of the galleried display rack.*

Materials List for Galleried Display Rack

2 sides	26	×	5	×	1/2
2 shelves	26	×	4 1/4	×	1/2
2 shelf fronts	26	×	1	×	3/4
4 cleats	5	×	1/2	×	1/2
2 rails	26	×	3/4	×	1/2
12 spindles	3	×	1/2 diameter		

EASY CHAIR

For relaxing, a fully overstuffed chair might seem the ultimate in comfort, but making it is more an exercise in upholstery than a woodworking project, as the wood is usually almost entirely hidden. For a basic woodworking project, you can make a chair which is sprung and uses loose cushions to achieve almost the same degree of comfort. Moreover, it can show your woodworking skill instead of obscuring it.

This chair (FIG. 4-25) is not as complicated to make as it might first appear, if the step-by-step instructions are followed. Note that it is built up of several independently-made units; there is a frame for the seat and another for the back, both carrying rubber webbing to support cushions. These join together and fit between the two sides, which are made completely before assembly.

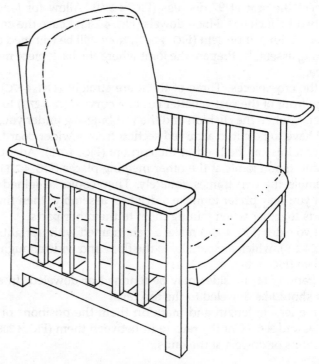

Fig. 4-25. *An easy chair with loose cushions.*

Finger joints are advised for some parts, but elsewhere you could use mortise and tenon joints or dowels. Construction should be of hardwood; although, if you want to match pine furniture, softwood is possible. A clear finish on the wood and suitably-colored cushions should make an attractive piece of furniture.

Sizes (FIGS. 4-26 and 27) are based on two cushions, 24-inches square and about 3-inches thick. Get rubber or plastic foam cut to this size and cover it yourself; or you might be able to buy cushions close to these sizes. Remember to adapt the suggested sizes to suit. In any case, you might find it worthwhile to check the general sizes with your needs, or compare then with a favorite existing chair. Slight alterations to the dimensions will not affect the methods of construction.

Besides deciding on the cushions to be made or bought, get the rubber webbing and the metal clips for its ends (FIG. 4-29A). A clip is squeezed over the cut end of webbing (FIG. 4-29B); then it is pressed into a groove in the wood. The groove may be cut square (FIG. 4-27A), but if you can cut it at an angle (FIG. 4-27B) that will give it a slightly better grip (FIG. 4-29C). If you get the clips first, tailor the groove size to suit, although a probable size is shown (FIG. 4-27A).

Start with the two frames that make the seat and back (FIG. 4-28A). Cut the wood long enough for the two pairs of sides (FIG. 4-28B and C). Cut grooves to take the webbing clips.

Mark the positions of the crosspieces. The bottom of the back side pieces meet the seat at 97 degrees (FIG. 4-28D). Allow for tenons (FIG. 4-28E) or two 1/2-inch or 5/8-inch dowels (FIG. 4-28F). Leave the ends of the seat sides overlong at present (FIG. 4-28G); they will be trimmed to the leg edge during assembly. Prepare the joint where the back piece meets each side piece.

Cut the crosspieces. Three of them are straight (FIG. 4-27C), but the one at the front of the seat is better cut to a curve (FIG. 4-27D) to give you leg clearance when the cushion and the webbing sag under your weight. This will have to be cut to a curved section from a wider board.

Finger joints can be used at the corners (FIG. 4-27E). Adapt these to mortise and tenon joints at the other meeting places (FIG. 4-27F).

Assemble the two frames squarely. They could be joined together now, but you may prefer to make a dry trial assembly; then finally glue these parts together when joining them to the other parts.

The two sides (FIG. 4-26A) make a pair, framed with uprights and flat tops (FIG. 4-26B), which are parallel to the floor and wide enough to take a cup or plate (FIG. 4-30).

The framing of the sides may be tenoned or doweled. In any case, the arms should be doweled to the top rails.

Cut the legs to length and mark on them the positions of the rails (FIGS. 4-26C and 30A). Cut the rails to fit between them (FIG. 4-30B), allowing for tenons or dowels at the ends.

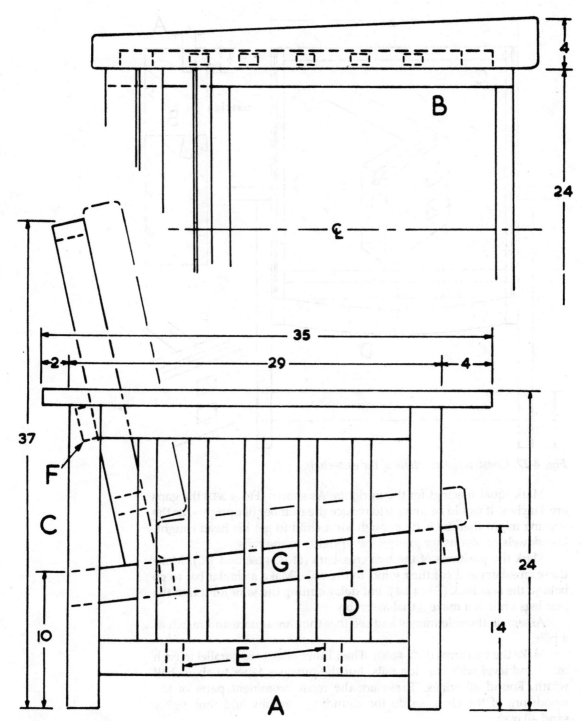

Fig. 4-26. *Sizes of the easy chair.*

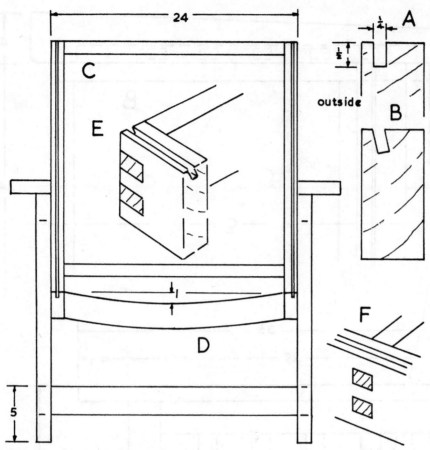

Fig. 4-27. *Constructional details of the easy chair.*

Mark equal spacings for the uprights. As shown (FIG. 4-26D) the gaps are 3 inches. It would be unwise to reduce the number of uprights, as the spacing might then be wide enough for a child to get his head caught. Use dowels or tenons for joining the uprights to the rails.

Mark the positions of the two crossbars (FIGS. 4-26E and 30C). Make these crossbars and cut their joints to the rails. Make a similar bar to go behind the seat back (FIG. 4-26F), but delay cutting the joint for it into the rear legs until you make a trial assembly.

Assemble the side frames and see that they are square and match as a pair.

Make the two arms (FIG. 4-30D). Their inner edges are parallel to each other and level with the side rails, but the outsides taper to about half width. Round all edges. These are the most prominent parts of the woodwork of the chair, so do the rounding carefully and thoroughly **sand** all over.

Join the arms to their side frames with 1/2-inch dowels at about a 6-inch spacing.

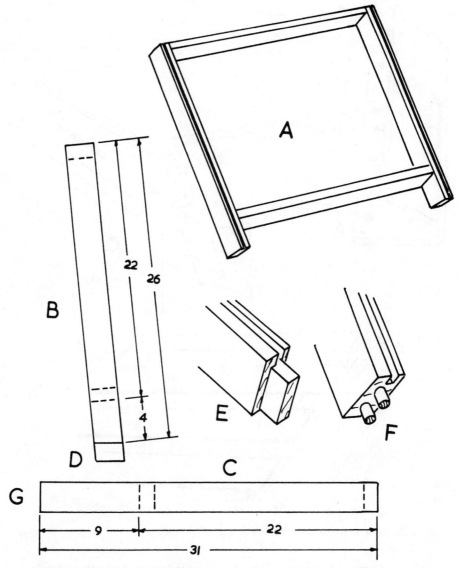

Fig. 4-28. *Parts of the easy chair.*

Put the seat and back assembly against one side frame in the position indicated (FIG. 4-26G). This will allow you to mark on the rear leg the position of the crossbar that supports the seat back (FIG. 4-26F). You may have to move the assembly, or alter the tilt of the back slightly to get this bar positioned. When you have it correct, mark this joint and where the seat side crosses the legs. Transfer the markings to the other side frame. Cut the mortises or drill for dowels for the rear crossbar. Drill for screws to be driven from inside the seat sides into the legs. Two or three screws with glue at each place should be sufficient.

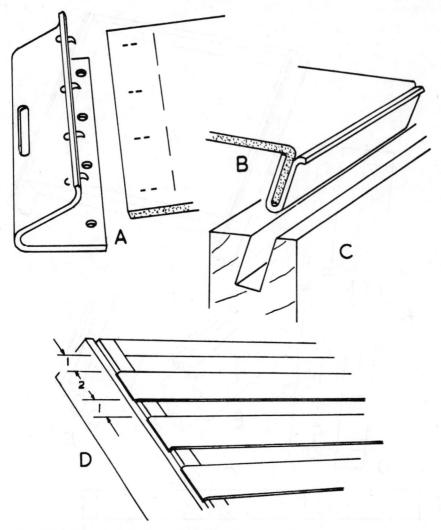

Fig. 4-29. *How to fit rubber webbing to the easy chair.*

Have the crossbars ready. Glue the joints between the back and seat frames. Screw and glue the seat frames to the side frame legs, and at the same time join the crossbars to the sides. The frames should pull the chair square, but check that it stands level without twist. Screw the rear crossbar to the back frame. Trim the rear ends of the seat frame at the legs.

The spacing and tension of the webbing depends on its choice. If it is not very elastic, you might space wider and not stretch as much in fitting as you would with more flexible material. With the usual 2-inch rubber webbing you may space pieces 1-inch apart across both frames (FIG. 4-29D).

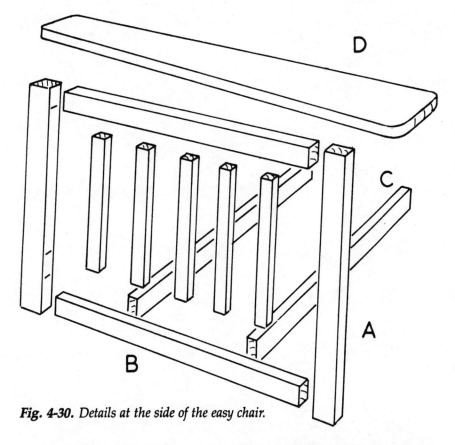

Fig. 4-30. *Details at the side of the easy chair.*

To get the tension you want, experiment with one piece; then cut all pieces to the same length. On this 24-inch width of frame, you will probably cut the webbing between 1-inch and 2-inches short of the distance between the grooves. Because there is more weight on the seat than the back, make the seat pieces shorter than the back pieces (for more tension), but keep all pieces in a frame the same. Cut sufficient pieces of webbing, and fit the end clips tightly; squeezing in a vise is suggested.

Apply stain and a clear finish to the woodwork before finally fitting the webbing and adding the cushions to complete the chair.

Materials List for Easy Chair

2 seat frame sides	35	×	$2^1/_2$	×	$1^1/_4$
2 back frame sides	30	×	$2^1/_2$	×	$1^1/_4$
3 frame crosspieces	26	×	$2^1/_2$	×	$1^1/_4$
1 front frame crosspiece	26	×	$3^1/_2$	×	$1^1/_4$
4 legs	25	×	$2^1/_2$	×	$1^1/_4$
4 side rails	29	×	$2^1/_2$	×	$1^1/_4$
10 side uprights	20	×	$1^1/_2$	×	$3/_4$
2 arms	37	×	4	×	1

5
Dining Room

One activity that takes place in every home at frequent intervals is eating. Certain furniture is related to this. According to the size and layout of the house, the dining room may also be the living room, or the dining area may be part of the kitchen. For the purpose of this book, it is assumed that there is a separate dining room. Even if there is not, there will be furniture associated with meals, from the quick snack to a banquet.

Some of the furniture described in this chapter might have uses in other rooms and they might be taken onto a deck or patio for outside eating. Some pieces of furniture could also have uses in a kitchen or in the transfer of food from one place to another. Furniture for dining will be used often because it is utilitarian, decorative, and attractive.

SHAKER SIDE TABLE

The Shakers made furniture which was functional, yet its fitness for purpose gave it an attractive appearance. This side table (FIG. 5-1) was originally intended as a sewing table, which it could still be, but it might have other uses. The two drawers may be pulled out from either side. Shaker tables can be identified by the central turned pillar and three legs; each with a single curve instead of the double curve to form shaped feet, typical of some other designs. There are three legs; although the top is square, when four legs might have been considered a more acceptable match. The advantage of three legs is that they will stand firm even if the floor is not level, where four legs might rock. Modern floors are level enough to suit four legs, so you could have a four-leg configuration, if you wish, but the table would not be so authentically Shaker.

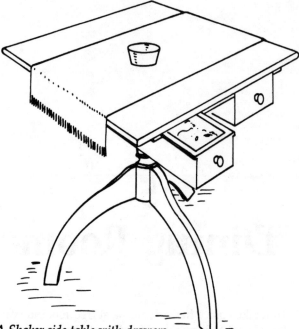

Fig. 5-1. *A Shaker side table with drawers.*

Some Shaker furniture was painted, so it was possible to use woods of different appearance, but if you want to apply a clear finish all parts should be made of the same wood. The Shakers would have used available local hardwoods, probably cherry or maple. Although it would be possible to make the table of softwood, a hardwood is more appropriate. Oak would be effective, but something with a closer grain would be better. You may wish to have a wood to match existing furniture.

For a good reproduction, all the parts should be solid wood, but otherwise you could use veneered particleboard or plywood for the top; edge it with solid wood molding. The drawer bottoms might be plywood in any case, as its choice will not be apparent. Thin, solid wood bottoms should have the grain across the short way.

Turning the pillar is essential for a good reproduction, but a four-leg table could be made with a square pillar and should be just as serviceable, if you do not mind departing from the Shaker appearance.

The sizes shown (FIG. 5-2) are close to those of a Shaker original, but alter them to suit your needs. If you make the top much larger, increase the spread of the legs for stability. If you choose four legs, arrange them squarely with the ends almost as great a spread as the top.

For a solid wood top, glue together sufficient boards to make up the width. With modern glue alone and closely fitting edges, the strength should be sufficient, but it is a help in keeping the boards level during assembly to have three or four dowels in each joint. If you have a suitable tool, use plates or biscuits instead of dowels.

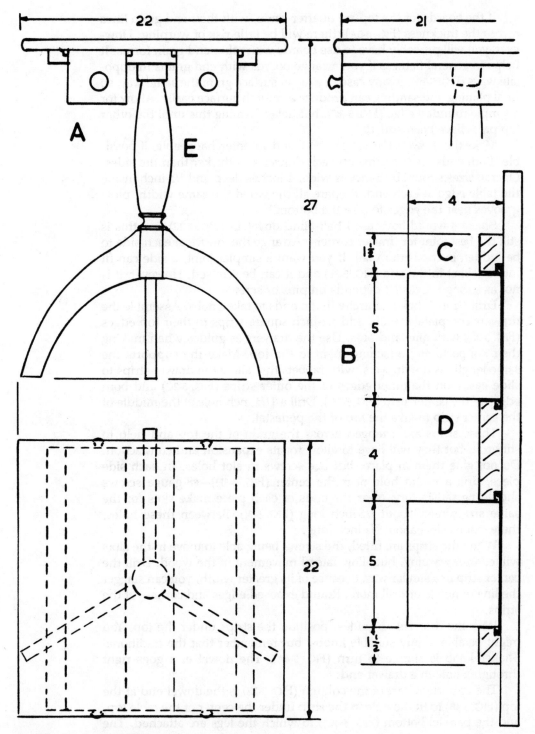

Fig. 5-2. Sizes and details of the Shaker side table.

If the boards for the top are quarter-sawn, with their end grain lines across the thickness (FIG. 5-3A), there will be little risk of warping. However, you will probably have to use boards with other end grain forms. It helps in general flatness if you arrange boards with end grains in opposite ways (FIG. 5-3B). In any case, try to get surface grain the same way, so final planing and sanding can produce a smooth surface easily. Allow for a simple rounded edge (FIG. 5-3C), but delay forming this until the other top parts have been added.

Make the drawers (FIGS. 5-2A and B and 3D) interchangeable, if possible. Both ends are the same on each drawer and thicker than the sides. Overall sizes should be 5-inches wide, 4-inches deep and 1/2-inch inside the table edge at each end. Prepare all the wood the same width; plow grooves near the edges to take the bottom.

Shakers would have used half-blind dovetails (FIG. 5-3E) and this is still the best joint for drawer corners. Arrange the groove at each side to be hidden in the bottom tail. If you want a simpler joint, a side can fit into a rabbet in the end (FIG. 5-3F) and it can be screwed. However, it is not as strong because it depends on pins or screws.

Drill 1/2-inch holes centrally in the ends to take knobs. Assemble the drawers completely; then, add 1/4-inch square strips to their top edges (FIG. 5-3G) with glue and pins. Use the drawers as guides when making their supports and attaching them to the top. Make the supports the same length as the drawers, with rabbets that allow the drawer strips to slide easily on the inner edges of the outer strips (FIG. 5-2C) and both edges of the center strip (FIG. 5-2D). Drill a 1 1/2-inch hole at the middle of the center strip to take the top of the pedestal.

These strips are arranged across the grain of the top and help to stiffen it, but they will have to allow for its expansion and contraction. Do not glue them in place, but use screws in slot holes. In each side piece, drill a round hole near the center (FIG. 5-3H)—#8-gauge screws should be satisfactory. Near the ends of each piece make slots for the same size screws about 1/2-inch long (FIG. 5-3J). Between these holes, there can be slots about 3/8-inch long.

When the strips are fitted, the screws being able to move in the slots will control warping, but allow lateral movement in the wood. Drill the center strip in a similar way. Because of its greater width, you can stagger the line of holes, or drill more. Round exposed edges and corners of the strips.

With the drawers as guides, position the strips under the top. You might be able to buy suitable knobs, but remember that the traditional Shaker knob is simple to turn (FIG. 5-4A). The dowel end goes right through a hole in a drawer end.

The important part of the column (FIG. 5-2E) is the dowel end at the top (FIG. 5-4B) to fit the hole in the strip under the center of the table top, and the parallel bottom (FIG. 5-4C), to which the legs are attached. The

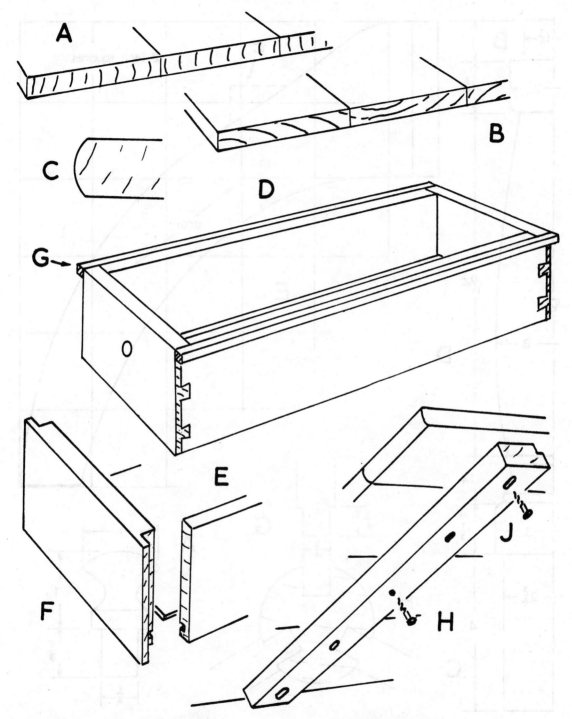

Fig. 5-3. *Constructional details of the top and drawers of the Shaker side table.*

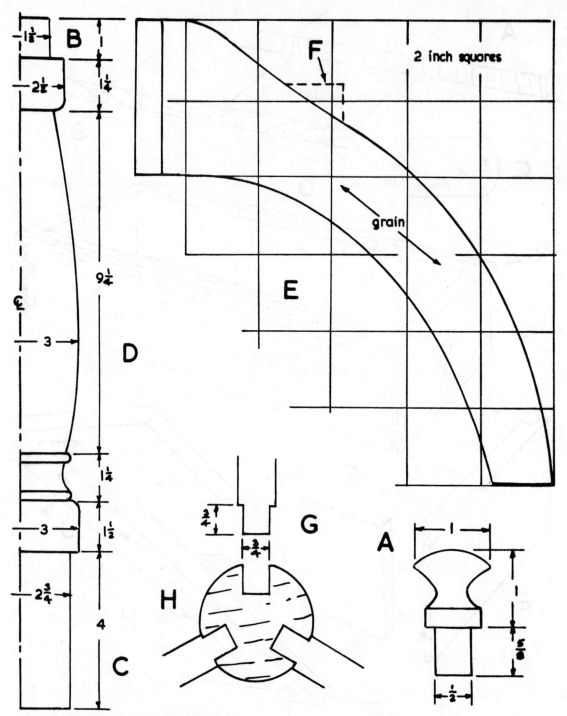

Fig. 5-4. *Leg details of the Shaker side table.*

part between can be turned as you wish; originals vary, but a typical form is shown (FIG. 5-4D).

Make three matching legs (FIG. 5-4E). In order to use a clamp to pull each leg tightly into its mortise, leave a lug on it (FIG. 5-4F); then, cut that off and trim the edge after the glue has set. Cut tenons (FIG. 5-4G). Be careful that the narrow shoulders are true, because they control the angle of each leg.

Mortises in the column have to be spaced evenly around the circumference (FIG. 5-4H). If you have a three-jaw chuck on your lathe, squeezing that on will mark the positions. If the lathe has a dividing head, that can be used while you draw the positions with a pencil along the tool rest.

Another simple way of dividing the circumference into three equal divisions is with a strip of paper. Wrap the strip round and push a spike through the overlap. Open the paper flat, and divide the distance between the pierced holes into three. Then, put the strip back and transfer the marked positions.

At the bottom parallel part of the column flatten each marked position for the width of each leg. Cut the mortises. If you use a router, square the end of each slot against the turned shoulder. Make each mortise slightly deeper than its tenon, so the leg will pull tightly to its shoulders.

Glue and clamp the legs to the column. It is easier to achieve accuracy if you do this one at a time, with the glue of one leg allowed to set before clamping another. Cut off the lugs and smooth the outsides of the legs. Check that the column stands upright. If necessary, trim the bottom of a leg to get it to stand true. Glue on the table top and check that it is parallel with the floor.

Almost any finish is suitable for this table. A Shaker table may have been painted or given coats of wax. Use varnish or a polish. Whatever the finish of other parts, wax in the drawer slides will aid easy movement.

Materials List for Shaker Side Table

1 top	$3/4$	×	22	×	22
2 drawer supports	1	×	$1^1/2$	×	22
1 drawer support	1	×	4	×	22
4 drawer ends	$5/8$	×	4	×	6
4 drawer sides	$1/2$	×	4	×	22
2 drawer bottoms	$1/4$	×	5	×	22
4 drawer runners'	$1/4$	×	$1/4$	×	22
4 knobs from	$1^1/4$	×	$1^1/4$	×	8
1 column	3	×	3	×	20
3 legs	1	×	5	×	18

RUDDER TABLE

Many folding dining tables have a central section of top which does not fold, and two flaps which can be held up by swinging frames. Because of the forms the usual swinging frames take, these are often called gateleg tables. Another way of supporting the flaps is with brackets that look like boat's rudders, and these tables are sometimes called rudder tables. They might also be called butterfly tables. This project is a rudder table (FIG. 5-5). One advantage of this design over the gateleg construction is that there is more freedom for your legs under the table. A disadvantage is that rudder supports are unsuitable for long flaps, as they do not provide floor support to the extended flap. However, when the top forms a circle (FIG. 5-6A) there is not enough extended flap on either side to cause the table to become unstable.

Fig. 5-5. *The rudder table has supports like a ship's rudder.*

This table is 29-inches high, which is a convenient height for dining; it opens to a top of 36 inches in diameter. When both flaps are hanging down, the top is about 36 inches × 14 inches. With one flap up, there is a width of 25 inches (FIG. 5-6B).

It might be possible to build the table from softwood, but hardwood is more suitable, and attractive. Most of the main parts are 1-inch thick. Use mortise and tenon joints, but it is easier and just as satisfactory to use dowels, which may be 1/2 inch in diameter and spaced not more than 3-inches apart. As much as possible, use wood of the full widths required, but you might have to glue boards together for parts of the top. Some shaping is shown on edges, but the table would function just as well if the edges are left straight; this might better match other furniture.

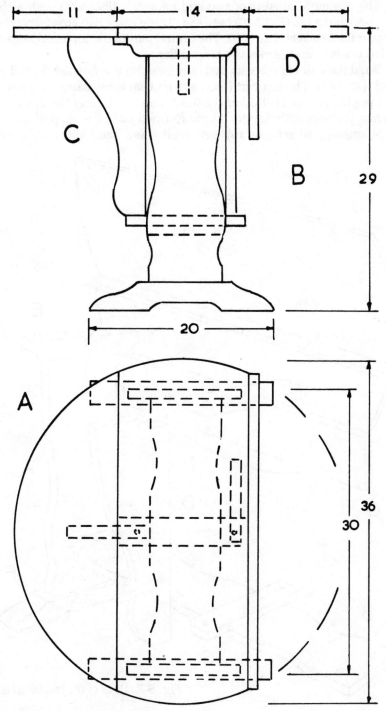

Fig. 5-6. *Sizes of the rudder table.*

The assembly consists of two end pedestals (FIG. 5-7A) with a shelf (FIG. 5-7B) and a rail (FIG. 5-7C) between. These carry two crossbars which support the brackets (FIG. 5-7D). The central part of the top overhangs the folded brackets and carries the hinged flaps.

Build the pair of pedestals first. Mark on the positions of the rail and shelf (FIG. 5-8A). The top part (FIGS. 5-7E and 8B) is the same thickness as the upright. The foot is thicker (FIGS. 5-7F and 8C). Center the upright on it when you join with dowels. In the finished table the shaped feet will be prominent, so remove any saw marks and sand the curved ends

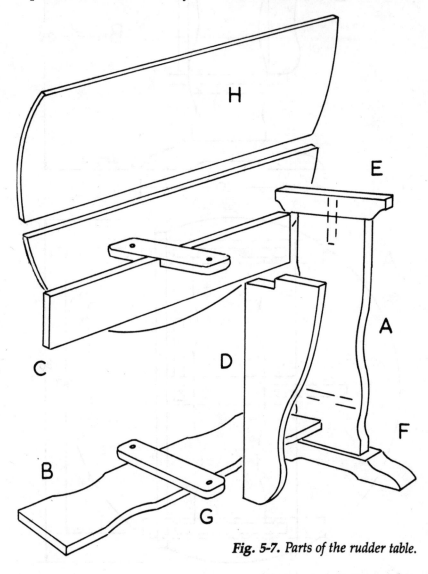

Fig. 5-7. *Parts of the rudder table.*

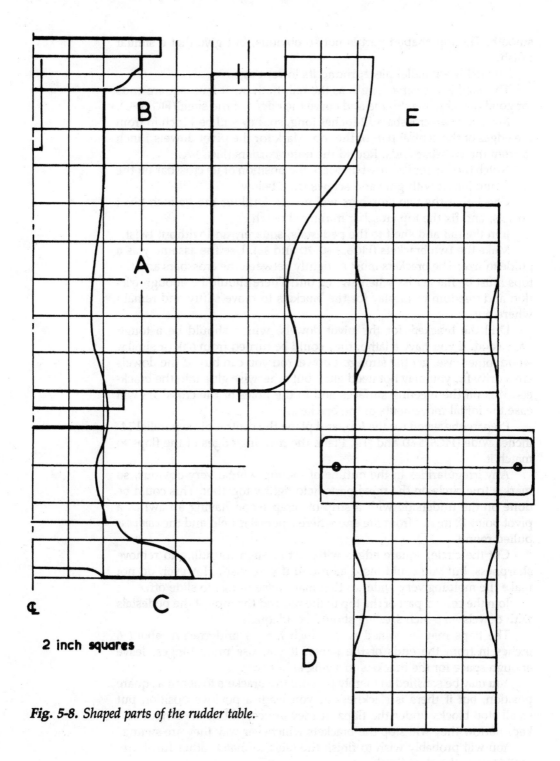

2 inch squares

Fig. 5-8. *Shaped parts of the rudder table.*

smooth. The top shaped part is not so obvious, but give that a similar finish.

The rail is a parallel piece; round its lower edge.

The shelf is the same length as the rail. Both must have square ends for good dowel joints. Shape and curve the edges of the shelf (FIG. 5-8D).

Make the two crossbars 12-inches long, so they will be 1 inch in from the edges of the central part of the top. Mark for the pivot dowels 1 inch in from the crossbar ends. Round the outer corners (FIG. 5-7G).

Notch the rail for its crossbar. Mark the position of its crossbar on the shelf, and join it with glue and screws from below.

Check that the two crossbars will match. Drill for the 1/2-inch pivot dowels, and fix the top crossbar in the rail notch.

Join the rail and shelf to the pedestals, squarely and without twist.

Make the two brackets (FIGS. 5-6C, 7D and 8E). Use the assembly as a guide to size. The brackets must fit tightly between the crossbars and the tops must be flat across when swung out. There should be enough friction and freedom from play for the brackets to move stiffly and remain where put.

Drill the brackets for the pivot dowels, which should be a tough hardwood. If you have a lathe, they could be turned from oak or similar wood; otherwise, get the strongest dowel rod you can buy. If the dowels are a drive fit, you may not need glue, but otherwise glue into the brackets. Wax on the meeting surfaces and in the holes of the crossbars will ease the initial movements of the brackets.

Prepare the wood for the top, and plane the central piece parallel 14-inches wide (FIGS. 5-6D and 7H). Plane the meeting edges of the flaps to match it.

Any irregularities in the outline of the top will be very obvious, so mark a true circle on the three parts held tightly together. This could be done on the underside with a strip of scrap wood having an awl as a pivot point 18 inches from the end where a pencil is held and the *compass* pulled round.

Cut the circle; square edges with just enough rounding to remove sharpness, but you could mold all round if you wish. However, do not make the molding very wide, as that may cause things to slide off.

Join the central part of the top to the rail and the tops of the pedestals with dowels—a 6-inch spacing should be adequate.

The flaps may be joined with 3-inch hinges underneath, about 6 inches in from the ends of the joints. If you use more hinges, leave enough space for the brackets to swing either way.

You may be satisfied to merely pull out the brackets to about a square position, but if there is slackness or you want a positive position put small stop blocks under the flaps. If they are central in the length and kept narrow they will stop the brackets whichever way they are swung.

You will probably wish to finish the table to match other furniture, with stain and a clear finish.

Materials List for Rudder Table

2 pedestals	26	×	8	× 1
2 pedestal tops	14	×	2	× 1
2 feet	20	×	3	× 1½
1 shelf	30	×	8	× 1
1 rail	30	×	6	× 1
2 crossbars	14	×	3	× 1
2 brackets	20	×	9	× 1
1 top	38	×	14	× 1
2 tops	38	×	11	× 1

BAR STOOL

If you want to sit at a bar, work surface or shelf built at a height to suit standing, your seat must have fairly long legs. This applies particularly at a breakfast or drinks bar. There could be just a plain tall stool, but a back is an improvement. This bar stool (FIG. 5-9) is at a suitable sitting height and has a low back. The legs are parallel, so construction is easy. Lower rails provide stiffness and act as footrests.

Hardwood should be used, including the dowel rods for the rails. The seat and back are plywood. They could be left plain, or one or both may be upholstered in the manner described for the kitchen stool (FIGS. 6-10 and 11).

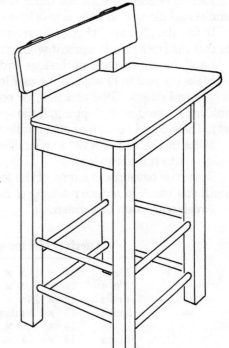

Fig. 5-9. *This bar stool has a low back and double rails for rigidity.*

You might wish to experiment with sitting heights at your particular bar. If you have any doubts, make the legs too long and cut off the bottoms after trying the seat heights.

Mark the four legs (FIG. 5-10A) together with the positions of the top rail and lower dowel rods. To get a good depth of hole for strong glued joints, the lower rails are shown with the side rails higher than those at front and back. Bevel and round the tops of the long legs (FIG. 5-10B).

Cut the four top rails (FIG. 5-10C) all the same length. Use mortise and tenon joints, but 3/8-inch dowels are suggested (FIG. 5-10D).

Mark out and drill for these dowels in the rails and legs. Drill the holes in the legs far enough to meet. Miter the ends of dowels to get the maximum penetration.

Drill holes for the round rails about 1-inch deep. Be careful to pair the legs.

Cut the round rails to lengths that will not quite reach the bottoms of the holes, to allow adjustment when you assemble.

Sand all parts and take off sharp edges.

Assemble a pair of sides first. See that they match each other. The top rails will set the distance across the legs. Check near the bottom that the legs are parallel. They will probably need moving in or out slightly. When you have set this, drive thin nails through the dowel end joints from what will be the inside of the stool.

Join these frames with the other rails, again checking that legs are parallel and using thin nails across lower joints.

Before the glue sets, check squareness when viewed from above and see that the stool stands upright when viewed from several directions.

Level the top surfaces of the legs and top rails, if necessary.

Make the seat to fit around the rear legs (FIG. 5-10E). Round the outer corners and edges. Glue and nail, or screw it in place. Heads may be sunk and covered with stopping, if the seat will not be covered by upholstery. There could be a loose cushion tied to the rear legs with tape.

Make the back (FIG. 5-10F) in a similar way, with rounded edges and corners. Attach it to the legs.

Round or bevel the bottoms of the legs when you have them to the length you want, to reduce marking of floor covering.

Finish with paint or varnish.

Materials List for Bar Stool

2 legs	34	×	1 1/2	×	1 1/2
2 legs	28	×	1 1/2	×	1 1/2
4 rails	12	×	2 1/2	×	3/4
8 rails	13	×	3/4 diameter		
1 seat	14	×	15	×	1/2 plywood
1 back	14	×	4	×	1/2 plywood

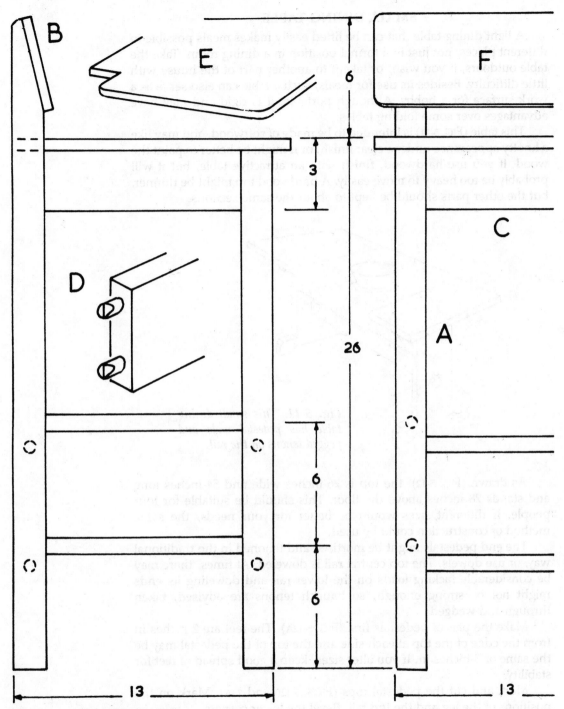

Fig. 5-10. Sizes of the bar stool.

SMALL DINING TABLE

A light dining table that can be lifted easily makes meals possible in different places, not just in a formal position in a dining room. Take the table outdoors, if you wish, or take it to another part of the house with little difficulty. Besides its use for meals, such a table can also serve as a work surface for a hobby. Although portable, it is rigid and may have advantages over some folding tables.

This table (FIG. 5-11) is intended to be made of softwood. You may like a knotty appearance under a clear finish, or it might be better to paint the wood. If you use hardwood, finish with an attractive table, but it will probably be too heavy to move easily. A hardwood top might be thinner, but the other parts should be kept to about the same sections.

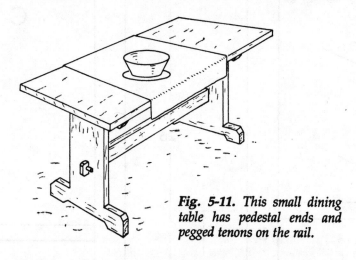

Fig. 5-11. This small dining table has pedestal ends and pegged tenons on the rail.

As drawn (FIG. 5-12), the top is 26-inches wide and 54-inches long and stands 28 inches above the floor. This should be suitable for four people. If different sizes would be better for your needs, the same method of construction could be used.

The end pedestals might be mortised and tenoned in the traditional way, or use dowels. The top central rail is doweled. At times, there may be considerable racking loads on the lower rail and doweling its ends might not be strong enough, so haunch tenons are advised, taken through and wedged.

Make the pair of pedestals first (FIG. 5-12A). The feet are 2 inches in from the edge of the top at each side and the top of the pedestal may be the same or 3-inches in. If you alter sizes, keep a good spread of feet for stability.

Mark and cut the pedestal tops (FIGS. 5-12B and 13A). Mark on the positions of the leg and the top rail. Bevel the lower corners.

Mark and cut the feet (FIGS. 5-12C and 13B). Mark the positions of the leg and bevel the upper corners. If you will be making mortises, leave

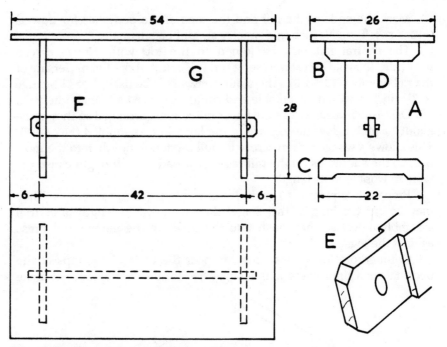

Fig. 5-12. *Sizes of the small dining table.*

cutting away the undersides until they have been finished, as the flat edge gives better support while working on them.

Mark the two legs (FIGS. 5-12D and 13C). For tenons, allow 1¹/₄ inches. Mark the position of the lower rail.

Cut the mortises for the lower rail. They will be the full depth of the rail, but allow for shoulders ¹/₄ inch each side of the tenon (FIGS. 5-12E and 14A). Mark the mortise on each side, so you can cut in each way and minimize the risk of grain breaking out around the hole.

If you are using dowels, mark out for ³/₄-inch dowels on all parts (FIGS. 5-13D and E and 14B). Allow for the dowels projecting about 1¹/₄ inches into each part.

If you intend to use mortise and tenon joints, mark the tenons (FIG. 5-14C) and the matching mortises on the other parts. Tenons should project 1¹/₄ inches.

Assemble the pedestals. Clamp tightly for strong joints. See that they match and are without twist.

The distance between the shoulders of the lower rail (FIG. 5-12F) settles the length of the assembly. Mark the shoulders and add a further 3¹/₂ inches each end for the tenons (FIG. 5-14D).

Cut the tenons to be a close push fit in their mortises. It is unlikely that the fits will be equally good either way, so mark the matching joints.

Make the top rail (FIG. 5-12G) the same length as the lower rail between its shoulders.

Mark the ends of the rail and the tops of the pedestals for dowels (FIG. 5-13F). Two, 3/4 inch in diameter should be adequate.

The central rail may be joined to the top with screws driven upwards. To avoid excessively long screws, counterbore the underside of the rail deeply (FIG. 5-14E). Any stout screws may be used, but #12-gauge × 2 1/2 inches would be suitable and could be spaced at 9-inch intervals.

Drill 1-inch holes across the lower rail tenons, arranged so they come about 1/8 inch below the surface of the leg when assembled (FIG. 5-14F). This allows a wedge driven across to pull the tenon tightly into the mortise, so the shoulders on the rail resist any loads which might cause the table to wobble in its length.

Prepare two pieces of 1-inch dowel rod (FIG. 5-14G) as wedges. They may be cut too long at this stage, then trimmed to length after trial assembly. Bevel so they push into the holes in the tenons and press against the legs.

Counterbore for screws upwards near the ends of the tops of the pedestals in a similar way to that suggested for the central rail, but make

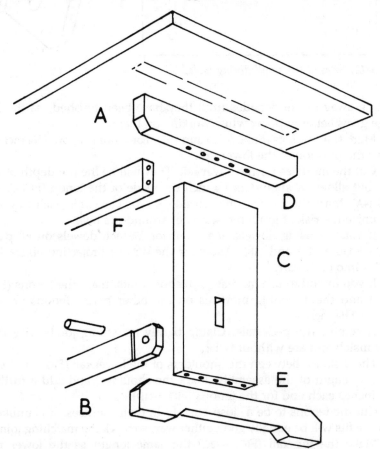

Fig. 5-13. *How the parts of the small dining table are assembled.*

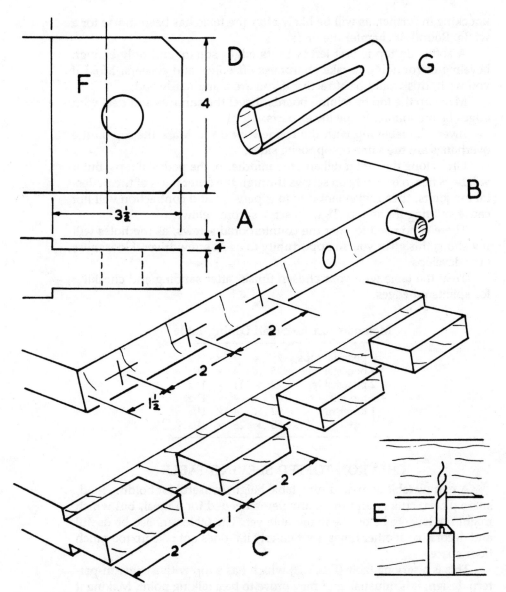

Fig. 5-14. *Details of joints for the small dining table.*

the holes a loose fit on the screws, so they can move slightly if the table top expands or contracts. One screw at each corner should be sufficient.

Put the lower rail in position in its mortises without glue. Join the top rail to the pedestals with glued dowels. Drive the wedges temporarily through the holes in the tenons. Leave for the glue to set while the assembly stands squarely on a flat surface.

Adjust the wedges by planing more off the bevels, if necessary; then, trim them so they project about 1¹/₂ inches each side, but allow for knocking in further, as will be likely after the table has been in use for a while. Round or chamfer the ends.

A softwood top is best left with its edges square and only enough beveling or rounding to take sharpness off edges and corners. Mold if you wish; this would be attractive if you are using hardwood.

Make up the top by joining boards. Level the surfaces and deal with edges before joining to the lower parts.

Invert the table top with the framework on it. Mark the top so the overhangs are the same on opposite sides.

Glue along the center rail and the middles of the pedestal tops, but it will be better to only rely on screws through the outer parts of the pedestal top joints; then movement due to expansion and contraction will not cause splitting in the top. Tighten screws from below.

There is no need to plug the counterbored screws, as the holes will not show; this gives you an opportunity to use a screwdriver if looseness ever develops.

Treat the table with your chosen finish, after sanding and checking for splintered edges.

Materials List for Small Dining Table

2 pedestal tops	26	×	4	×	$1^{1}/_{2}$
2 pedestal feet	28	×	4	×	$1^{1}/_{2}$
2 pedestal legs	22	×	11	×	$1^{1}/_{2}$
1 top rail	42	×	4	×	$1^{1}/_{2}$
1 lower rail	52	×	4	×	$1^{1}/_{2}$
1 top	58	×	26	×	$1^{1}/_{2}$

CHEVRON-TOPPED SERVING TABLE

A narrow table at main dining table height is useful for holding food, spare plates, cutlery and the many items needed for a meal, but which might not have to be on the main table yet. The table can also be useful and decorative at other times, particularly if it does not take up too much floor space.

This is a serving table (FIG. 5-15) which has a top with a chevron-pattern design; it is unusual, and may prove to be a talking point. Making it is not as difficult as might appear. If you are a careful woodworker, you can make it. Besides the top at a useful height, there is a drawer with a capacity for cutlery and table cloths. Lower down the framing is a shelf that has a good capacity and is enclosed so the contents are prevented from falling out. This will take bottles, large containers and all the items not required immediately on top.

The wood should match that of furniture already in the room, if possible. In any case, use a hardwood for the framing. The top pattern could be made of softwood, if you wish, with a hardwood border to match the wood below it. However, variations are possible, as described later.

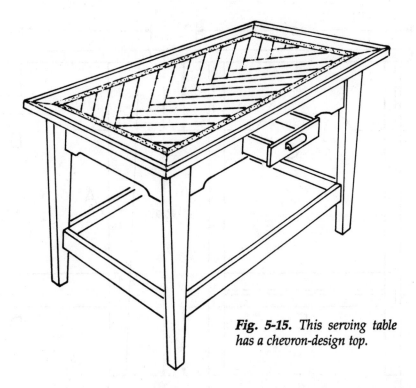

Fig. 5-15. *This serving table has a chevron-design top.*

If you are an enthusiastic cabinetmaker, you will choose to use mortise and tenon joints for the rails into the legs, but dowels are suggested; their use is described below. If you use tenons, allow extra length on the rails for them. The drawer could be made in the traditional way with dovetails, but a simple assembly is described and that should have ample strength.

Cut the four legs (FIG. 5-16A). Their inner edges will be parallel in the length as well as the width, and these edges will stand upright. The outsides taper from the full 3-inch width at the top to 1¹/2 inches at the bottom. Leave a little extra at the top to trim off after assembly. Mark on the positions of the rails in both directions.

Cut the long rails (FIG. 5-16B). Reduce their centers to a 4-inch width by curving from 3 inches in from the ends. What will be the front rail has to be cut away for the drawer 12 inches wide × 3 inches deep (FIG. 5-17A). Although this will be strong enough when assembled into the table, it would weaken the part for handling during other work. Therefore, mark the shape, but delay cutting out until the main parts are ready for assembling.

Cut the short rails (FIG. 5-16C) with shaped lower edges to match those on the long rails.

Make the bottom long rails (FIG. 5-16D) and short rails (FIG. 5-16E) to the same lengths as the top rails. Put strips inside (FIGS. 5-17B and 18A) all pieces to support the shelf.

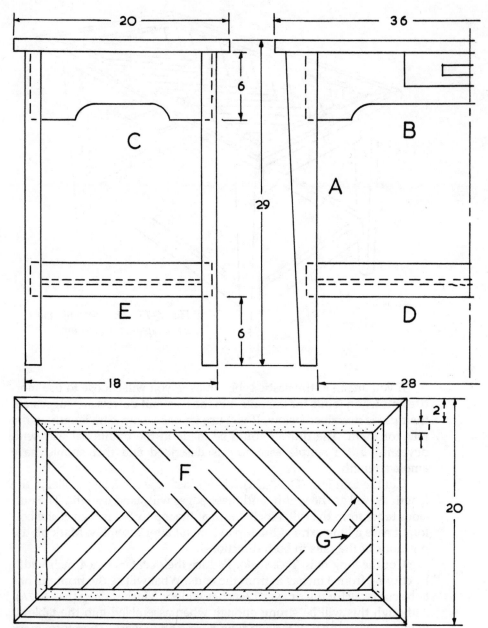

Fig. 5-16. *Sizes of the chevron-topped serving table.*

The rails will join the legs so their inner surfaces are level with the corners of the legs (FIG. 5-18B). Mark and drill for three 3/8-inch or 1/2-inch dowels in the top rail joints and two in the bottom rail joints. Stagger the hole spacing, so the holes will miss each other in the legs, by making hole centers 1/2-inch higher in one rail than in the other rail that joins to the same leg.

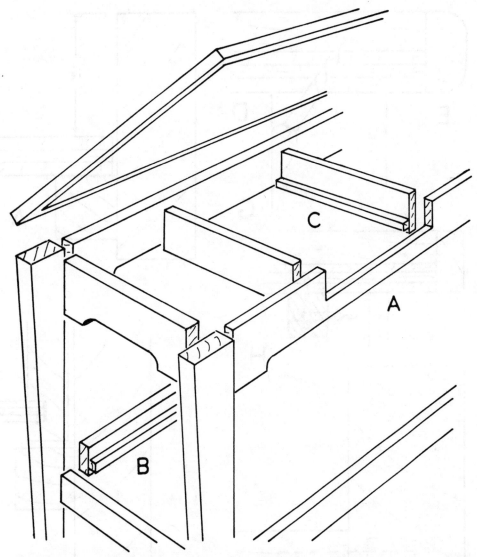

Fig. 5-17. *Parts of the framework of the chevron-topped serving table.*

The two drawer guides (FIG. 5-17C) will be the same length as the short rails and as deep as the cutaway parts of the long rails. Put strips (FIG. 5-18C) on with their top surfaces level with the cut-out parts of the front rail, so they act as drawer runners. Drill the strips and rails for dowels.

Assemble the two long sides (after cutting out the drawer opening, if it has been left until this stage). Check that they are square and match as a pair; then join across with the short rails and drawer guides. See that this assembly stands level and the legs are upright when viewed from several directions.

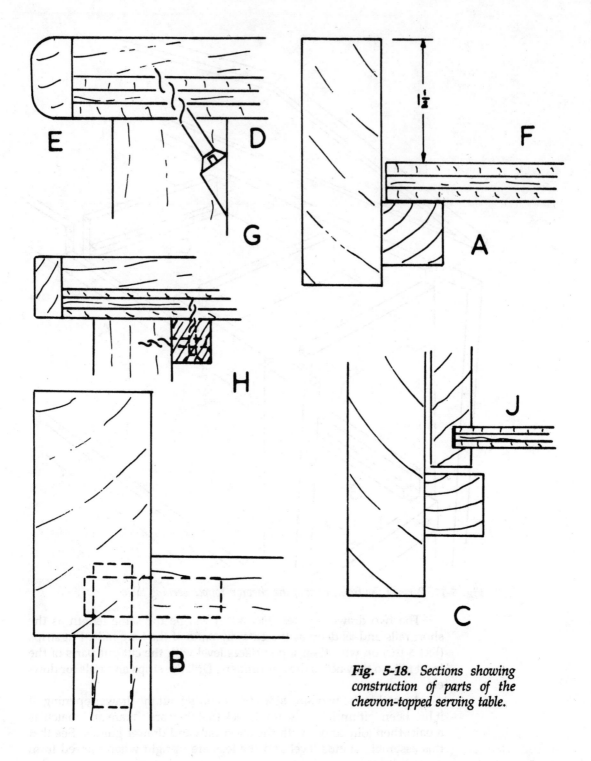

Fig. 5-18. *Sections showing construction of parts of the chevron-topped serving table.*

The base of the table top is a piece of 1/2-inch plywood (FIG. 5-18D). Cut it to come at least 1/2-inch outside the leg top corners. The decorative top goes on it and there is a further 1/2-inch thickness of border to go around it.

The top design shown (FIG. 5-16F) has a 1 1/2-inch border with a 1-inch strip inside it, then the chevron pattern. This arrangement looks good if the 1-inch strip is stained darker than the border outside and the pattern inside. The 1-inch strips should be cut, and stain allowed to dry on them, before assembly.

The decorative top could be made with strips of 1/2-inch plywood, or use solid wood 1/2-inch thick. The exact thickness is not so important as getting all pieces the same and all parts that should be the same width exactly so. You can cut your own strips on a fine-toothed table saw, all at one setting, or you might buy strips planed to width.

Mark out the plywood top base with the widths of the borders and a centerline with other lines at 45 degrees to it at one end (FIG. 5-16G). These marks provide the data, or information, for your layout of the chevron pattern.

There are at least two ways you can set about making the chevron pattern—you can glue on the borders to the base and fill in the chevron pieces after, or you can fix the chevron pieces and fit the border strips around later. In both cases, you need to work carefully and avoid leaving excess glue to harden where another piece will have to be fitted. This is particularly important if you leave the top partly made at the end of a work session, to resume some time later when the glue used so far will have set. Scrape away surplus glue before it hardens.

If you glue the borders first, fit them to their lines, with mitered corners. Clamp them while the glue sets and remove any glue which spreads into the inner space. Excess glue outside will not matter so much because it will be removed when you plane these edges ready for the outside strips.

Cut a pair of chevron strips to fit against the datum lines, so they meet closely at the center and against the borders. Cut more pieces to fit between these pieces and the corners. You might cut another pair of fullsize pieces as part of this first group.

Glue all the pieces cut so far, clamping them under boards to spread the pressure.

Cut and fit more long pieces in this first gluing session, but with a large number and your first effort it is difficult to bring and hold each edge joint close and maintain parallel lines. Much depends on your skill and the available clamping equipment.

If you choose to fit the chevron pieces first and leave the border strips until later, make sure the markings on the base plywood are accurate and clear. Cut the first pair of chevron pieces, as in the first method, and make an adjoining pair as well as the ones to fill the corners. Cut them to fit closely together and pay particular attention to getting the outer mitered ends level with the drawn border lines. Clamp this group; then follow on with further groups to complete the pattern.

It is difficult to trim the outsides of this pattern straight if you do not get it correct and there are irregularities, so care in cutting and assembling the chevron pieces is important. If you have to make corrections to the edges, use a chisel or rabbet plane. It does not matter if you cut slightly into the surface of the plywood. When you are satisfied with the edges of the pattern, glue on the border strips.

There are a few possible variations in the pattern. The pieces in the first design are shown with an overlapping pattern along the centerline; miter them there (FIG. 5-19A). The pattern does not have to be symmetrical—the meeting line could be off center or even at an angle (FIG. 5-19B), but still with the pieces at 45 degrees to it. Another interesting variation is to mix the woods. Alternating light and dark colors is effective (FIG. 5-19C). Differences in widths of strips are possible, but do this with restraint if the appearance is to be neat—a pair of narrow pieces of a different color wood between groups of ordinary pieces gives an interesting effect (FIG. 5-19D). You could abandon the chevron arrangement of meeting pieces and merely arrange diagonal strips (FIG. 5-19E).

True the edges of the top assembly and glue and pin on the outside strips (FIG. 5-18E).

If you have to do any leveling of the top surface, be careful of the differences in grain direction, which may cause tearing out or roughness with too-heavy cuts or blunt tools. Thorough sanding may be all the leveling needed if you have used wood of the same thickness and have clamped joints tightly. If all you have to do is remove surplus glue, a scraper along each joint may precede sanding.

You will probably want to give the top a clear finish and this will need more coats of polyurethane or other polish than the rest of the table, so it may be worthwhile applying one or two coats now before assembly. This will prevent the grain absorbing dirt during further work.

The bottom of the tray inside the lower rails (FIG. 5-18F) is a piece of 1/2-inch plywood. It could have a veneer to match the other wood or its top surface may be painted a neutral color. Notch it around the legs. Glue it down to its supports, or leave it loose to lift out for cleaning.

Make and fit the drawer before joining the table top to its framework. The suggested method of construction consists of two sides grooved to take a thin plywood or hardboard bottom, a back and a front which fit above the bottom, and a second front which overlaps the opening in the rail (FIG. 5-20).

Make the pair of drawer sides (FIG. 5-20A). Their depth should be an easy fit in the opening, so they clear the top when it is fitted. The length may go almost to the rear rail, or you could shorten the sides if such a

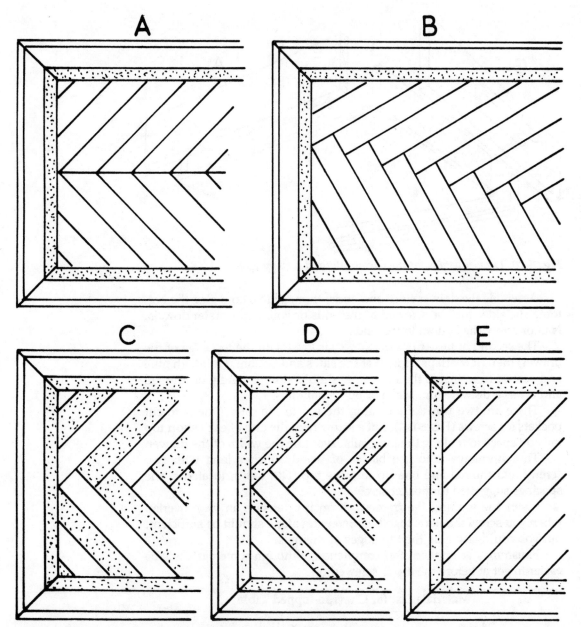

Fig. 5-19. *Alternative top layouts for the chevron-topped serving table.*

drawer would better suit your needs. Groove near the lower edges for the bottom (FIG. 5-18J).

The back and front of the drawer are the same (FIG. 5-20B). Depth should come to the tops of the grooves in the sides. The overall width of the drawer should be an easy fit between the drawer guides.

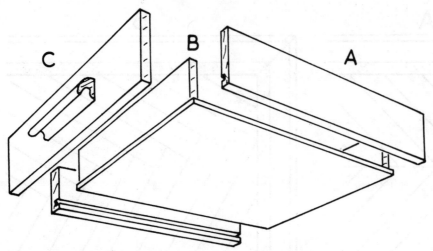

Fig. 5-20. *Drawer details for the chevron-topped serving table.*

Assemble the drawer sides and ends; then, slide in and glue the bottom. The sides may be screwed to the ends or you might prefer dowels. Nail or screw the bottom to the ends.

The second or false front (FIG. 5-20C) is level with the top edge of the drawer; then, it overlaps 1/2 inch at the sides and bottom. Fit it with glue and screws from inside the drawer. It should close squarely on the rail and act as a drawer stop. Make or buy a handle.

There are two ways of attaching the top to the rails. One is to cut pockets for screws (FIG. 5-18G). Put a screw near the end of each short top rail and space four along the long rails, avoiding the width of the drawer.

The alternative is to use blocks of wood 3-inches long with two screws into the rail and one up into the top (FIG. 5-18H), located at the spacings suggested for pocket screws.

Invert the top and the framework on it to ensure an even overlap when you screw the parts together. Screwing alone should be sufficient, but you could also glue the top edges of the rails.

Finish may be applied after completion, although some parts will be easier to get at before the top is screwed on.

Materials List for Chevron-topped Table

4 legs	30	×	3	×	1¹/2	
2 rails	34	×	6	×	1	
2 rails	18	×	6	×	1	
2 rails	34	×	3	×	1	
2 rails	18	×	3	×	1	
2 drawer guides	18	×	5	×	3/4	
2 drawer guides	18	×	3/4	×	3/4	
2 shelf supports	34	×	3/4	×	3/4	
2 shelf supports	18	×	3/4	×	3/4	
1 shelf	34	×	18	×	1/2 plywood	

Continued

2 drawer sides	18	×	4	× $1/2$
2 drawer ends	13	×	4	× $1/2$
1 drawer front	14	×	$4^{1/2}$	× $1/2$
1 drawer bottom	18	×	13	× $1/8$ or $1/4$ plywood or hardboard
1 top base	37	×	20	× $1/2$ plywood
2 top borders	37	×	$1^{1/2}$	× $1/2$
2 top borders	34	×	1	× $1/2$
2 top borders	20	×	$1^{1/2}$	× $1/2$
2 top borders	18	×	1	× $1/2$
2 outside strips	37	×	1	× $1/2$
2 outside strips	21	×	1	× $1/2$
chevron strips from				
twenty-six	13	×	2	× $1/2$

REFECTORY DINING TABLE

This is a table of traditional construction made in the traditional way (FIG. 5-21). The name of the type comes from the massive tables used in the refectories, or dining halls, of the great monasteries of Europe, where the end supports were trestles made in this way. Some of the large tables were joined with wedged tusk tenons so they could be disassembled, which was probably necessary to get the tables from room to room. This table is not intended to take apart and is of a size that could pass through modern doorways.

Fig. 5-21. A refectory dining table of traditional form.

The table has a top 30-inches wide × 42-inches long, standing 29 inches above the floor. This accommodates four people comfortably or six rather closely, but make the table any length if you want it to regularly suit six or more people. Keep height and width the same—or check the sizes of doorways if you want to make it much wider.

Although it would be possible to use softwood, to match other furniture, this is really a table to be made in a quality hardwood; then, give it a good finish by polishing. It would then be a piece of furniture to be proud of and worth the cost of the fairly large pieces of wood needed.

The structural joints are mortises and tenons. This is not an assembly where dowels might be substituted for satisfactory results. Sizes are given for joints, which might be cut by hand or machine. Alter them to suit your equipment, but do not vary sizes too much. There is some stopped chamfering, or grooving, which could be worked by hand, but is most easily done with a suitable cutter in a router. A table top of this width is liable to expand and contract enough to matter, even if you start with properly seasoned wood, so it is held down by buttons which can slide.

Construction is done in stages. First, make the two pedestals completely; then prepare the lengthwise parts. Assemble them to the pedestals; finally make the top and attach it. It is best to sand and prepare each part for finishing as it is made, taking care not to damage joints, rather than wait until after assembling sections or the whole table before thinking about the finish.

Make the tops of the pedestals (FIGS. 5-22A and 23A). Taper and round the ends. Cut grooves for the buttons along what will be the inside top edges (FIG. 5-23B). Mark where the upright will come (FIG. 5-23C).

The feet are very similar (FIGS. 5-22B and 23D). Cut similar tapers to rounded ends. Mark where the mortises will come on the top surface. Mark where the cutout will be underneath (FIG. 5-23E), but it will probably be better to leave this uncut until after you have made the mortises, so as to have a flat supporting surface.

On the uprights (FIG. 5-22C) allow for tenons $1^{1}/2$-inches long at each end (FIG. 5-23F). Mark where the rails will come. The lower rail is 2-inches up from the joint (FIG. 5-23G). The top rail has to overlap the pedestal top (FIG. 5-23H).

Mark out the tenons on both ends of the upright. There are four tenons with a wider gap at the center (FIG. 5-22D) in order to give clearance for the tenon on the top rail; use the same arrangement at the bottom. Make the tenons one-third the thickness of the wood.

Be careful to have clean lines on the shoulders when you cut the tenons. Mark the line with a knife cut; then the joints will close neatly.

Cut the mortises to match; then do the shaping under the feet.

Chamfering edges lightens the appearance and gives a high-quality effect. It it not essential, but if you have suitable equipment, it is worth doing. A chamfer or groove, about $3/8$ inch is appropriate. Go all round the projecting curved ends and up to 1 inch of the joint. Do the same on the edges of the upright (FIG. 5-24A).

Assemble the pedestals, and see that they match.

The two lengthwise rails (FIG. 5-22E) are the same between shoulders (FIG. 5-24B), but they differ in the tenon arrangements. They have curves on the undersides; these might have chamfers worked to match those on the pedestals, but do not carry the chamfers along the parallel parts.

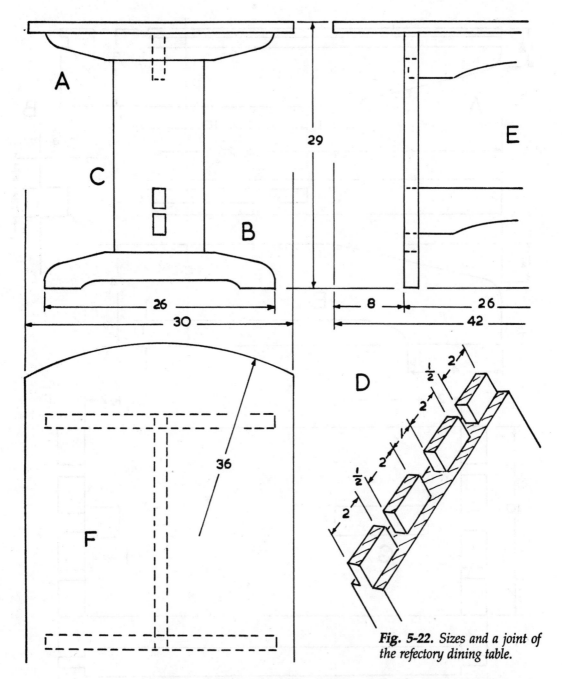

Fig. 5-22. *Sizes and a joint of the refectory dining table.*

Cut grooves for buttons along both sides of the top rail, (FIG. 5-24C), the same size as those on the pedestal.

The tenons on the bottom rail will go right through the pedestal upright. Mark and cut them as shown (FIG. 5-24D). Make them slightly too long at first to allow for leveling with the uprights after assembly.

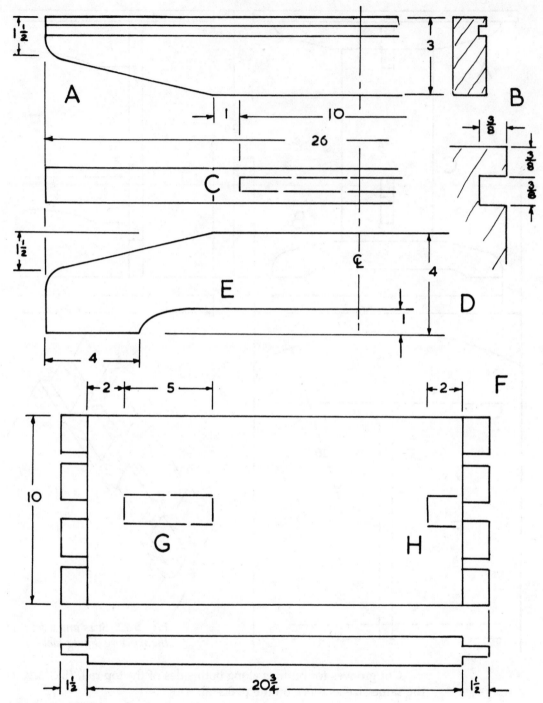

Fig. 5-23. *Sizes of parts of the refectory dining table.*

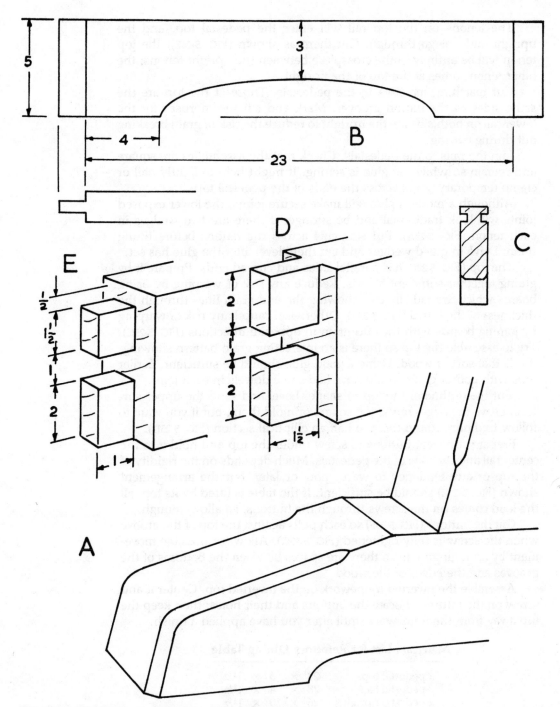

Fig. 5-24. *Shaped parts and joints of the refectory table.*

The tenons on the top rail will enter the pedestal top, and the upright and not go through. Cut them as shown (FIG. 5-24E); the top tenon will be entirely in the crosspiece between the upright tenons; the other tenon comes at the top of the upright.

Cut matching mortises in the pedestals. Those at the top are the same sides as the button grooves. Mark and cut the mortises for the lower rail on both sides of the upright to reduce the risk of grain breaking out during cutting.

Join the rails to the pedestals. Check that the assemblies are square and remain so while the glue is setting. It might help to lightly nail or clamp temporary strips across the ends of the pedestal tops.

Although a modern glue will make secure joints, the lower exposed joints will look traditional and be stronger if there are two wedges in each tenon (FIG. 5-25A). Put saw cuts across the tenons before fitting them; Drive in glued wedges and cut them level after the glue has set.

The top (FIG. 5-22F) has parallel sides and curved ends. Prepare it by gluing together sufficient boards. Reduce any risk of warping by using boards which are radially cut, showing the end grain lines through the thickness of the board (FIG. 5-25B). Otherwise, cancel any risk of warping by joining boards with the end grain in opposite directions (FIG. 5-25C). Try to assemble the top so there is an interesting grain pattern showing, if it is that sort of wood. Using a good glue should be sufficient. Earlier tops with poorer glues would have had some dowels in each joint.

Cut the outline of the top to shape. Level and sand the upper surface. Leave the edges of the top square or mold them, but if you want to follow tradition, round them to half an elliptical section (FIG. 5-25D).

Prepare sufficient buttons to screw under the top and hold it to the center rail and the tops of the pedestals. Much depends on the rigidity of the top or any tendency to warp, now or later, but the arrangement shown (FIG. 5-25E) should be sufficient. If the table is lifted by its top, all the load comes on the screws through the buttons, so allow enough.

Cut the buttons (FIG. 5-25F) so each pulls against the top of the groove when the screw is fully tightened (FIG. 5-25G). Allow for possible movement by arranging them so there are spaces between the bottoms of the grooves and the edges of the wood.

Assemble the inverted framework on the inverted top. Center it and screw on the buttons. Locate the buttons and their holes; then keep the top away from the framework until after you have applied a finish.

Materials List for Refectory Dining Table

2 pedestal tops	28	×	3	×	1$1/2$
2 pedestal feet	28	×	4	×	1$1/2$
2 pedestal uprights	26	×	10	×	1$1/2$
2 rails	28	×	5	×	1$1/2$
1 top	44	×	30	×	1$1/4$
buttons from	33	×	2	×	$3/4$

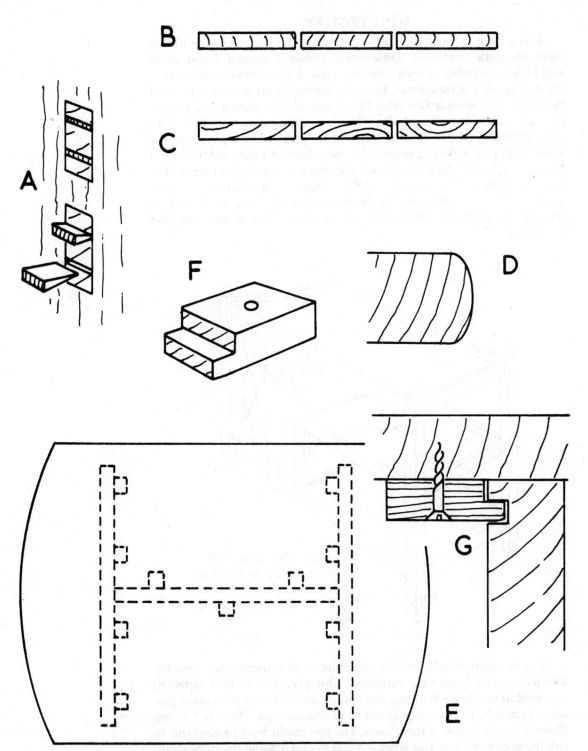

Fig. 5-25. *Leg joint (A) and details of the top (B-E) and buttons (F and G).*

WINE TROLLEY

If you have to move food and drink from the kitchen to the dining room, the patio or further, some sort of trolley is needed if you are to avoid a large number of trips carrying trays. A plain trolley with two or three trays on it is functional, but not necessarily an attractive piece of furniture. This wine trolley (FIG. 5-26) is intended to transport plenty of food and drink, but it might also stand in the dining room to fit in with other furniture. Also, it functions as a serving table. The top is about the same height as a dining table. The glass-fronted cupboard will hold plenty of soft and alcoholic drinks, and the trays are quite roomy. The upper two have ledges around, but the bottom one is without projecting edging, so heavy containers may be slid in or out. There are casters on the legs. In short, the whole trolley is mobile as well as attractive and functional.

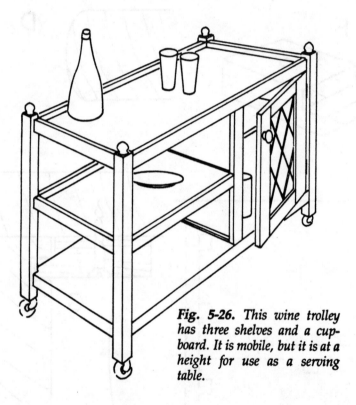

Fig. 5-26. *This wine trolley has three shelves and a cupboard. It is mobile, but it is at a height for use as a serving table.*

Construction should be of a furniture-quality hardwood, possibly selected to match existing furniture. The plywood is best obtained veneered to match the framing, but you might be able to stain other plywood to match. The tray tops could be plastic-covered. There is 2 inches allowed for the depth of the casters, but you might have to alter this to suit the ones you have. Use wheels if you intend making the trolley suitable for pushing along outside paths. The tops of the legs are shown decorated with turned knobs, which you may make or buy, but the trolley would still look good with the leg tops just rounded.

Most of the joints are mortise and tenon. With the need for grooves and rabbets for the plywood, there is little space at the end of some rails for the two dowels that would be required as an alternative; moreover, they would not be as strong. There is considerable mutual support from the many parts when the whole trolley has been assembled, but care will be needed in handling some of the sub-assemblies.

Prepare sufficient wood for all parts before marking out and cutting joints. Use the actual plywood to get the sizes of grooves which have to be cut. The legs are 1^1/$_2$-inch square pieces without grooves. All the rails and the intermediate uprights are ^{3}/$_4$ inch × 1^1/$_2$-inch section; each has one or more grooves to suit ^{1}/$_2$ inch or ^{1}/$_4$-inch plywood. Substitute ^{3}/$_8$-inch plywood in both cases, but details on the drawings are for the first two sizes.

Cut all pieces a few inches longer than shown (FIG. 5-27).

Cut the wood for the four legs, and mark on them the positions of the rails (FIG. 5-29A).

Groove the wood for the top and middle trays (FIGS. 5-27A and B and 28A/B). The grooves are ^{3}/$_8$-inch deep and ^{1}/$_4$ inch from the bottom edge.

For the bottom four rails, cut rabbets to let the ^{1}/$_2$-inch plywood in ^{3}/$_8$ inch (FIGS. 5-27C and 28C).

The rail that goes across the top of the closed end also needs a groove ^{1}/$_4$-inch deep and ^{1}/$_4$ inch from the outer edge (FIG. 5-28D).

The rail that goes across the bottom of the closed end needs a matching groove (FIG. 5-28E).

Cut ^{1}/$_4$-inch grooves ^{1}/$_4$ inch from the edge in the rail that will hold the inner end of the middle shelf (FIG. 5-28F).

The outer panel is divided at the same level; this needs grooves at the top and bottom (FIG. 5-28G). When the trolley is finished a shelf may rest on these two rails.

The two uprights (FIG. 5-27D) have to be grooved for ^{1}/$_4$-inch plywood (FIG. 5-28H) forming the inner side of the cupboard.

The top and bottom of this cupboard side come against the plywood trays, which cannot be grooved. Instead, prepare strips of ^{1}/$_2$ inch × ^{3}/$_4$-inch section with ^{1}/$_4$-inch grooves (FIG. 5-28J) to glue to the plywood and take the edges of the panels.

A piece of plywood forms the back of the cupboard. If you have the means of making stopped grooves you can let the plywood into the rails, legs and uprights, but otherwise it will be simpler to use similar strips to those across the plywood trays (FIG. 5-28K and L).

The joint between the rails and the legs are barefaced tenons on the rails into mortises in the legs, arranged so the inner surfaces of the rails meet at the corners (FIG. 5-28M). Allow for the mortises meeting (FIG. 5-28N), so the tenons can be as long as possible and meet with miters. When you assemble, the plywood must have small notches around the legs.

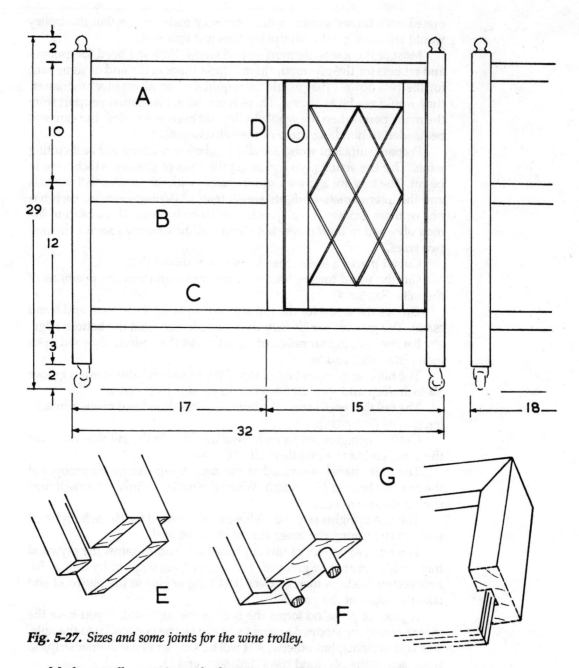

Fig. 5-27. *Sizes and some joints for the wine trolley.*

Mark out all parts in each direction together to ensure that they match. It is the length between shoulders which is important, but allow extra for the tenons.

All rails across the trolley between legs are the same length (FIG. 5-29B). The intermediate center rail is longer, to allow for the uprights being thinner than the legs.

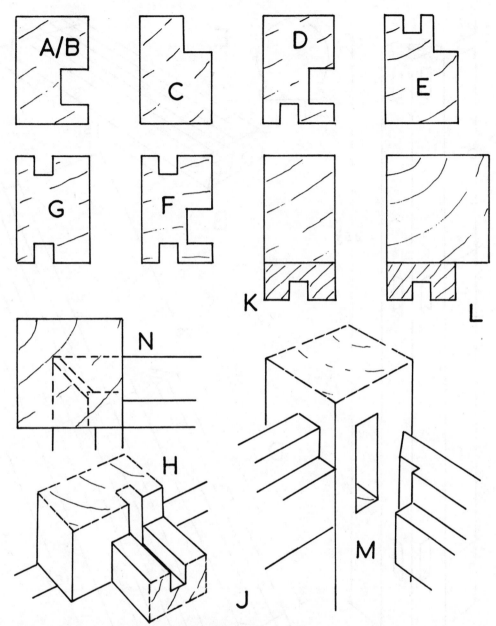

Fig. 5-28. *Sections of parts to prepare for constructing the wine trolley.*

Mark all the lengthwise rails the same (FIG. 5-29C), with the positions of the uprights marked.

The middle side rails reach the upright (FIG. 5-29D).

Cut all the tenons that will join the legs, and miter their ends. Cut matching mortises in the legs.

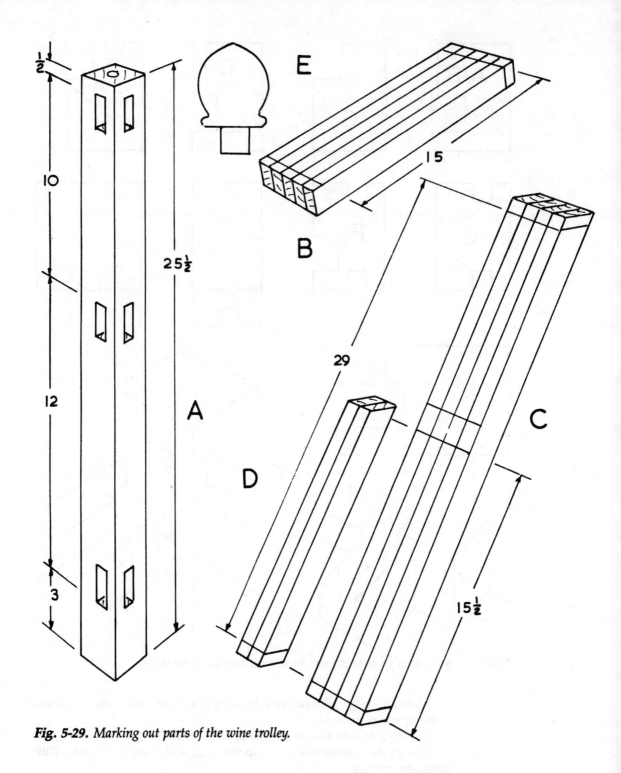

Fig. 5-29. *Marking out parts of the wine trolley.*

Get the lengths of the uprights from the relevant marks on the legs. Join the uprights into the rails with thin central tenons (FIG. 5-27E), or use 1/4-inch dowels (FIG. 5-27F). Join in the middle side rails, using one of these ways.

Prepare the decorative knobs for the tops of the legs (FIG. 5-29E), and drill the legs to suit. Prepare the bottoms of the legs for the casters, which may screw on or fit into holes.

Ready the two pieces of plywood for fitting into the closed end. When you fit them, plane their edges, so they go in without quite touching the bottoms of the grooves; then they will not tighten before frame joints are closed.

Lightly round the upper edges of tray rails. Sand all parts. The legs at the open part could be chamfered between the trays, if you wish. In any case, take sharpness off there.

Assemble the open end; then assemble the closed end with its plywood panels. Check that these ends are square, without twist; also, they must match each other as a pair.

Carefully fit the parts in stages as you assemble the rest of the trolley, which should be done in one operation; however, the back cupboard panel and its framing can be left until later and, obviously, the door will come at a later stage. Have the plywood tray pieces ready, but slightly oversized, until you know the exact dimensions, as assembly progresses.

Join the middle rail across the uprights and slide in its plywood panels, allowing for the grooved 1/2-inch × 3/4-inch strips that will come at top and bottom.

From the end frames and the long rails, get the sizes of the bottom plywood panel to fit in rabbets, and cut it to size, including the small notches at the corners. This will also provide a guide to the sizes of the other tray bottoms. Keep them a little undersize, so they do not quite reach the bottoms of their grooves when fully tightened.

Fit all three pieces of plywood, using glue and pins in the rabbets. Join with the uprights and their panels and grooved strips; then, bring this assembly into the legs, using clamps as much as possible for really tight joints. The end frames will ensure squareness in that direction, but check that the assembly is square when viewed from   front. It should stand level, without twist.

Make the back of the cupboard to fit in as one assembly. Miter the corners of the grooved strips (FIG. 5-27G) and cut the plywood slightly undersized. Bevel the outer exposed edges of the strips. Fit the assembly with glue and a few pins driven through the strips inside.

A shelf inside might be a loose piece of plywood resting on the rails. If you make it only about 10-inches wide, there will be space in front of it for tall bottles. However, if you are only storing canned drinks, it may be wider.

The door could be made with a plywood panel, but a glass panel looks better, particularly if it is given a leaded pattern. Make the door to fit inside the opening, not on the surface, for the best appearance.

The door will be about 12 inches × 19 inches (FIG. 5-30A), but get the actual sizes from the opening. It should have square corners, but if your opening is slightly out of true, you must make the door to suit. Allow sufficient clearance for the door to fit easily. Remember that a test of good cabinetmaking is to make door clearances no more than is necessary.

Make the framing of the door of 1-inch × 2-inch section wood. Cut rabbets two-thirds of the thickness of the wood and 3/8-inch deep (FIG. 5-30B). Tenons should be one-third the actual thickness of your wood, or as near to that as your equipment will cut. The tenon edge should be in line with the rabbet, so check before rabbeting your strips (FIG. 5-30C).

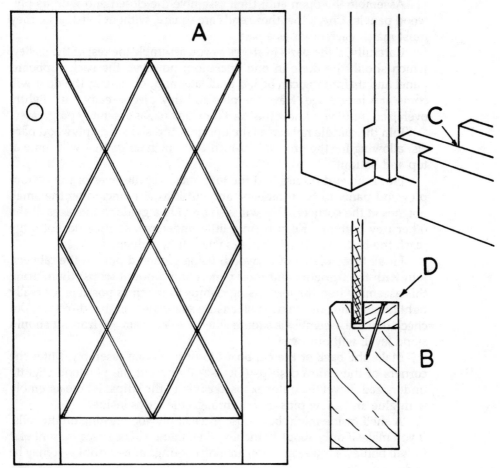

Fig. 5-30. *Details of the door of the wine trolley.*

The sides of the door are the full height; the other pieces tenon into them. Mark the lengths of the side pieces, but leave a little extra on the ends until after the mortises have been cut. The tenons need not enter the sides more than 1 inch.

Mark and cut the tenons. From them, mark the mortises and cut them.

Join the door parts and cut off the side extensions after the glue has set. Remove any surplus glue inside the rabbets. Do any planing necessary to make the door fit the opening.

Cut glass to fit and prepare fillets to go round the rabbets and hold it in place (FIG. 5-30D).

If you want to give the door a leaded appearance, this can be done with self-adhesive strip lead about $3/16$-inch wide. Draw the outline of the opening on a piece of paper and find the middle of each side. Join these points and the corners to obtain the pattern. Put this under the glass and stick on strips of lead over the lines. Stop the ends of the lead at the edges of the wood.

Fit the glass in the door with just enough pins to hold the fillets and no glue; then if the glass ever has to be replaced, you can remove it without difficulty or damage to the frame.

Let in two, 2-inch hinges, preferably brass. Add a knob or handle, fairly high so it is easy to reach. Use a spring or magnetic catch. If the trolley is to be used over a rough surface, make sure the catch is strong enough to resist the contents falling against the door and opening it, or fit a lock as well. If the catch does not also act as a stop, put a small block of wood on the upright near its center.

The finish will have to be chosen to suit the wood and any other furniture it has to match. Start with stain, especially if the plywood is a different color; then use several coats of a clear finish.

Materials List for Wine Trolley

4 legs	28 ×	$1^{1}/_{2}$ ×	$1^{1}/_{2}$
4 rails	32 ×	$1^{1}/_{2}$ ×	1
7 rails	18 ×	$1^{1}/_{2}$ ×	1
2 uprights	22 ×	$1^{1}/_{2}$ ×	1
2 frame strips	18 ×	$3/_{4}$ ×	$1/_{2}$
2 frame strips	22 ×	$3/_{4}$ ×	$1/_{2}$
2 frame strips	14 ×	$3/_{4}$ ×	$1/_{2}$
2 door frames	22 ×	2 ×	1
2 door frames	14 ×	2 ×	1
knobs from	14 ×	$1^{1}/_{2}$ ×	$1^{1}/_{2}$
2 tray panels	32 ×	18 ×	$1/_{2}$ plywood
1 tray panel	17 ×	18 ×	$1/_{2}$ plywood
4 cupboard panels	18 ×	12 ×	$1/_{4}$ plywood
1 cupboard back	20 ×	14 ×	$1/_{4}$ plywood
1 cupboard shelf	14 ×	12 ×	$1/_{2}$ plywood

6
Kitchen

Although most modern kitchens have equipment and worktops built in and all of a cook's needs are apparently provided, there is always scope for adding other items that aid the food preparation processes, improve comfort and give an individual touch to a kitchen. You can make containers and racks that fit on or above the worktops; there can be things to sit on or stand on to reach higher; there may be space for extra working positions, and you will be able to fill otherwise unused areas. Kitchens are often quite compact; you will be able to exercise your ingenuity in making furniture and accessories to make the best use of the space.

Some furniture for other rooms described elsewhere in the book may be brought into the kitchen, but the items that follow are particularly appropriate to this room.

PLYWOOD WINE BOTTLE RACK

Wine stores best when the bottles are nearly horizontal. In most homes there are not many bottles to store at one time; this and the following rack are intended to stand on a worktop or shelf and hold just a few bottles. This rack is made of 1/2-inch plywood, nailed or screwed together and finished with paint. A hardwood plywood, would also look well, with a clear finish.

The design is for a rack (FIG. 6-1) to hold two rows of four bottles not much more than 4 inches in diameter, with necks about 1 1/2 inches in diameter. These are common sizes, but if you have bottles of another size, the rack can be adapted to suit. Also, use the drawings to make a rack of a different length. For the arrangement suggested (FIG. 6-2) the finished rack is about 23-inches long, 10-inches high, and 8-inches wide, but allow for the length of bottles (about 13 inches) across the width. Check these sizes against the available space.

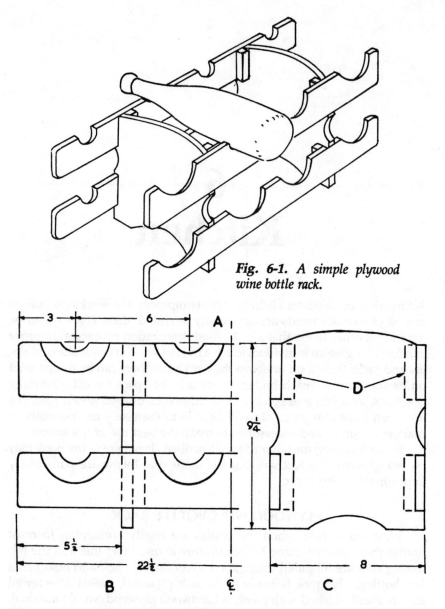

Fig. 6-1. *A simple plywood wine bottle rack.*

Fig. 6-2. *Sizes of the wine bottle rack.*

The curved cutouts are not complete semicircles, but the centers are 1/4-inch above the strip edge (FIG. 6-2A). Using these points as centers for a compass, the curves on two strips are a 2-inch radius and 3/4 inch on the other two strips (FIG. 6-3A). If you have a suitable hole saw, you might mark out each pair on one piece of plywood, with 1/2 inch to cut away

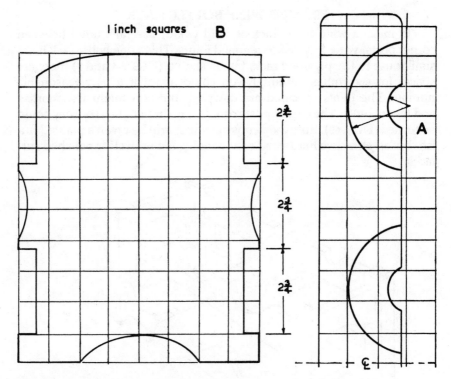

Fig. 6-3. *Shaped parts of the wine bottle rack.*

between after drilling. Otherwise, cut the curves with a bandsaw or jig-saw. The strips are 2³/4-inches wide. Round the outer corners and take the sharpness off all edges. Mark on the positions of the uprights (FIG. 6-2B).

The two uprights (FIGS. 6-2C and 3B) are notched around the strips. Cut away the bottoms to form feet and round the tops. Take sharpness of all edges that will be exposed.

Do any sanding of surfaces and edges that is necessary before assembly. Have blocks ready to glue into the angles (FIG. 6-2D); they could be softwood. Round their ends and the edges that will project or be exposed.

Assemble with glue and fine screws or nails. Check that the rack stands level and is square. Glue the blocks in the inner corners. Finish with several coats of paint.

Materials List for Wine Bottle Rack

4 rails	24 ×	2³/4 ×	1/2 plywood
2 uprights	11 ×	8 ×	1/2 plywood
blocks from	24 ×	5/8 ×	5/8 softwood

FRAMED WINE BOTTLE RACK

To make a wine bottle rack of solid wood, use rails fitted between corner posts, with doweled or tenoned joints. This wine bottle rack has a similar use to the plywood rack, but as shown (FIGS. 6-4 and 5) there are spaces for six bottles, although you could adapt it to any reasonable number. The joints specified are doweled, but you might use mortise and tenon joints. The corner posts could be plain (FIG. 6-6A) or they could be turned (FIG. 6-6B). Softwood construction might be given a painted finish, but an attractive hardwood would look good with clear polished surfaces.

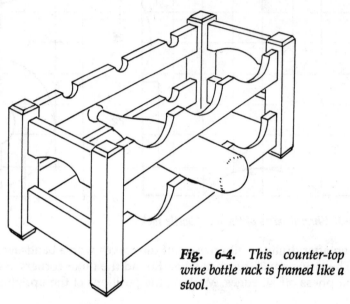

Fig. 6-4. This counter-top wine bottle rack is framed like a stool.

The long rails are laid out with similar curves to those in the plywood rack (FIGS. 6-2 and 3). Cut the ends squarely and mark for dowels (FIG. 6-6C). Round all the other edges.

The other rails are made the same size (FIG. 6-5A). They are shown with the same depths as the long rails, but they could be narrower. If the top rails are hollowed (FIG. 6-5B), they may be used as handles for moving the rack.

Mark the legs for dowels. Plain legs should have chamfers at the top and bottom (FIG. 6-6D).

If you turn the legs, leave sufficient square sections for attaching the rails (FIG. 6-6E).

Drill for dowels. Their diameters should be about half the thickness of the rails, so they would be 5/16 inch for the recommended sections. There should not be much strain on the finished rack, but you will get maximum strength by taking the dowels into the legs so they meet with mitered ends (FIG. 6-5C).

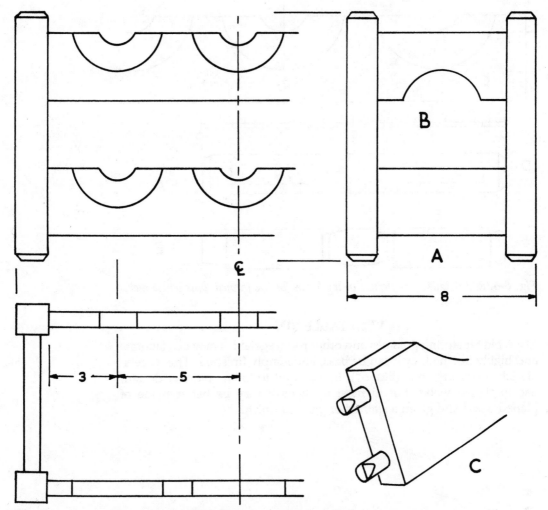

Fig. 6-5. *Sizes and joint details of the framed wine bottle rack.*

Assemble the two long sides first. Check that they match and are square and without twist.

Add the rails the other way. Check squareness in all directions and see that the rack stands level.

Apply the chosen finish.

Materials List for Framed Bottle Rack

4 legs	11	×	1¼	×	1¼
4 rails	17	×	2¾	×	⅝
4 rails	6	×	2¾	×	⅝

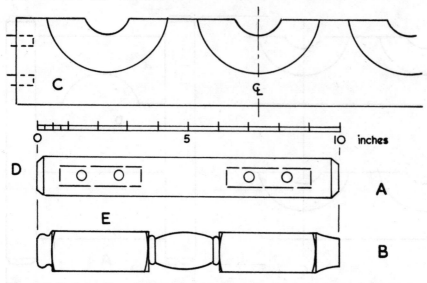

Fig. 6-6. *Rail details and alternative leg forms for the framed wine bottle rack.*

VEGETABLE BIN

A bin for storing potatoes and other root vegetables may be elaborate and highly finished, or it can be basic and simply finished. This vegetable bin is country style (FIG. 6-7). If you want to follow pioneer design, use unplaned wood, but in most kitchens it may be better made of planed wood and given a stained or painted finish.

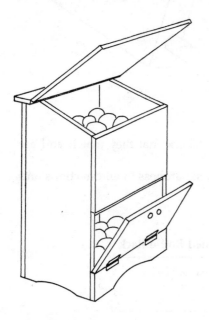

Fig. 6-7. *This vegetable bin provides storage in two compartments.*

Softwood is suitable. If it has a few knots, they may help to give the country appearance. All joints are nailed, but you could also use glue. Drill for most nails, to reduce the risk of splitting.

Make the pair of sides (FIGS. 6-8A and 9A). Mark the positions of the two shelves. Cut away the lower edges for feet.

Back and front parts all overlap the sides, so the shelves (FIGS. 6-8B and 9B) are the same width as the sides. Make them. Put a strip as a stop for the door under the upper shelf (FIG. 6-8C), although the bin sides will also act as stops.

Nail the shelves between the sides.

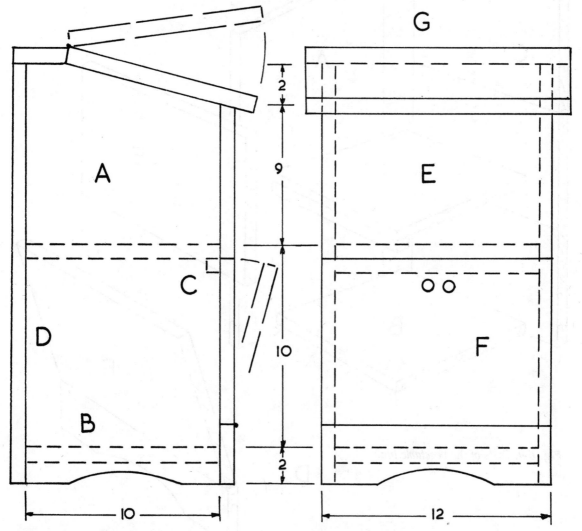

Fig. 6-8. *Sizes of the vegetable bin.*

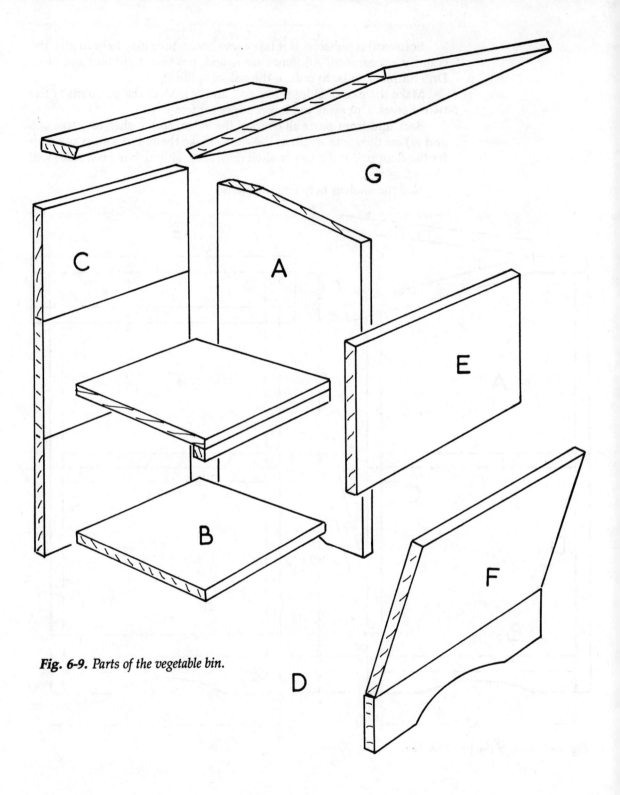

Fig. 6-9. *Parts of the vegetable bin.*

Nail pieces across to form the back (FIGS. 6-8D and 9C). They can be any width to make up the length. Hollow the bottom edge to form feet. Check that the sides are kept parallel as you nail on the back. Boards can be slightly too long, to be planed level after nailing.

Put a strip across at the front (FIG. 6-9D), with a hollowed lower edge.

Put on the front upper part (FIGS. 6-8E and 9E), level with the underside of the top shelf and beveled to match the slope of the top.

Make the bottom door (FIGS. 6-8F and 9F) to fit in the space. Drill two, 1-inch holes near its top edge for two finger openings.

Use two, 2-inch hinges on the surface. Add a spring or magnetic catch to keep the door closed.

The top and its flap extend 1 inch (FIGS. 6-8G and 9G). Miter their meeting angle. Round projecting corners and the edges. Nail the top on and hinge the flap to it.

For a country finish, darkening with stain may be all that is required, but you might wish to seal the wood with varnish, polyurethane, or a colored painted finish.

Materials List for Vegetable Bin

2 sides	22	×	10	×	3/4
3 backs	13	×	8	×	3/4
1 front	13	×	3	×	3/4
1 front	13	×	7	×	3/4
2 shelves	12	×	10	×	3/4
1 door stop	12	×	3/4	×	3/4
1 door	13	×	9 1/2	×	3/4
1 top	15	×	3	×	3/4
1 flap	15	×	10	×	3/4

KITCHEN STOOL

A busy cook will be glad of something with a little comfort to sit on. The kitchen stool may also be needed to stand on; this cannot be done on an upholstered top without risk to damage to the seat or the user. This stool (FIG. 6-10) is a square, at a comfortable height for sitting at a table and with two alternative seats. For normal use, there is an upholstered seat and a plywood shelf, but for standing or using the stool as a small table, the seat may be removed and the shelf put in its place.

Hardwood is advisable for the framework. Softwood would probably not have enough strength in the joints for rough use. It would be possible to dowel the joints, but mortises and tenons are described. The stool will take a standard seat pad 12-inches square; however, any plastic or rubber foam about $1 1/2$-inch thick might be cut to suit.

Mark out the four legs together with the positions of the rails (FIG. 6-11A). Round the tops when the mortises have first been cut.

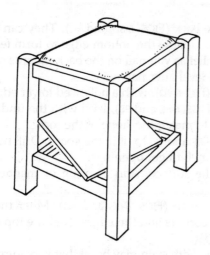

Fig. 6-10. *This kitchen stool has a top and shelf which can be changed over when you need a firm top in place of the upholstered one.*

The eight rails are the same (FIG. 6-11B). Mark them together so the lengths between shoulders are the same. Allow ³/₄-inch each end for the tenons.

The tenons are barefaced, which means they have shoulders at one side only (FIG. 6-11C). Mark them and the mortises at the same time, so they match.

Cut the mortises so they meet in the legs, and miter the ends of the tenons so they almost meet. This will give the maximum glue area (FIG. 6-11D).

Round the tops of the legs. Sand all parts and take sharpness off the edges.

Assemble opposite sides first, to get them square and matching; then, join them with the rails the other way. Check squareness in all directions.

Glue and screw strips inside the rails, ¹/₂-inch down from their top edges (FIGS. 6-11E and F), to form bearers for the seat and shelf.

Seat and shelf are squares of ¹/₂-inch plywood that will drop easily into position; they should fit into either place.

Use cloth or plastic-faced material to cover the foam pad for the seat. If you cut foam from a larger piece, make it about ¹/₄-inch too large, and bevel the underside all round. This allows for compressing and curving the edges. Pull the cloth underneath, and tack far enough in for the tacks to come inside the bearers (FIG. 6-11G). Pull over near the centers of opposite sides first; then work outwards towards the corners, where you may have to make V cuts in the cloth underneath. In this way, it can be neatly tacked with an overlap. Trim surplus cloth away below. Make the plywood base a suitable size to allow for the thickness of the cloth around the edges, so the seat will fit in without force or undue slackness.

Finish with paint or a clear varnish.

4 legs	19	×	1½	×	1½
8 rails	15	×	1½	×	¾
8 bearers	13	×	1	×	½
2 seats	13	×	13	×	½ plywood

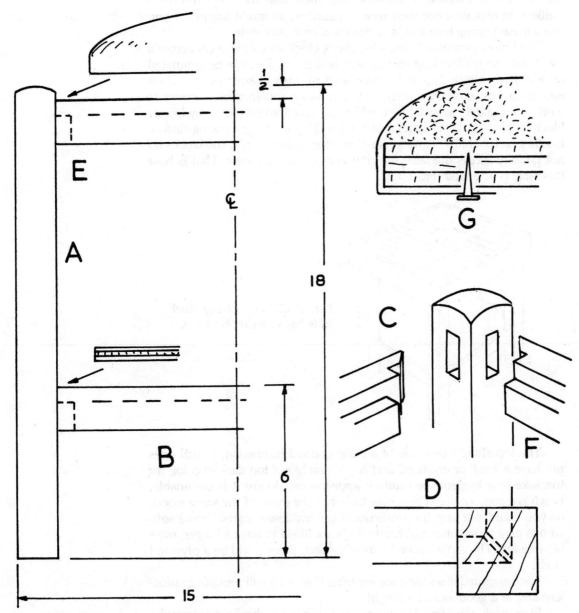

Fig. 6-11. *Sizes and details of the kitchen stool.*

BUTCHER BLOCK TABLE

For the enthusiastic cook, one of the finest food preparation surfaces is a table with a traditional butcher block top. This is substantial and it will resist all kinds of cutting and chopping. The wood surface, with its multiple grain pattern, is kind to cutting tools, so they do not quickly blunt. There is a feeling of stability. You know that whatever you do is unlikely to rock or move your working surface, as might happen if you use a loose cutting board on a surface where it may slide.

In its most primitive form, a butcher's block was a piece cut across a tree trunk, so the working surface was end grain. This can be simulated on a table by gluing together a very large number of squares with their end grain upwards. Obviously, that involves a considerable amount of work in accurately assembling the blocks. An alternative is to lay longer blocks sideways; this is easier and quicker. The resulting working surface is side grain, but it will give years of service. Traditionally, the blocks do not go fully across the table top, but are in shorter pieces. That is how this table is arranged (FIG. 6-12).

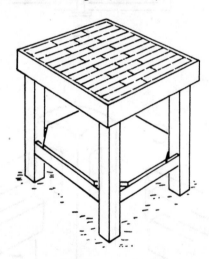

Fig. 6-12. This strong work table has a butcher block top.

The top should be made of a close-grained hardwood, which does not have a smell or exude oil and is preferably not too dark in color, for the sake of a hygienic or sanitary appearance. Where it is obtainable, beech is a good choice. The whole table may be made of the same wood, or you could use any furniture wood for the lower parts. Some softwoods may be suitable, but hardwoods are likely to have a longer, trouble-free life. The top is backed with plywood; there could be a plywood shelf.

The suggested sizes for a square table (FIG. 6-13) will provide a sufficient area at a good working height.

Start with the top. All wood for the blocks should be carefully planed to a square section that is the same throughout, even if it is not exactly 2 inches. If there is a difference, make sure you put the blocks

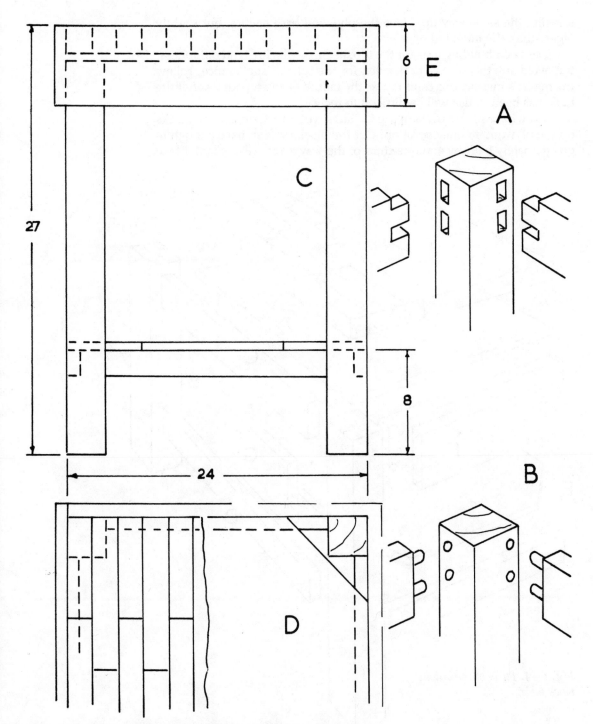

Fig. 6-13. *Sizes and alternative joints for the butcher block table.*

together the same way up. Have the plywood base square, but slightly bigger than the intended final size.

Use a boatbuilding glue for the top, as this will withstand dampness, but avoid any that dries a dark color, for the sake of appearance. Follow the maker's instructions carefully, as the failure of any top joints after the table has been in use will be difficult to rectify.

If you have plenty of clamping facilities, you can assemble the blocks on the plywood in one operation. Cut the blocks so you have enough to go alternately halfway and one-third of the way across (FIG. 6-14A). Make

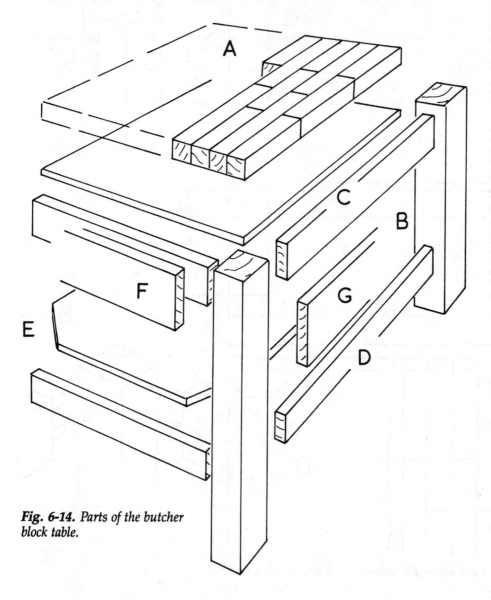

Fig. 6-14. *Parts of the butcher block table.*

sure the meeting ends are square and they will butt together closely. Where ends come at the outside, leave them long, for trimming to length later.

Use ample glue between the blocks and each other as well as the plywood. Start at one side, rubbing the joints together and filling the plywood in a fairly quick operation; then clamp in all directions. Put paper over the blocks to absorb some of the glue which squeezes out.

If you do not have sufficient clamps, or you are doubtful about being able to get a complete assembly true in one operation, it is safer to glue up the blocks in groups. Then join the groups together before finally gluing to the plywood.

Glue together groups of three or four rows. Check that surfaces are as level as you can get them, to reduce the amount of planing later.

When the glue in these groups has set, glue pairs of groups together, and so on until you have made up the full width.

Remove surplus glue, and level the block surface that has to meet the plywood; then glue together.

Whichever method of building the top has been used, remove surplus glue and level the top surface. Trim the edges to a square. Make sure the edges are square across. Use this top as a guide when making the lower parts. It does not matter if sizes are slightly different from the drawing, providing they match the top.

The lower parts are made like a conventional table. The legs are shown square, turn between and below the rails, if you wish. There is a choice of joints. Use barefaced tenons (FIG. 6-13A) or dowels (FIG. 6-13B). Mortise and tenon joints are traditional, but neither type of joint will show. Use whichever you prefer.

Mark out the four legs (FIGS. 6-13C and 14B) with the positions of the rails, which will be level with the outside surfaces. Leave a little extra at the top until after the joints have been cut.

Cut the rails (FIGS. 6-14C and D) to length. Allow 3/4 inch at each end for the tenons, if that is your chosen joint. Be careful to get ends square if they are to be doweled.

Cut the joints or drill for dowels. When the table is assembled, the top of the framework must match the block and plywood top. If there is any difference, it is better for the framework to be slightly smaller than the top, which is easier to plane and match than to try to get an oversize framework to fit.

Assemble two opposite sides of the framework first; then join with the other rails, at all times checking squareness and freedom from twist. Also, check squareness above with the top.

Join the top rails to the plywood top with a few pocket screws driven upwards from outside, where they will be covered. Two at each side should be sufficient, because the joints will be further strengthened with the top frame.

There could be a shelf on the lower rails. A piece of plywood cut at the corners is shown (FIGS. 6-13D and 14E). A different shelf could be made from a number of strips laid across with narrow gaps between. Pieces about $5/8$ inch × 2 inches would be suitable.

Frame the top with strips outside (FIGS. 6-13E and 14F and G). They have to finish level with the surface of the blocks, and be level with the lower edge of the top rail. Miter the corners, but it will be more in keeping with the design to appear to have doweled the corners. Actually, it is better to pull the overlapping corners together with counterbored screws and cover their heads with short pieces of dowel. Do the same to attach the framing pieces to the surfaces of the top rails and blocks, using plenty of glue. When finished, the joint lines around the edges should show a tightly glued line. Round the outer edges and corners of the top framing.

It is usual to leave the working surface of the blocks and their frame untreated. The lower parts could be painted or given a clear finish.

Thoroughly sand the untreated wood. After the table has been in use and scrubbed a few times, some grain fibers may have been raised. These are better treated by scraping than sanding.

Materials List for Butcher Block Table

blocks from twelve	26 ×	2 ×	2
1 top	25 ×	25 ×	$1/2$ plywood
1 shelf	25 ×	25 ×	$1/2$ plywood
4 legs	26 ×	3 ×	3
4 rails	23 ×	$3^{1/2}$ ×	1
4 rails	23 ×	2 ×	1
4 top frames	28 ×	6 ×	1

WELSH DRESSER

This is a traditional piece of furniture which might have a place among your modern kitchen cabinets and appliances. In this context, the word *dresser* means a place to keep all the things needed for food preparation and serving. The design comes from Wales and Welsh immigrants, who would have made these dressers for their new homes, where kitchen and dining room were probably the same place. Using a good hardwood and given a high finish, could result in a piece of dining room furniture. It might be made in that way for the kitchen, although if it is to withstand fairly hard utilitarian use, it could be painted softwood, possibly with a laminated plastic counter top for the working surface.

In an early home, the shelves would have displayed special plates and other treasured possessions, with cutlery and the everyday crockery and all that went with day-to-day cooking and serving, hidden from view in the drawers and cupboard. The sizes and proportions are such that this Welsh dresser (FIG. 6-15) should fit into a kitchen with its working surface level with that of fitted cabinets. Check the suggested sizes (FIG. 6-16) against your available space. For the usual proportions, which produce a good appearance, the dresser should be *higher* than it is *wide* and the depth back-to-front may be about *half* the width.

Most of the main parts are made of boards 1 inch × 8 inches, which will probably be between 3/4 inch and 7/8 inch after planing. Anything thinner would be inadvisable. The early makers did not have the advantage of plywood. The broad expanse of back was made up in several ways, but a popular one was tongued and grooved boards with a bead over each joint (FIG. 6-17A). If you are able to make or buy suitable boards these will make the most authentic reproduction. Otherwise, fit a plywood back (FIG. 6-17B). The door panels would also have been solid wood, but plywood panels are suggested, as these smaller pieces will not look very different, particularly in a painted dresser. If you have the equipment to make fielded solid wood panels, they would be attractive.

The method of construction described includes some traditional joints, while others are doweled. It would be possible to use dowels for more joints, if you wish, but in a piece of furniture of this size, strong joints are needed to give strength and rigidity. If you substitute dowels for other joints, they should be large enough and close enough for strength. Fortunately, modern glues are much stronger than those available to the original makers. Good, close joints should resist all the loads likely to be put on your Welsh dresser.

Collect sufficient boards for all the main parts and select pieces according to their uses. Shelf pieces should be straight-grained, so as to resist warping. If widths have to be built up, you might select other boards, where there will be a mutual resistance to internal movement.

The key parts, which control the sizes of several other pieces, are the pair of ends (FIGS. 6-16A and 17C). Glue together pieces to make up the width. The long piece should be 8-inches wide, but the lower part could be made up from other widths.

Cut rabbets in the rear edges for the back (FIGS. 6-17A and B).

Mark on the positions of the crosswise parts with lines spaced to suit the actual thickness of the wood.

Glue boards together to make the counter top (FIG. 6-16B and 17D); it should be long enough to extend 1 inch at each end, and wide enough to meet the rabbet at the back and overhang the front by 1 inch.

The counter top rests on the extended parts of the ends, and it is cut to fit into grooves in the long part (FIG. 6-17E). Cut the grooves and notch the top to fit. Round the extending edges and corners of the top.

Where the counter top rests on the ends it will be attached later by pocket screws. Cut the pockets and drill the holes in the ends now at about 6-inch intervals, with the first one near the front edge.

Make the two shelves (FIG. 6-16C); they should be fitted to the ends with stopped dado joints (FIG. 6-17F). Lightly round the front edges.

Fig. 6-15. *A Welsh dresser of traditional design.*

The top (FIG. 6-16D) overlaps the back, and extends 1 inch at sides and front. It rests on top of the sides, where it could be doweled. Because it is above the normal sight lines and screw heads will not show, it can be screwed downwards later. A strip underneath it will support the back

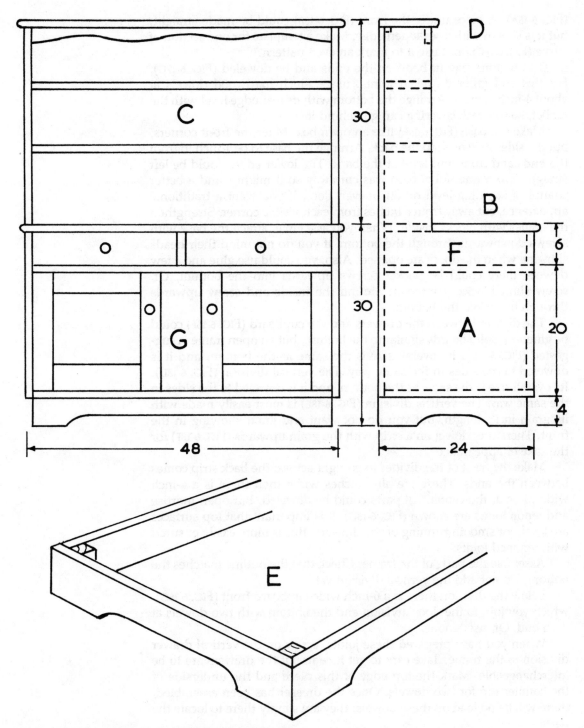

Fig. 6-16. *Sizes and base details of the Welsh dresser.*

(FIG. 6-18A). A piece under the front (FIG. 6-18B) could be made straight, but it is shown with a scalloped edge. Make a template for one section of curve (FIG. 6-18C), and use it to mark an even pattern.

The bottom may fit between the ends and be doweled (FIG. 6-17G). For this and other dowelled joints, use 1/2-inch hardwood dowels at about 4-inch centers. Arrange the bottom with its rear edge level with the rabbet, so the back covering can go behind it.

Make the base (FIG. 6-16E) like an open box. Miter the front corners, but the sides may overlap the back. Arrange the base to be 1-inch in from the ends and front, but level at the back. The lower edges could be left straight, but a traditional base was cut away so it might stand a better chance of standing level on an uneven floor. If you want a traditional appearance, cut away from 6 inches from each visible corner. Strengthen the angles with blocks inside. When you assemble, attach the base with screws downwards through the bottom, if you do not mind their heads showing when the doors are opened. Also, you could use glue and a few dowels; there could be pocket screws upwards into the bottom. Or, screw short blocks at intervals around the inside and screw upwards through them into the bottom.

The divider between the drawers and the cupboard (FIG. 6-16F) could be glued-up solid boards similar to the bottom, but an open frame is suggested (FIG. 6-18D). Its overall size is the same as the bottom, and it is doweled to the sides in the same way. The vertical division (FIG. 6-18D). Its overall size is the same as the bottom, and it is doweled to the sides in the same way. The vertical division (FIG. 6-18E) is most easily made with its grain in its length, but you do not want end grain showing in the front. Therefore, dowel on a strip with the grain upwards (FIG. 6-18F) for the sake of appearance.

Make the front of the divider to go right across; the back strip comes between the ends. These are all 2-inches wide; then there is a 4-inch wide piece at the center. All parts could be doweled, but open mortise and tenon joints are shown (FIG. 6-18G). It is important that top surfaces are level, for smooth running of the drawers; this is more easily ensured with tenoned joints.

Assemble the parts of the frame. Check that the outline matches the bottom. Do not add the vertical division yet.

Below the division there is a 6-inch wide cupboard front (FIG. 6-16G), which you join to the door division and the bottom with two dowels at each end. Or, use tenons.

When you have prepared these joints, screw on the vertical drawer division to the frame. Take care to get it central if the drawers are to be interchangeable. Mark the top edge of this piece and the underside of the counter top for two dowels. Once the dresser has been assembled, there will be no load on these dowels; they are simply there to locate the parts.

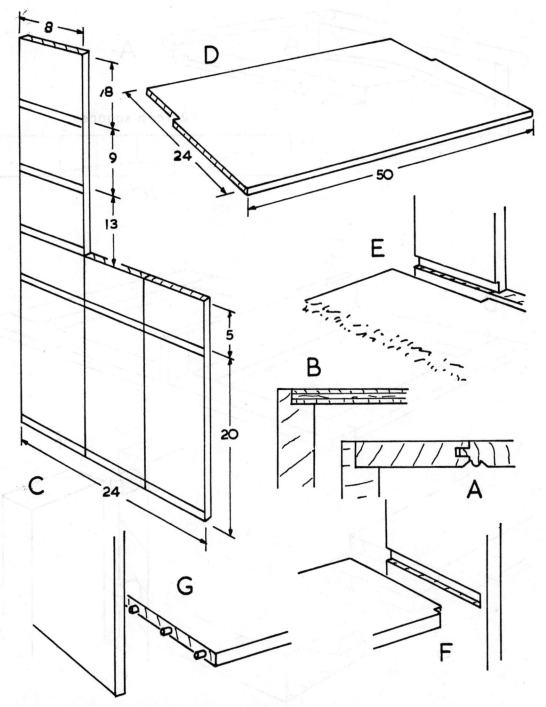

Fig. 6-17. *Main parts and joint details of the Welsh dresser.*

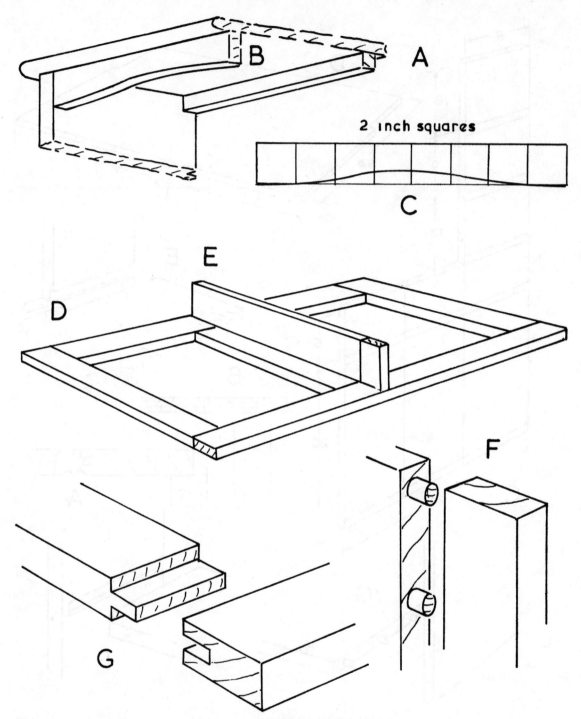

Fig. 6-18. *Constructional details of the framework of the Welsh dresser.*

2 inch squares

This completes the preparation of all parts for the main framework. Check that dowel holes are all drilled and their dowels are ready. See that all screw holes that can be drilled in advance have been drilled. Do any rounding of edges and sanding that might be difficult after assembly. Ready the material for the back.

Make the base completely, and prepare it for attaching to the bottom. Ready the drawer division and its vertical piece. Join the pieces that go under the top.

Start the main assembly with the back of the dresser on the floor. All of the crosswise parts have to go in at the same operation. Join the drawer division under the counter top. Glue in all the crosswise pieces. Clamp across the bottom; then, when you have slot-screwed the counter top and the top piece above the shelves, all other parts should be held close.

Compare diagonals at the front and back to ensure squareness. Stand the assembly on a flat surface, and add the back with glue and screws to anything crossed. Add the base after you have squared the main assembly.

In traditional Welsh dressers, the doors and drawers fit flush to their frames; that is how they are described here, in the traditional way. It is easier to make the fronts stand forward and overlap their frames, and there are simpler constructions. Therefore, choose if you want to be as authentic as possible, or adopt a similar construction to some of the projects described elsewhere.

Make each door to fit its opening, with no more clearance than is necessary for operation. Work to the actual sizes of the opening. door frames are made of 3-inch strips on three sides, and a 4-inch strip at the bottom (FIG. 6-19A), which looks better than having the same width all round.

Groove the inner edges of all pieces for the plywood panel. For 1/4-inch plywood this could be 1/2-inch deep.

Mark out the tenons first (FIG. 6-19B). Cut back to the bottom of the groove, and allow stubs the groove depth at the outside. Tenons may be 1 1/2-inches long.

Leave the door sides too long at first. Mark out and cut the mortises (FIG. 6-19C).

Cut the plywood panel, so it will fit with a little clearance. It should not touch the bottoms of the grooves, or it might prevent he joints being pulled tight.

Clamp the doors tightly when gluing; then, cut the ends off the sides. Trim if necessary, to fit the opening.

Many old Welsh dressers had ornamental hinges on the surface. You might wish to follow this practice, or insert two, 2-inch ordinary hinges into the door edges. It is usual to hinge on the outsides, but if hinging in the middle would suit your needs better, that is possible.

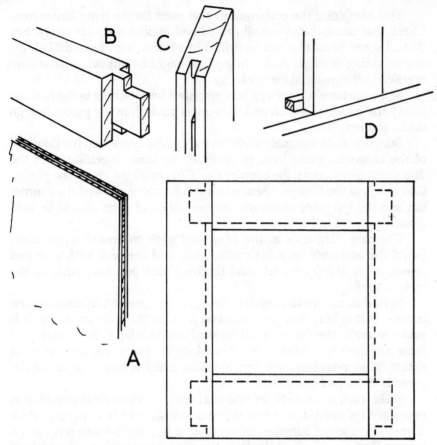

Fig. 6-19. *Construction of the doors for the Welsh dresser.*

Turned knobs are appropriate, or use other handles. Locate them above the centers of the doors.

Make door stops with strips projecting behind the center piece (FIG. 6-19D) at the top and bottom. Use spring or magnetic catches.

The drawers (FIG. 6-20A) have half-blind dovetails at the front corners and through dovetails at the rear corners with a thin plywood bottom fitting into grooves in the sides and the front. The front is 1-inch thick, and the sides and back are 5/8-inch thick. Prepare these strips with grooves near the bottom edges for the plywood bottom. Grooves for 1/4-inch plywood, 1/4 inch from the bottom edge and 1/4-inch deep would be satisfactory.

Make the drawer sides first to a depth that will slide in easily. Mark the length back to front of the openings.

Make the fronts to fit the openings with very little clearance.

Mark the half-blind dovetails (FIG. 6-20B). Arrange the bottom half tail, so it includes the groove (FIG. 6-20C); then, it will be hidden after

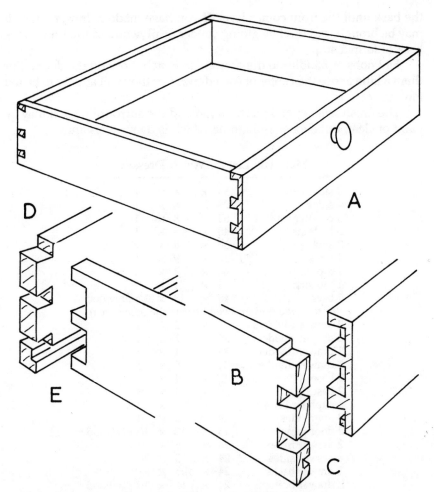

Fig. 6-20. *Construction of the drawers for Welsh dresser.*

assembly. Cut the tails in the sides, and use them to mark the sockets in the fronts.

Mark the dovetails at the back (FIG. 6-20D), so the tails will project slightly after assembly. Cut away parallel to the top edges of the grooves. The back fits above the plywood with pins going through immediately above the grooves (FIG. 6-20E).

Assemble these parts of each drawer; then, slide in the bottom from the back. It need not be glued, but should have screws upwards into the back at about 3-inch intervals. The plywood might extend a little at the back at first.

Try a drawer in position. Edges or sides might need lightly planing. A drawer must finish with its front level with the surrounding frame, when it is pushed in. It will probably project slightly at first. That can be corrected by planing off parts of the extending tails or plywood bottom at the back until the front comes level. If you have made a drawer short, it may be brought out level by gluing veneer or plywood to the framework back to form a stop.

Fit knobs or handles to the drawers to match those on the doors. Put them a little above the center of each drawer, or they will appear to be too low.

The finish will depend on the wood and the surroundings. It may be paint or clear, but choose something which is damp-resistant.

Materials List for Welsh Dresser

2 sides	58 ×	8 ×	1
4 sides	28 ×	8 ×	1
3 counter tops	52 ×	8 ×	1
3 bottoms	48 ×	8 ×	1
2 shelves	50 ×	8 ×	1
1 top	52 ×	9 ×	1
1 top strip	48 ×	2 ×	1
1 top strip	48 ×	1 ×	1
1 back	48 ×	48 ×	1/2 plywood
(or tongued and grooved boards the same area)			
2 drawer dividers	48 ×	2 ×	1
2 drawer dividers	24 ×	2 ×	1
1 drawer divider	24 ×	4 ×	1
1 drawer divider	24 ×	5 ×	1
2 bases	48 ×	4 ×	1
2 bases	24 ×	4 ×	1
1 cupboard front	20 ×	6 ×	1
8 door sides	20 ×	3 ×	1
2 door panels	18 ×	18 ×	1/4 plywood
2 drawer fronts	24 ×	5 ×	1
4 drawer sides	24 ×	5 ×	5/8
2 drawer backs	24 ×	41/2 ×	5/8
2 drawer bottoms	24 ×	24 ×	1/4 plywood

7
Bedroom

You may not consider making all the major pieces of furniture for a bedroom, although it is possible and might not be as difficult as you expect. In a modern home some things are better built in. Even if you have your bedroom equipped with the essential furniture, there are many, usually smaller, items which you can make to add to the comfort and convenience of the room.

Some of these smaller pieces of furniture may also have uses elsewhere, but they are primarily for the room where you spend almost one-third of your life so why not make it more comfortable?

DRESSER STOOL

Somewhere to sit in front of a dresser mirror will be appreciated. Many modern dressers are unsuitable because the mirror is inconvenient from a standing position. For a prolonged session, sitting is the obvious posture.

This dresser stool (FIG. 7-1) has a flat top with rounded edges, and it might be used as it is or with a cushion. There is a shelf below; the sides extend upwards with hand holes, to keep a cushion in place and to provide an easy means of moving the stool.

Construction could be with hardwood or softwood. Boards may have to be joined to make up widths. The seat and shelf have tenons taken through the sides and projecting with curved ends. Besides providing strength, the projecting *tusk* tenons are a design feature. Although it would be simpler to dowel the parts together, they might not be strong enough to stand up to long use, when the stool may be stood on or taken for other uses elsewhere.

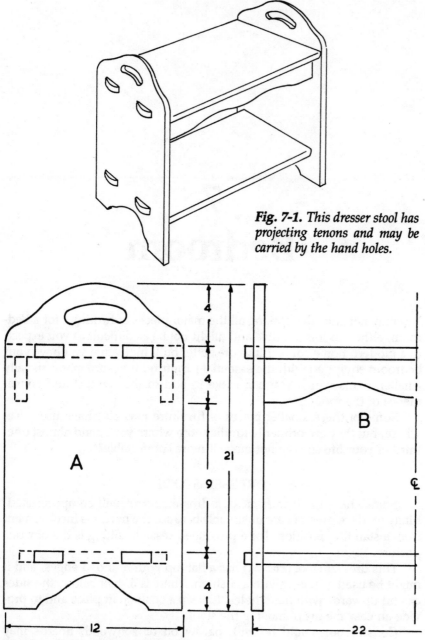

Fig. 7-1. *This dresser stool has projecting tenons and may be carried by the hand holes.*

Fig. 7-2. *Sizes of the dresser stool.*

Mark out the pair of ends (FIG. 7-2A) with the positions of the top and shelf, which is kept 1-inch in from the edges.

Mark and cut the shaped tops of the sides (FIG. 7-3A). Drill the ends of the hand holes, and cut away the waste between them. Thoroughly round the edge of the hole and all of the shaped top edge.

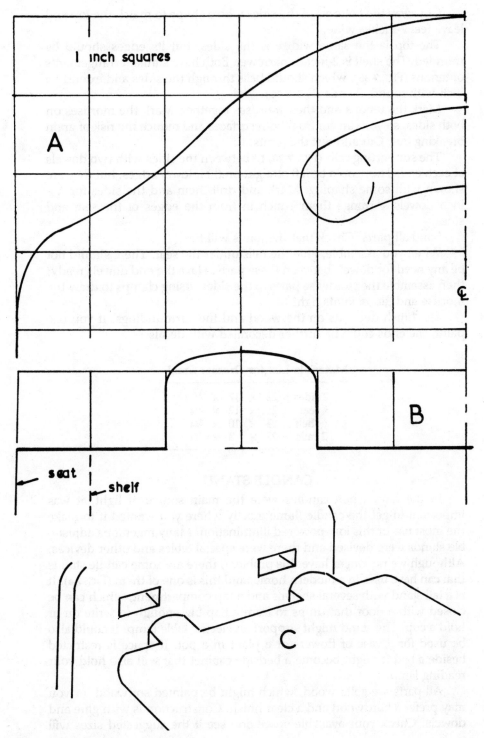

1 inch squares

A

₵

seat

shelf

B

C

Fig. 7-3. *Shaped parts of the dresser stool.*

Cut away the bottoms of the sides with a shape to match the top and leave feet 2-inches wide.

The top is the same width as the sides, but its edges should be rounded. The shelf is 2-inches narrower. Both have similar arrangements of tenons (FIG. 7-3B), which should pass through the sides and extend $1/2$ inch with rounded ends (FIG. 7-3C).

Mark the tenons and their mortises together. Mark the mortises on both sides, so you can cut from both surfaces and reduce the risk of grain breaking out. Cut and test the joints.

The supporting rails (FIG. 7-2B) fit between the sides with two dowels at each end. They could be left straight on their lower edges, but they are shown with some shaping. Mark and drill them and the sides for $3/8$-inch dowels. Arrange them 1-inch in from the edges of the seat and sides.

Sand all parts. Check that the joints will fit.

When you assemble, glue the rails under the seat. There should not be any need for dowels between these parts. Have the end dowels ready; then assemble the crosswise parts to the sides, using clamps to draw the mortise and tenon joints tight.

The finish depends on the wood and the surroundings. If you use paint, the ends could be further decorated with decals.

Materials List for Dresser Stool

2 sides	22	×	12	×	$3/4$
1 seat	25	×	12	×	$3/4$
1 shelf	25	×	10	×	$3/4$
2 rails	22	×	3	×	$3/4$

CANDLE STAND

In the days when candles were the main source of light, it was important to get the candle flame exactly where you wanted it to make the most use of this low-powered illumination. Many ingenious adjustable stands were devised and there were special tables and other devices. Although we no longer have this problem, there are some candle stands that can have uses in a modern home, and this is one of them (FIG. 7-4). It is a tall stand with several shelves and a top compartment, which can be closed with a door that drops to form a flap big enough to write on or hold a cup. The stand might support an electric table lamp. It could also be used for a vase of flowers or a plant in a pot. If space is restricted beside a bed it might become a bedside cabinet that will also hold your reading lamp.

All parts are solid wood, which might be painted softwood, or you may prefer a hardwood and a clear finish. Construction is with glue and dowels. Check your available space and see if the suggested sizes will

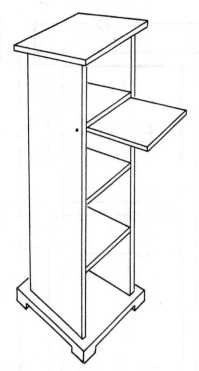

Fig. 7-4. *This traditional candle stand is tall enough to carry a bedside lamp; the flap will take a cup, or it can be used for writing.*

suit (FIG. 7-5) or need to be modified. If you alter sizes, make sure there is a good spread of feet to give stability.

Mark out the back (FIGS. 7-5A and 6A) with the positions of the shelves.

From this, mark the pair of sides (FIGS. 7-5B and 6B). Note that the top shelf (FIGS. 7-5C and 6C) has to be set back enough to clear the flap.

Make the shelves with the grain across and their lengths the same as the width of the back.

Mark all these parts for dowel holes, which could be 5/16 inch. Between back and sides they could be about 12-inches apart; have two in each end of each shelf. Drill pairs of holes in both ends of the upright parts for attaching the top and bottom.

Join the back and shelves to one side; then add the other side. There should be no difficulty with squareness, as the parts will pull each other square.

Top and bottom are the same (FIG. 7-6D) and should overlap the other parts the same amount all round. Mark to match the dowel holes in the ends of the uprights. Drill carefully.

Put square blocks as feet under the corners of the bottom (FIG. 7-5D).

Make the door flap (FIGS. 7-5E and 6E) to fit easily between the sides and in front of the top shelf. Extend about 2-inches below that shelf.

Put a small strip across under the top (FIGS. 7-5F and 6F) to act as a door stop.

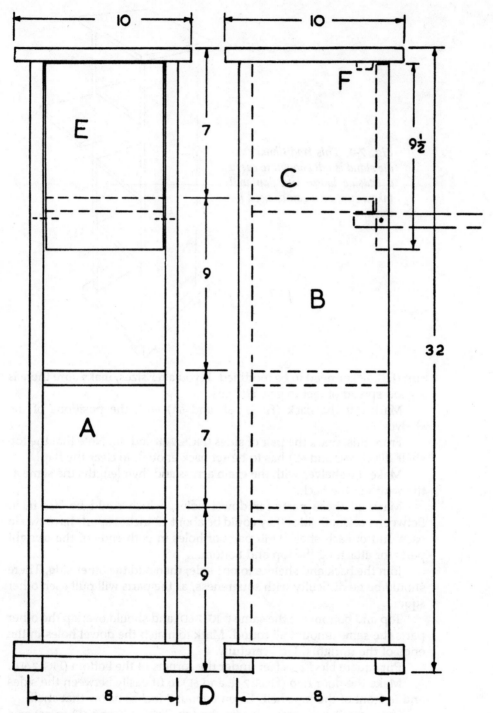

Fig. 7-5. *Sizes of the candle stand.*

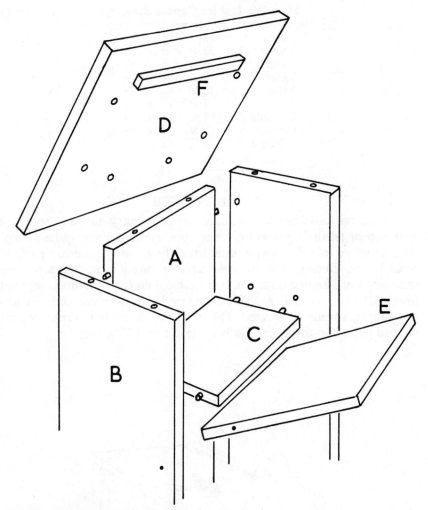

Fig. 7-6. *Assembly of the candle stand.*

Mark and drill for screws through the sides to act as door pivots. They have to be located so the door closes squarely, but when it is open it lodges under the shelf and remains level. Although the pivots will be fairly large screws (#10-gauge × 2-inch roundhead are suitable), it is best to start by drilling holes for fine nails first. Try pivoting the flap on two nails. For slight alterations, make corrections as you drill for the screws.

You could put a knob or handle on the door, but that is not essential, as you can open it by pushing its bottom edge, and close it by pushing the top edge.

Sand all parts before applying a finish. Round the corners of the feet to minimize marking a carpet. Glue cloth underneath if you wish.

Materials List for Candle Stand

1 back	32	×	$6^3/4$	×	$5/8$
2 sides	32	×	8	×	$5/8$
2 shelves	8	×	$7^3/8$	×	$5/8$
1 shelf	8	×	$6^3/4$	×	$5/8$
1 flap	10	×	$6^3/4$	×	$5/8$
1 top	11	×	10	×	$5/8$
1 bottom	11	×	10	×	$5/8$
feet from	12	×	2	×	$5/8$
1 door stop	7	×	$3/4$	×	$3/8$

SMALL DRESSER

In a large bedroom the facilities for combing your hair, applying make-up or leisurely preparing your appearance may be quite a large dresser, either free-standing or built-in. If the room is more compact, so must be the dresser; this dressing table or vanity is intended for use where space is limited (FIG. 7-7). It is a table with classical lines, without lower framing, so a stool can be pushed underneath or you can sit without your legs being obstructed. The mirror in its frame is supported on shaped pillars, so the general effect is traditional Victorian.

Fig. 7-7. *This small dresser is made of a table with a hinged mirror.*

Construction should be hardwood, preferably matching existing furniture. With a traditional appearance it would be appropriate to use traditional mortise and tenon joints, but no one will see the leg joints, so you could use dowels between rails and legs. The pillars could also be doweled to the table top, but tenons are better there.

Exact sizes are not important. The table top will have to be made by gluing boards together. If this results in a slightly different width, it does not matter, unless your table has to fit a particular position. If you have a mirror of a different size, that could be used, unless it is vastly different. However, if you make a frame and take it to a glass merchant, he will have stock mirror glass and will cut what you need. Check the thickness of available mirror glass before cutting rabbets in the frames.

The suggested sizes (FIG. 7-8) are for a table with its top 16 inches × 28 inches, standing 27-inches above the floor. The tilting mirror projects about 20-inches above the table top. If your situation requires the table to be a different size, alter measurements at this stage. Do not make the top too narrow, or this may make the table unsteady.

Prepare the wood for the four legs (FIG. 7-8A). Mark their lengths, but leave a little extra at the tops until after the joints have been cut. They are shown with tapers on the inner surfaces only, so the outsides will be square to the top in both directions. Mark the tapers from 6-inches down. Reduce to 1^{1}/4-inch squares at the feet. Cut the tapers both ways.

Mark out the rails (FIGS. 7-8B and C). If they are to be doweled to the legs, cut the ends square to fit against the legs. If you want tenons, allow for about ^{5}/8 inch into each leg (FIG. 7-10A). Use double tenons ^{3}/8-inch thick (FIG. 7-10B).

Mark matching mortises on the legs. Cut them to meet (FIG. 7-8D) or be slightly deeper, so the tenon corners will have to be mitered.

If you use dowels, they may be ^{3}/8 inch or ^{1}/2 inch, arranged three on each rail end. Drill the legs, so the dowels meet and are mitered.

Cut away the lower edges of each rail (FIG. 7-10C) 3 inches from each leg. Take sharpness off all edges which will be exposed.

It will be best to hold the top on with buttons, to allow for expansion and contraction, so cut grooves on the inner surfaces of the rails (FIG. 7-8E). A suitable size is a groove ^{3}/8-inch wide and deep, ^{3}/8 inch from the rail edge.

Assemble two long sides first. Pull the joints tight, and check that the legs are square to the rails, and the outside measurements are the same at top and bottom. If necessary, to hold the shape while the glue sets, nail strips across under the feet. See that the two assembled sides match.

Join the rails in the other direction in the same way. Check squareness of the assembly when viewed from above.

Trim the tops of the legs level with the rails. Sight across the rails to look for high spots or twist.

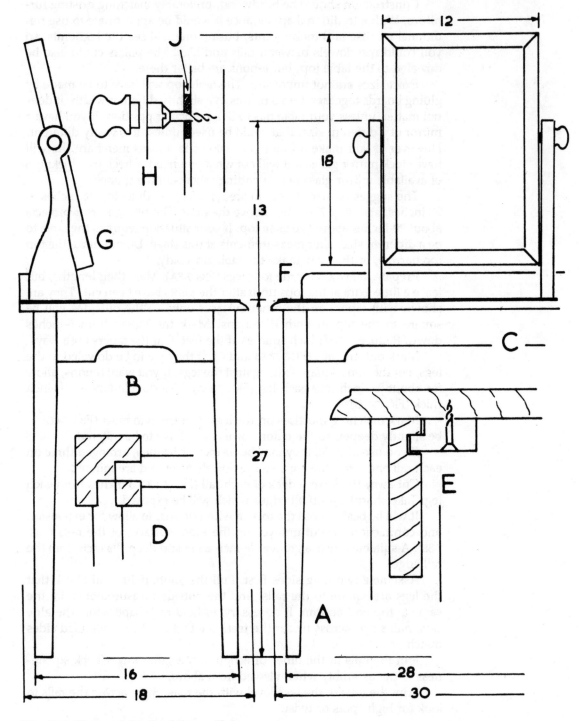

Fig. 7-8. Sizes and details of the small dresser.

Glue and level boards to make the top. Make it to extend 1-inch outside the legs all round.

Leave the rear edge square, where the ledge will fit, but the other three edges may be molded. A simple rounding might be all that is needed. The molding could match other furniture, or use any molding cutter available (FIG. 7-10D).

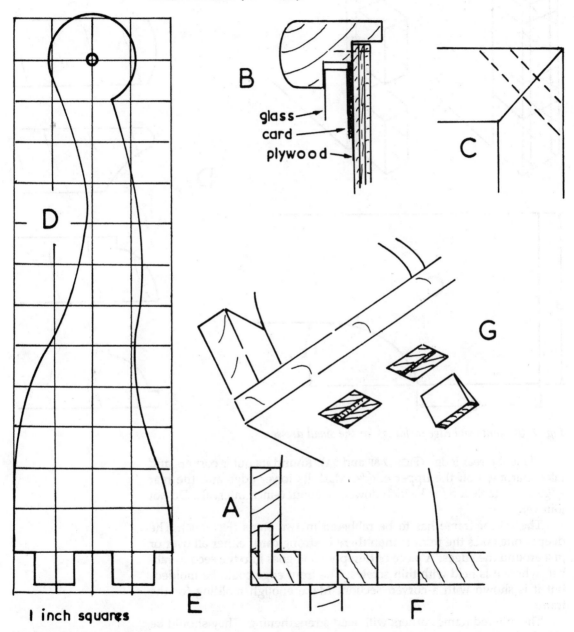

B

glass
card
plywood

C

D

G

A

E

F

1 inch squares

Fig. 7-9. *The mirror supports and joints for the small dresser.*

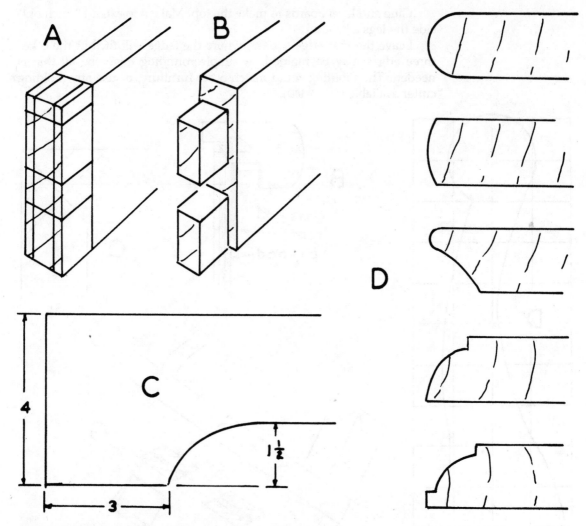

Fig. 7-10. *Joints and edge moldings for the small dresser.*

Make the rear ledge (FIGS. 7-8F and 9A). Round its outer corners and take sharpness off the upper edges. Mark its lower edge and the rear edge of the table top for ³⁄₈-inch dowels at about 6-inch intervals. Do not join yet.

The mirror frame has to be rabbeted in two steps (FIG. 7-9B). The deeper one takes the mirror; then there is strong card, either all over or just around the edges. A piece of thin plywood goes into the second rabbet, where it is held with thin screws. The front edge could be molded, but it is shown with a curved section. Make enough molding for the frame.

The mitered frame corners will need strengthening. They should be glued; the back plywood will provide some strength, but one way of reinforcing is with 1/4-inch dowels arranged diagonally (FIG. 7-9C). Glue them in and plane the ends level after the glue has set.

Cut the two pillars (FIGS. 7-8G and 9D). Use straight tapered pillars, if you wish, but those shown enhance appearance. Remove all saw marks from the shaped edges and take the sharpness off, or fully round them. Tenons are advised (FIG. 7-9E); or arrange three, 1/2-inch in diameter dowels in each pillar.

At the top of each leg drill for a stout screw #10-gauge would be suitable. Counterbore to about half thickness (FIG. 7-8H).

To hold the mirror at any angle by friction there may be rubber or soft fiber washers between the pillars and the mirror frame (FIG. 7-8J). Allow for the thicknesses of these when arranging the spacing of the pillars on the table top.

Mark the mortises in the table top (FIG. 7-9F) at a spacing that will allow the pillars to be upright when the screws are tightened through the rubber washers into the mirror frame.

To hold the mirror at any angle by friction there may be rubber or soft fiber washers between the pillars and the mirror frame (FIG. 7-8J). Allow for the thicknesses of these when arranging the spacing of the pillars on the table top.

Mark the mortises in the table top (FIG. 7-9F) at a spacing that will allow the pillars to be upright when the screws are tightened through the rubber washers into the mirror frame.

Cut the mortises. Join the ledge strip at the same time as the pillars. Put saw cuts across the tenon ends; then, drive wedges from below when you glue the joints (FIG. 7-9G). Check that the pillars are upright and match the mirror before the glue has set.

Attach the top to the leg and rail assembly with buttons (FIGS. 1-3 and 7-8E). There might be three on each long rail and one at each end. Assemble the table inverted, so you get the overhang the same all round.

Make knobs with dowel ends that will press into the counterbored holes over the screws through the pillars. They should be left as push fits without glue, so you can withdraw them if you need to tighten the screws. Do not finally assemble and fully tighten the screws until after staining and polishing the wood.

Materials List for Small Dresser

4 legs	28 ×	1³/4 ×	1³/4
2 rails	28 ×	4 ×	3/4
2 rails	16 ×	4 ×	3/4
1 top	32 ×	18 ×	3/4
2 pillars	14 ×	4 ×	1¹/4
2 frames	19 ×	1¹/2 ×	7/8
2 frames	13 ×	1¹/2 ×	7/8
1 back	18 ×	12 ×	1/4 plywood

FENCE RAIL BED

Beds come in an enormous range of sizes and designs. Fortunately for anyone building a bed, modern foam or internally-sprung mattresses have all the softness required without the need for a supporting spring mattress. This means that you can build a bed with solid supports and the mattress will provide all the comfort you need with simplicity of construction.

This bed (FIG. 7-11) is a country-style design with the head and foot arranged very similarly to a farm fence. Mattress support is arranged by a number of boards across. The bed is made in three parts, so it can be taken through doorways and up stairs. It is then screwed together and can be disassembled if ever necessary.

Construction may be with hardwood or softwood. The design is particularly suitable for softwood, which could be painted, but it would look attractive clear if surrounded by other knotty pine or similar furniture.

The bed could be made any size. As drawn (FIG. 7-12), a mattress 36 inches × 78 inches is assumed, but if you get your foam or internally-sprung mattress first, fashion the woodwork to suit.

The head is shown 30-inches high, and the foot is 20 inches. Alter these and you might wish to lower the foot so sheets go over it, but for an authentic country look there should be a foot high enough to see.

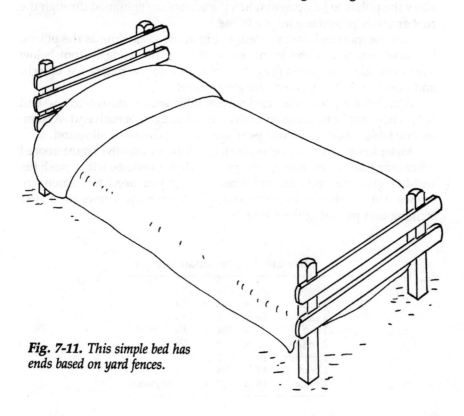

Fig. 7-11. *This simple bed has ends based on yard fences.*

Start with the bed frame (FIG. 7-12A). This should be the same width as your mattress and about 1-inch longer. Use straight-grained wood without large knots, even **if** elsewhere you regard knots as decorative features.

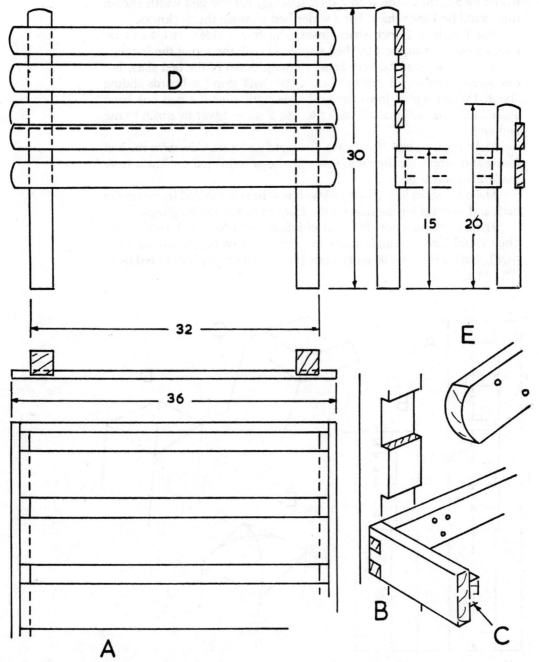

Fig. 7-12. *Sizes and details of the fence-end bed.*

Make the bed frame like an open box. The corners could be screwed, or dovetailed; also, finger joints (FIG. 7-12B) are simple and secure with screws both ways.

Cut enough bed slats to fit across between the sides. A suitable size would be 5-inches wide with 1-inch spacing. For the bed width shown they could be 1-inch thick. For a wider bed increase the thickness.

Put 1 inch × 2 inch strips inside the frame sides (FIG. 7-12C) far enough down to support the bed slats level with the top of the frame.

There is no need for very firm fastening down of the bed slats, but one screw in each end into the 2-inch strip will stop the boards sliding about. Do not screw down the end slats until after the bed has been assembled; this will make it easier to use a screwdriver to attach to the bed ends.

Make the long legs (FIG. 7-13A). Cut notches 1/2-inch deep for the bed frame and others for the rails. Leave the tops untreated until you have made the short legs.

Make the short legs (FIG. 7-13B) with notches for the bed frame on the back and notches for the rails on the front to match the long legs.

There are several possible ways of finishing the tops of the bed posts. They could have a simple rounding (FIG. 7-11) or be chamfered (FIG. 7-13C). Work a shallow flat-sided cone (FIG. 7-13D) or give it rounded faces (FIG. 7-13E).

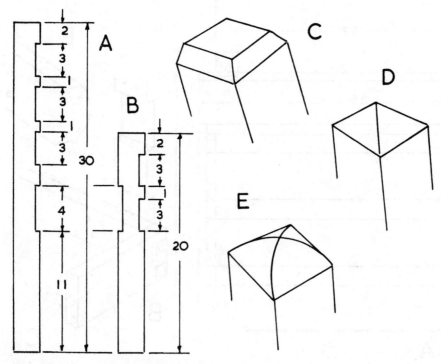

Fig. 7-13. *Legs for the fence rail bed.*

Make the rails (FIG. 7-12D) the same length as the width of the bed frame. Round the ends and take sharpness off all exposed edges. Mark for the legs 2-inches in from each end.

To maintain a country appearance, any screws used may be left exposed. If you prefer to hide them, counterbore and cover with plugs. The rails might be attached to the legs with #8- or #10-gauge × 1³/₄-inch or 2-inch screws. With glue, it should be sufficient to arrange two screws diagonally (FIG. 7-12E). Assemble both ends, checking that they are square and match each other.

Try the ends on the bed frame. Mark the positions and adjust notches if necessary.

Drill the frame ends for screws into the legs. Three or four in each place should be sufficient. They could be #10 or #12-gauge × 2¹/₂-inch screws. Drill pilot holes and wax the screws before driving, if you expect to have to remove and replace them many times.

Make a trial assembly before applying a finish, by using a few screws. Apply paint or a clear finish; then move the parts to the bedroom and make the final assembly.

Materials List for Fence Rail Bed

2 legs	32	×	2¹/₂	×	2¹/₂
2 legs	22	×	2¹/₂	×	2¹/₂
5 rails	38	×	3	×	1
2 bed frames	80	×	4	×	1
2 bed frames	38	×	4	×	1
2 bed frames	78	×	2	×	1
13 bed slats	36	×	5	×	1

BEDHEAD SHELVES

When in bed, we need places to put a great many things, preferably where they can be reached without getting out of bed. This assembly of shelves on a backboard attached to the wall (FIG. 7-14) fits above and beside the bed without the bed position having to be altered. There are shelves 5-inches wide and two lower shaped ones projecting 8 inches.

The unit could be made with all edges straight and that might suit the decor in some bedrooms, but usually the curving shown will be more acceptable and fit in with the surroundings. The sizes suggested (FIG. 7-15) will fit round a bed 54-inches wide and are based on half a standard sheet of plywood, but the same design can be used for a bed of any width, by altering the center section to suit. If there have to be joins in the plywood, they can be behind one of the uprights.

Use softwood for the framing and softwood plywood for the back. Use hardwood to match existing furniture with veneered plywood for the back. For a special effect, cover the back with one of the self-adhesive

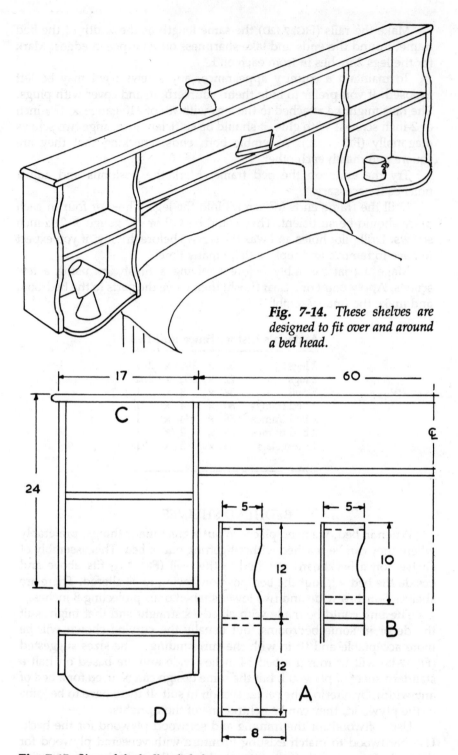

Fig. 7-14. These shelves are designed to fit over and around a bed head.

Fig. 7-15. Sizes of the bedhead shelves.

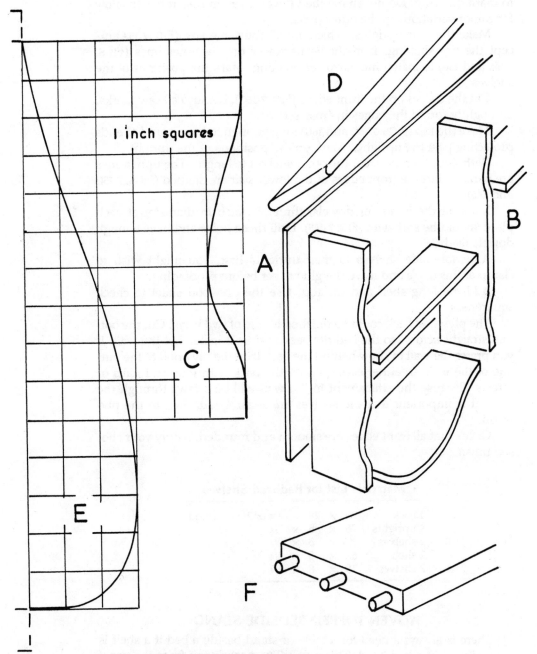

Fig. 7-16. *Shapes and assembly of the bedhead shelves.*

clothlike facings. It would be possible to use dado joints all round, but it will be simpler and strong enough to use dowels.

Lay out the design on half a sheet of plywood, which will become the back (FIG. 7-16A). This could be on the reverse side if you do not want to mark the front. Do not shape the plywood yet, in case it has to allow for minor variations in the other parts.

Make the four uprights, which are all the same size (FIG. 7-15A) except the top shaping; it might be narrower on the inner ones (FIGS. 7-15B and 16B) to match the narrower opening. Mark the positions of the shelves.

Cut the curves on the front edges (FIG. 7-16C). Remove all saw marks, and lightly round the edges in cross-section.

Make the top (FIGS. 7-15C and 16D) long enough to have rounded ends projecting past the uprights. Mark on the positions of the uprights.

With this as a guide, cut the other shelves to length. The upper ones are parallel, but the front edges of the lower pair are shaped (FIGS. 7-15D and 16E).

Mark all the joints for dowels; three, $3/8$ inch in diameter at each place should be sufficient (FIG. 7-16F). Drill these holes and have enough dowels ready.

Assemble side shelves to their uprights first. You might wish to clamp at this stage and leave the glue to set before proceeding.

Add the long shelf and the top. Use the plywood sheet to check squareness.

The plywood back could be finished in one of two ways. Cut the bottom straight across, so the bed fits back against it instead of the wall. If you prefer the wall to show behind the bed, trim the plywood to the outline of the unit. In either case, join on the back with glue and nails or screws. Because the attachment to the wall will be screws through the back, it is important that the shelves are securely attached to the plywood.

Check that all front edges are smooth and rounded. Apply your chosen finish.

Materials List for Bedhead Shelves

1 back	96	×	24	×	$1/4$ or $1/2$ plywood	
4 uprights	26	×	5	×	$3/4$	
2 shelves	18	×	5	×	$3/4$	
1 shelf	62	×	5	×	$3/4$	
2 shelves	18	×	8	×	$3/4$	

WOVEN-TOPPED BEDSIDE STAND

There is always a need for a table or stand beside a bed if a shelf is not included in a bed head. This stand (FIG. 7-17) differs from the usual table or cabinet in having a flat woven top, which gives adequate support to anything put on it. However, it has a soft appearance appropriate to a bedroom.

The top is a checker pattern of cord, seagrass or similar material, which could be all one color or bright contrasting colors. The woven top

Fig. 7-17. *This bedside stand has a tightly-woven top on a framework having a strip wood shelf.*

is done on a frame before mounting it on the legs. This avoids the often tedious work of dealing with the weave underneath when the legs and rails get in the way, on normal stools. Rigidity is provided by two sets of rails lower down and a shelf can be arranged on the upper of these rails.

All of the stand is best made of hardwood, which will probably match other furniture in the room. The knobs can be turned on a small lathe, or you might be able to buy drawer knobs which are similar. The top frame corners can be halved together. The lower rails as described are tenoned, but you could use two, 1/4-inch dowels in the end of each rail, although that may not be as strong.

Check sizes; make a stand of different size if that would better suit your available space. The stand is shown square, but it need not be.

Make the four legs (FIG. 7-18A). Mark the positions of the rails, which are all 1 1/2-inches deep. Drill the tops to take 5/8-inch dowels on the knobs (FIG. 7-18B).

Make the twelve rails (FIG. 7-18C). Mark across them all together so sizes match. Allow 3/4 inch at each end for tenons.

Mark the mortises and tenons. Allow for the tenons going far enough into the legs to almost meet with mitered ends (FIG. 7-18D).

Assemble opposite sides squarely; then join across with the other rails, checking squareness in all directions.

Use this assembly as a guide to the size of the top frame, which should come level with the outsides of the legs (FIG. 7-18E). If the frame is slightly bigger, that would be better than being slightly undersize.

Cut halving joints in the corners (FIG. 7-18F), but do not drill yet.

Glue the corner joints. If you feel additional fastening is necessary, drive screws from below where they will miss the holes that will be drilled through the joints.

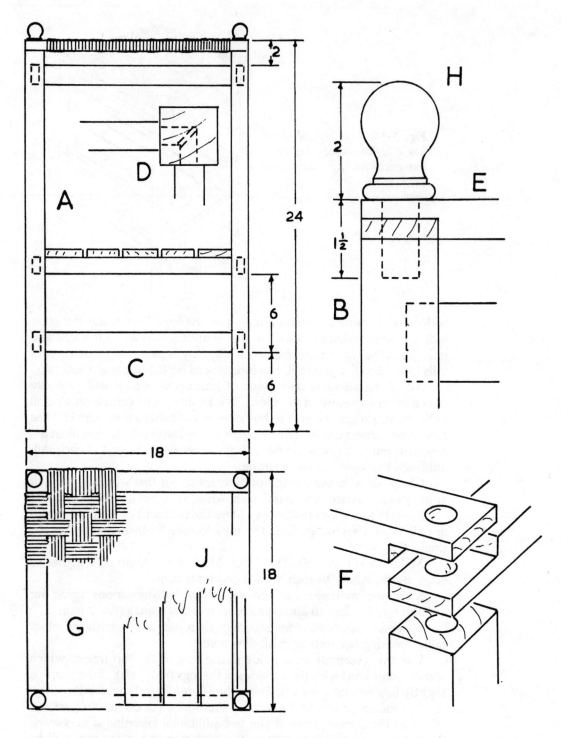

Fig. 7-18. *Sizes of the woven-topped bedside stand.*

Take sharpness off all edges of the frame and round what will be the top corners. For reasons of strength while working on the woven top, leave drilling the corners of the frame.

Any cord or cordlike material might be used for the top, in diameters up to 1/8 inch. Large size material is quicker to weave, but finer cord is neater.

The only tool needed is a wooden needle, preferably long enough to go right across the top, although you can work with a shorter one. This is a strip of wood about 1/4-inch × 1/2-inch section, with rounded edges and two holes in one end and a point at the other (FIG. 7-19A). This may get rough treatment, so use a strong straight-grained hardwood.

Arrange the pattern in various groups. It is suggested that you have two wraps between four or five strands across. With fine cord, you may

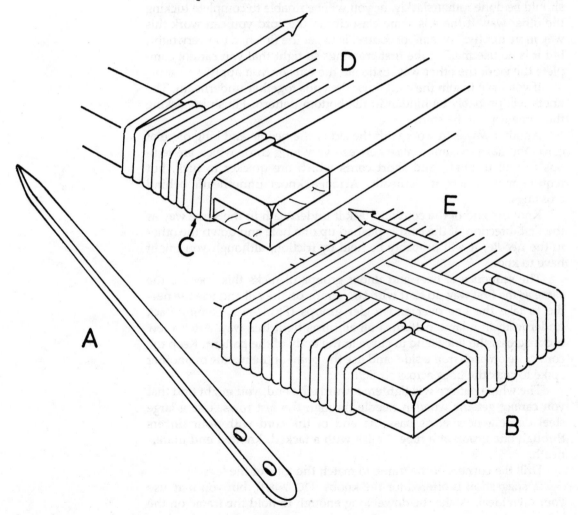

Fig. 7-19. *How to weave the top of the bedside stand.*

prefer a greater number in each group. On the top, the groups go over and under each other to make the checker pattern (FIGS. 7-18G and 19B). Work the same pattern on the underside, but it is simpler to work larger squares. Divide the distance across into approximately three or four sections, and go over and under these groups. The simplest way is to go across, underneath, without tucking over and under at all. However, that does not look very good if anyone inspects your work from below.

Start by knotting the end of the cord and driving a tack through it underneath the end of a side. Wrap the cord twice around the side (FIG. 7-19C); then go across and back underneath to put five lines across the top (FIG. 7-19D). Put two wraps on the far side, then, return underneath to add two wraps on the near side, and start across again.

The tension has to be judged. If the cord is without stretch, all of this should be done rather slackly, or you will be unable to complete tucking the other way. If there is some elasticity in the cord you can work this way more tightly. The aim, of course, is to get the finished top very tight, but it is no use making the first crossings so tight that you cannot complete the work the other way. Estimate the tension you apply.

If you have to join the cord, knot the ends together underneath. The knots will probably be hidden in the bottom pattern. Finish by tacking the same way as the start.

Another way is to work with the aid of the needle and long piece of cord. You have to compromise between very long cords which are tedious to pull through, and short cords which are quicker to tuck, but require more knots underneath. Arrange knots underneath behind crossings.

Knot the end of the cord and tack it underneath in the same way as the first direction. If the cord is pushed up one hole and down the other in the needle, it will probably be held by friction, although you might have to knot.

The sequence of over and under groups of tucks this way are the same as the first way, so start with two wraps on the rail and use the needle to take the line over and under groups (FIG. 7-19E), coming back underneath in a large pattern. Pull all turns tight this way. After a few tucks across, the lines tend to curve in the body of the pattern. Keep the cord close on each frame side, and use the point of the needle or another spike to coax the lines across straight.

The whole pattern will tighten; towards the end, you might find that you cannot get the wooden needle through the last rows. Use a large steel darning needle, or pass the end of the cord with your fingers through one group at a time. Finish with a tacked, knotted end underneath.

Drill the corners of the frame to match the tops of the legs.

A suggestion is offered for the knobs (FIG. 7-18H), but you may use your own ideas. Make the dowel long enough to hold the frame on the legs.

Glue the frame on with the knobs now, but it might be more convenient for applying a finish if you leave final assembly until later.

The shelf could be a piece of plywood, but several strips across with narrow gaps between are suggested (FIG. 7-18J). They can be glued and pinned to the rails.

Finish to suit your needs. Assemble all parts. If necessary, trim the bottom of one leg if there is a tendency to rock.

Materials List for Woven-topped Bedside Stand

4 legs	24	×	1¹/₂	×	1¹/₂
12 rails	18	×	1¹/₂	×	³/₄
4 frame sides	20	×	1¹/₂	×	³/₄
5 shelf strips	20	×	2³/₄	×	¹/₂
knobs from	20	×	1¹/₂	×	1¹/₂

TRIPLE MIRROR

For dressing hair, applying make-up and generally checking on appearance a mirror is necessary, but a single mirror is often not enough. It is a help to have side mirrors as well, with all three mirrors adjustable. This unit of three mirrors (FIG. 7-20) has a central mirror that can be tilted and two side mirrors hinged to it. It is built as a free-standing unit for use

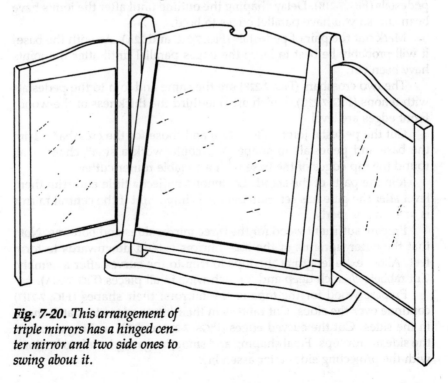

Fig. 7-20. *This arrangement of triple mirrors has a hinged center mirror and two side ones to swing about it.*

on any table or suitable surface, but it could also be screwed to a dresser as a more permanent arrangement.

The mirror framing is mostly pieces 1^1/8-inches square. This should be a hardwood with a reasonably straight grain, which would finish to make a high-quality piece of furniture. Softwood is not advised, but if it is used, you should increase the thicknesses slightly. Sizes are suggested (FIGS. 7-21 and 22). Mirrors will have to be cut to size, but if you can obtain stock mirrors near these sizes you could adapt the frames.

The assembly is made in four units. Parts are tenoned together. In most joints, there is insufficient space for dowels to be satisfactorily used as alternatives. The only possible places for dowels are the bottoms of the pedestals in place of the multiple tenons. In the small sections of wood used, tenons should be taken through. If neatly finished, they can be a design feature and evidence of your ability as a craftsman.

Make the stand first; use it as a guide to the sizes of the mirror frames. The main mirror is hinged to the top crossbar, and it has an adjuster mating with a peg at the center of the bottom crossbar. The two side mirrors hinge near the front edges of the pedestals. There is some shaping at the tops of the mirror frames and around the base. If other furniture in the room is made with more severe straight lines, you might prefer to finish edges straight.

The base (FIG. 7-21A) extends outside the pedestals and it has more in front than behind them. Mark out the shape and the positions of the pedestals (FIG. 7-21B). Delay shaping the outline until after the joints have been cut, so you have parallel edges to hold.

Mark out the pair of pedestals (FIG. 7-21C and 22A). As with the base, it will probably be best to leave the edges parallel until after the joints have been cut.

The two crossbars (FIG. 7-22B) are the same and join to the pedestals with tenons (FIG. 7-22C), which are one-third the thickness of the wood. Front edges are level.

Cut the pedestal joints (FIG. 7-22D) and those for the crossbars. Trim the base and pedestals to shape. You could work a small chamfer all round the top edges of the base with a suitable router cutter.

Join the parts of the stand. Let tenons project a little and trim them level after the glue has set. Squareness is important if the central mirror is to swing properly.

Prepare sufficient wood for the three mirror sides and bottoms. Note that the outer uprights of the side mirrors extend downwards to form feet. Allow extra length at the tops to trim to the curves after assembly. Cut rabbets ^{3}/8-inch deep and ^{3}/4-inch wide in all pieces (FIG. 7-23A).

Prepare wood for the tops of the mirrors; their shapes (FIG. 7-21D) continue over the sides. Cut rabbets in their lower edges to match those in the sides. Cut the curved edges (FIGS. 7-23B and C), making a pair of the side mirror tops. Final shaping and smoothing may be left to be done with the projecting sides after assembly.

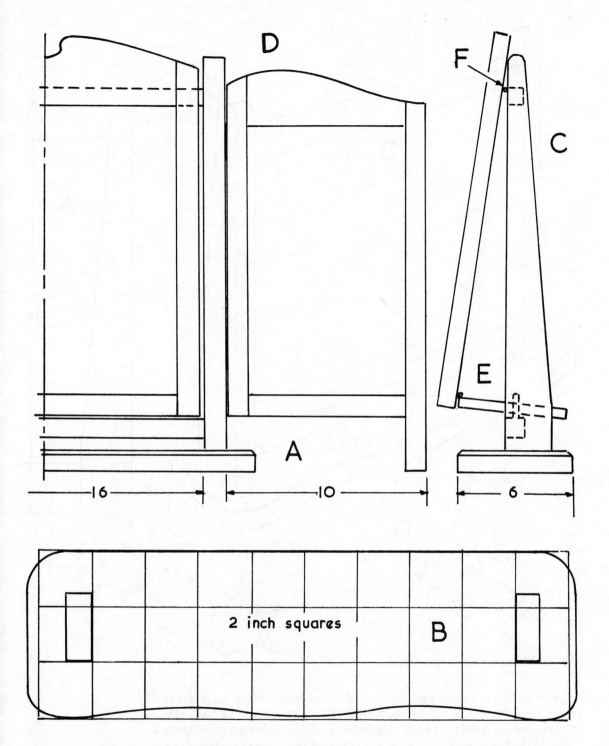

Fig. 7-21. *Sizes of the triple mirror and the shape of the base.*

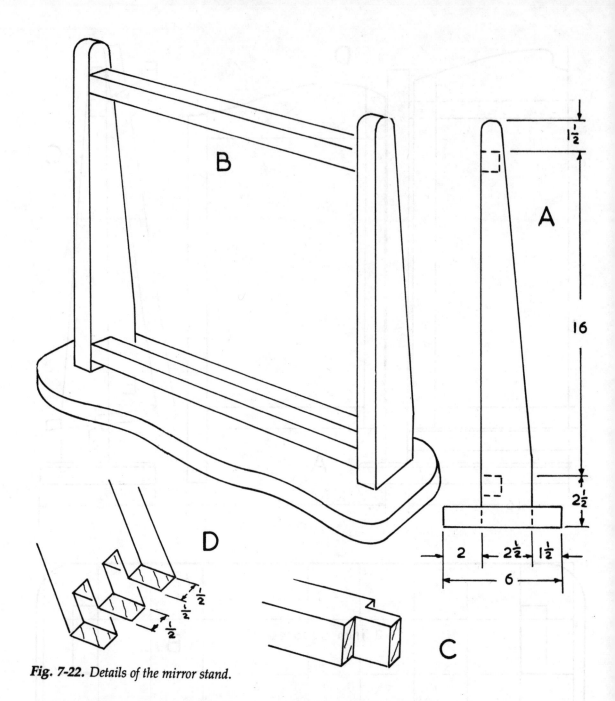

Fig. 7-22. *Details of the mirror stand.*

Join all frame parts with mortise and tenon joints. Have each tenon edge level with the inside of the rabbet (FIG. 7-23D), and cut back the shoulder on the front to fit neatly against the edge of the other piece (FIG. 7-23E). Make the tenons level with the rabbeted wood edge on the inner side, and 3/8-inch back from what will be the end. Leave on some excess

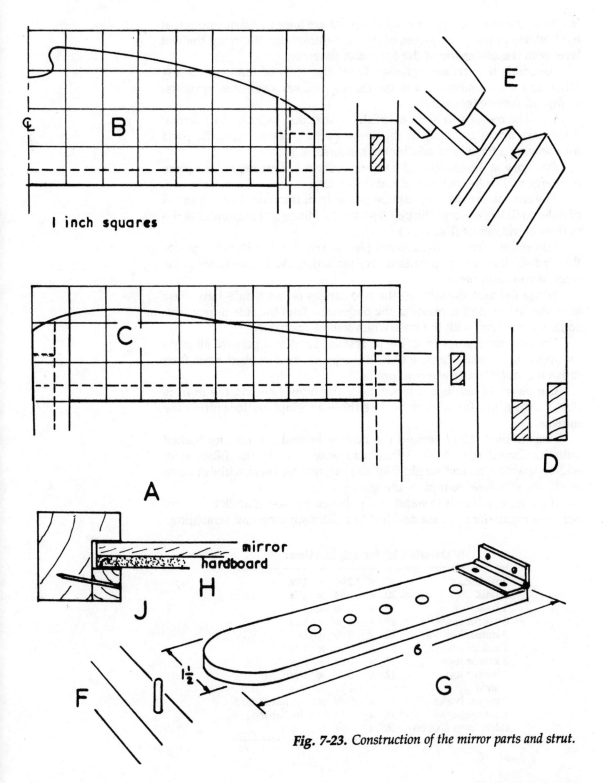

1 inch squares

mirror
hardboard

$1\frac{1}{2}$

6

Fig. 7-23. Construction of the mirror parts and strut.

length in the mortised piece until the parts are joined. Allow enough at the bottoms of the outer pieces of the side mirrors for trimming the feet level with the underside of the base after assembly.

Assemble the frames squarely. Level the ends of tenons and any other uneven surfaces. Continue the top curves over the uprights. Round all outer edges lightly.

It will be most convenient to finish construction without the mirrors; then make a trial assembly. If this is satisfactory, disassemble the parts for applying a finish and adding the mirrors.

Put a peg at the center of the lower crosspiece. This might be a piece of a large nail or 1/8-inch dowel rod (FIG. 7-23F).

The strut to provide adjustment is a strip of thin wood with a series of holes to fit loosely over the peg (FIG. 7-23G). Hinge it at the center of the bottom of the mirror (FIG. 7-21E).

Hinge the mirror to the top rail (FIG. 7-21F). Use 1 1/2-inch hinges for this and all other hinged positions. Try the action. Add more holes in the strut, if you need them.

Hinge the side mirrors, so the two hinges on each side have their knuckles level with the fronts of the pedestals. Trim the side mirror feet, so they come level with the base when folded against it.

Unscrew the frames from the pedestals. Sand and prepare all parts for applying a finish. Prepare to fit the mirrors, as described next; then finish the wood in the way you prefer.

Cut pieces of hardboard to fit inside the frames behind the mirrors (FIG. 7-23H). Allow for an easy fit. Use these as templates for cutting the mirrors.

Prepare fillets to fit around the rabbets behind the mirrors backed with hardboard (FIG. 7-23J). When you assemble, fit the fillets with widely-spaced pins and no glue, so you can remove them without damage if you ever have to replace the glass.

If the triple mirror is to stand on a polished surface, glue cloth or rubber sheeting under the base and feet to reduce slipping and scratching.

Materials List for Triple Mirror

2 pedestals	22	×	2 1/2	× 1 1/8
2 rails	20	×	1 1/8	× 1 1/8
1 base	22	×	6	× 1
6 mirror sides	19	×	1 1/8	× 1 1/8
2 mirror bottoms	12	×	1 1/8	× 1 1/8
1 mirror bottom	17	×	1 1/8	× 1 1/8
2 mirror tops	12	×	2 1/2	× 1 1/8
1 mirror top	17	×	3 1/2	× 1 1/8
1 strut	6	×	1 1/2	× 1/4
2 mirror backs	15	×	9	× 1/8 hardboard
1 mirror back	16	×	15	× 1/8 hardboard
fillets from sixteen	16	×	3/8	× 3/8

8
Children's Furniture

In most homes, the need for children's furniture is not ongoing in the same way as the need for adult furniture, particularly if there are only expected to be a few children in the family. This means you have to decide whether what you make is to be only temporary, or if you will make child-size furniture to the same standard and permanency as the furniture intended for general adult use. Only you can decide. However, if you are interested in craftsmanship, you are unlikely to be happy with something which is too obviously almost thrown together, even if that is justified by its temporary need. If you make good quality children's furniture it will almost certainly find an ongoing use, possibly continuing down the line to grandchildren.

Some children's furniture is scaled down from adult sizes; a child will enjoy having something like father uses. Other furniture may be built without an adult equivalent, and probably finished in bright colors. In short, the possibilities in the range of children's furniture are enormous. Many of the projects you can make are simpler than other furniture, so you might test your skill on furniture for a child before tackling something more ambitious.

There are complete books on making furniture for children, so the projects shown in this chapter are only a selection. Some furniture described in other chapters will have uses in a children's room, either as it is or scaled down.

Keep safety in mind. Make sure there is no risk of splintering or cracking; only use finishes which would be safe if chewed. Make sure that the furniture is stable in use. See that joints are unlikely to pull open in the rough use which may be inevitable with some children's activities.

CHILD'S CHAIR

A young child likes to have his or her own chair as early as possible. This chair (FIG. 8-1) is intended for a child who is just beginning to walk, and it should be suitable for up to age 2+ years. It may be particularly useful for sitting in front of a television set. It gives support while sitting up, but it is not intended for lounging. The sides are arranged so the child may position elbows or arms in the hollows for comfort, and to reduce the risk of falling forward.

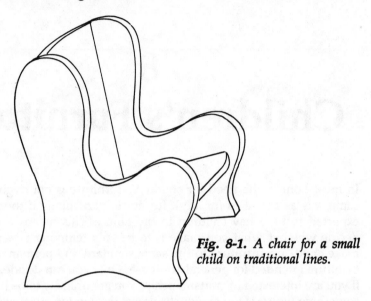

Fig. 8-1. A chair for a small child on traditional lines.

Construction is with 1/2-inch plywood, preferably hardwood. If you use softwood plywood, make sure all splintery edges are smoothed by well rounding the shaped parts and sanding surfaces as well as edges.

Mark out the two sides, with the positions of other parts on them (FIG. 8-2A). Cut the outlines to match; round all edges except those in contact with the floor.

The seat (FIG. 8-2B) is symmetrical and slightly narrower at the back. Shape and round the front edge.

Make the back (FIG. 8-2C) parallel and the same width as the rear edge of the seat. Round its top edge in the same way as the front of the seat. Make its length enough to go a short distance below the seat.

Fit the seat and back between the sides with glue and screws and thin nails. Use screws, which could be #4-gauge × 1 inch or 1 1/4 inch, near the ends of each joint, or nails could be used at about 2-inch intervals between them.

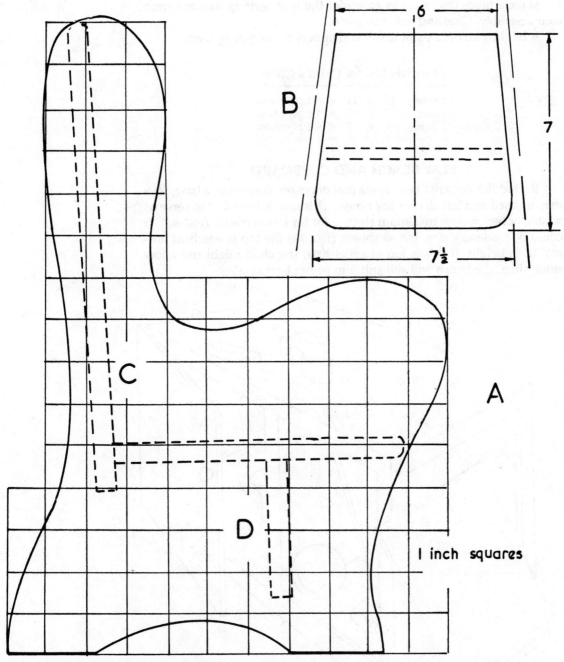

Fig. 8-2. *Shapes of parts of the child's chair.*

B

6

7

7½

A

C

D

1 inch squares

Make a brace (FIG. 8-2D) to go under the seat, getting its sizes from your assembly. Glue and nail it in place.

A brightly colored paint finish will appeal to the young user.

Materials List for Child's Chair

2 sides	15	×	11	× 1/2 plywood
1 seat	8	×	7	× 1/2 plywood
1 brace	8	×	3	× 1/2 plywood

PLAY BENCH AND CUPBOARD

If a toddler does not have some sort of center to serve as a base, toys may be used and left all over the house. This unit is intended to serve as a table or bench with maximum storage for toys underneath (FIG. 8-3). It could be made any size, but as shown (FIG. 8-4) the top is nearly at normal table height. If this is too much at first, the child might use a low stool; then, the bench will still suit him or her later on.

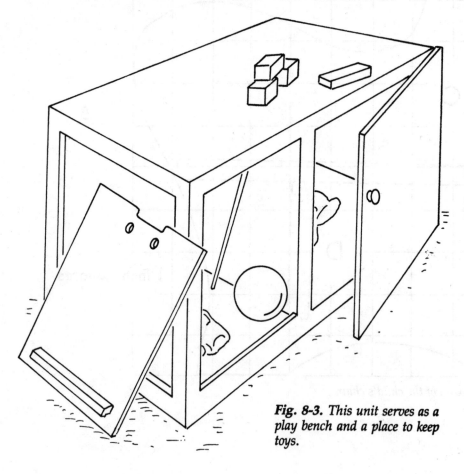

Fig. 8-3. *This unit serves as a play bench and a place to keep toys.*

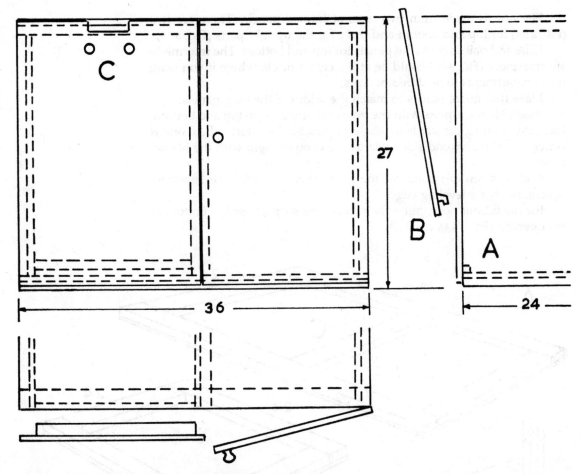

Fig. 8-4. *Suggested sizes for the play bench and cupboard.*

The accommodation is shown divided into two, with one hinged door and one that will lift out. You could fit both of the same type if you wish. The lift-out door gives clear access to the inside, while the loose door might have play uses.

Construction is of plywood framed with 1 inch × 2 inch-softwood strips, with the parts glued and joined together. The panels may be joined with nails or screws. If more children will follow on as the first child grows out of using the bench, it might be regarded as permanent. If not, move it for a further useful life into a storeroom or workshop. Otherwise, if the sections have been screwed together, they could be disassembled to be used in some other construction.

Softwood plywood 1/2-inch thick is suitable, but if you use hardwood plywood it could be thinner. A painted finish will probably appeal most to a child, so it does not matter if you mix the plywood and solid wood types.

The unit is made from two sizes of framed panels. There are two (FIG. 8-5A) for top and bottom and three for the upright parts (FIG. 8-5B).

Glue and nail strips to the panels for top and bottom. The intermediate crosspiece (FIG. 8-5C) could be at the center or elsewhere if you want the compartments to be different sizes.

Make the square panels to match the width of the long panels.

Assemble these parts with the plywood upwards on top and bottom. Have the framing outwards on the end panels; the intermediate one is better with the plywood side towards the compartment with the lift-out door.

Nail or screw plywood on the back; this will hold the assembly square, ready for leveling edges.

For the lift-out door, put a 3/4-inch square strip across the bottom of the opening (FIGS. 8-4A and 5D).

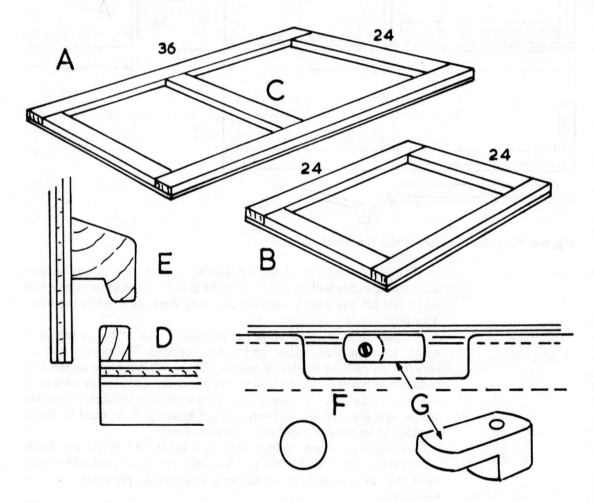

Fig. 8-5. Details of parts of the play bench and cupboard.

Cut the plywood lift-out door to a size that will come within 1/4 inch of the top and bottom of the bench. Its width may reach the outer edge and halfway over the intermediate upright.

Make a notched strip to fit easily between the sides of the door opening and over the strip across at the bottom (FIGS. 8-4B and 5E). It has to slip over when the door is tilted, so slope the inside of the rabbet. Make this solid, or join two strips.

Cut away 4-inches long and 1-inch deep at the center of the top of this door. Round the corners and drill two, 1-inch finger holes below it (FIGS. 8-4C and 5F). Round all corners and edges.

Attach the strip across the bottom of the door at a height that will bring the top edge of the door to about 1/4-inch below the top surface of the bench when closed.

Make a turnbutton (FIG. 8-5G). Position it so it can be turned both ways without obstruction. This would be better made of hardwood than softwood. Use a washer on a roundhead screw.

Make the other door to fit over the remaining space. Hinge it to the outer bench end; add a spring or magnetic catch, and a knob or handle.

If either door is not rigid enough, frame it inside with strips kept far enough in from the edges to go inside the openings.

Finish the bench with paint. A light color inside will make it easier to see what is kept there. The top might be covered with Formica. Brighten the outside with decals.

Materials List for Play Bench and Cupboard

2 panels	36	×	24	×	1/2 plywood
3 panels	24	×	24	×	1/2 plywood
1 back	36	×	27	×	1/2 plywood
2 doors	27	×	18	×	1/2 plywood
4 strips	38	×	2	×	1
18 strips	25	×	2	×	1
1 door stop	18	×	3/4	×	3/4
1 door stop	17	×	2	×	1 3/4

CHILD'S BED

When a child has grown big enough to move from a cot or crib to a proper bed, you have the problem of deciding if the bed is to be a scaled-down type or a fullsize one which can be converted to adult use later on. A small bed might be the choice if there are more children following on, and several years of use are anticipated. Otherwise, it may be better to have a bed long enough for later adult use.

This bed (FIG. 8-6) is designed around an internally-sprung or foam mattress 36 inches × 78 inches. Adapt the sizes to suit whatever mattress is available. Two guards are shown to prevent a child from falling out. If the bed is to go alongside a wall, you might only need one guard. When the bed moves on to become a more adult place of rest you can remove

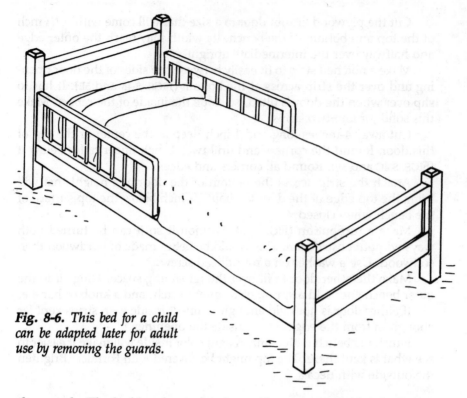

Fig. 8-6. *This bed for a child can be adapted later for adult use by removing the guards.*

the guards. The bed is a few inches lower than a normal adult bed. This may not matter for later adult use, but you could raise the legs on blocks, or if you fit casters they will raise the bed about 2 inches.

The bed is deliberately plain. A child may want to stick pictures to it, paint on it or use chalks. He or she may also treat it fairly roughly. If you keep it plain, it will stand up to hard knocks and the child's attempts at decoration, but eventually you can bring the woodwork back into presentable condition with a coat of paint. You could use hardwood and give it a clear finish, but softwood with paint might be better for a child. The panels are plywood.

The mattress fits into a frame over a piece of plywood. The head and foot are separate assemblies, so the parts may be taken through doorways or up stairs and assembled with bolts. The mattress and the plywood it rests on are also transported loose. With the mattress fitting inside its frame, there is less risk of a fidgeting child pushing all of his or her bedding over the side.

Get your mattress first, because it controls the sizes of the woodwork. They are not always exactly the size specified, so you can modify the frame to fit the actual mattress.

Make the mattress frame first (FIG. 8-7A). It is an open box with 4-inch deep sides. Corners could be screwed or you might use dovetails; however, finger joints screwed both ways are effective, as described for the

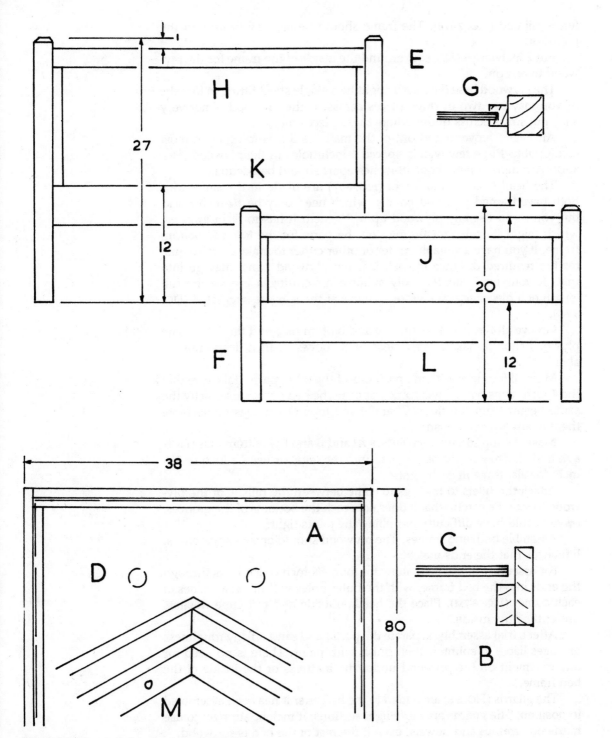

Fig. 8-7. Sizes and details of the child's bed.

fence rail bed (FIG. 7-12B). The frame should be an easy fit around the mattress.

Put 2-inch strips (FIG. 8-7B) around the inside of the frame for the plywood to rest on.

The plywood base (FIG. 8-7C) might be a single sheet fitting in loosely, or you may use two or three pieces across. If the plywood is not very stiff, put strips across under where these pieces meet.

Air has to move in and out of the mattress if it is to function most comfortably. Put a few widely spaced 1-inch holes in the plywood (FIG. 8-7D). Arranging them about 18-inches apart should be adequate.

The head (FIG. 8-7E) and foot (FIG. 8-7F) are made in the same way. Both have framed plywood panels, which need only be 1/4-inch thick, but you could use any plywood up to 1/2 inch. It has to fit in grooves, which might be cut right through on the parts for the top and bottom frame. If you have a suitable router or other cutter to make a groove just for the required distance in each leg, the plywood panel may go into that. If your equipment is only suitable for cutting a groove the full length of a piece, separate grooved fillets at the legs are suggested (FIG. 8-7G).

Groove all the wood for the top and bottom rails and the fillets. The plywood should make a fairly close fit. Grooves 1/2-inch deep are suitable.

Mark all four legs with the positions of the other parts. Take care that the 4-inch strips, which will come opposite the bed frame, are exactly the same height from the floor. Chamfer the tops of the legs or decorate them in any way you wish.

Make the top square rails (FIGS. 8-7H and J) and the bottom rails (FIGS. 8-7K and L). They might be tenoned into the legs, or use 3/8 inch or 1/2-inch dowels, three in each joint.

Attach the fillets to the legs to come between the rails. Cut the plywood to size. Be careful that it does not reach the bottoms of the grooves, or you could have difficulty in pulling the joints tight.

Assemble both end frames. The plywood should ensure squareness, but check that the ends match.

For assembly of the bed, allow for four, 3/8-inch coach bolts through the ends into the bed frame, with the outer holes within a few inches of each corner (FIG. 8-7M). Place the heads outside and put large washers under the nuts inside.

After a trial assembly, separate the parts, and sand off any roughness or edges liable to splinter; then finish with paint. There is no need for any treatment on the plywood under the mattress or the inside of the bed frame.

The guards (FIG. 8-8) are added to the bed after it has been assembled in position. The guards are fairly light sections; it may be stronger to use hardwood frames and dowels, even if the rest of the bed is softwood.

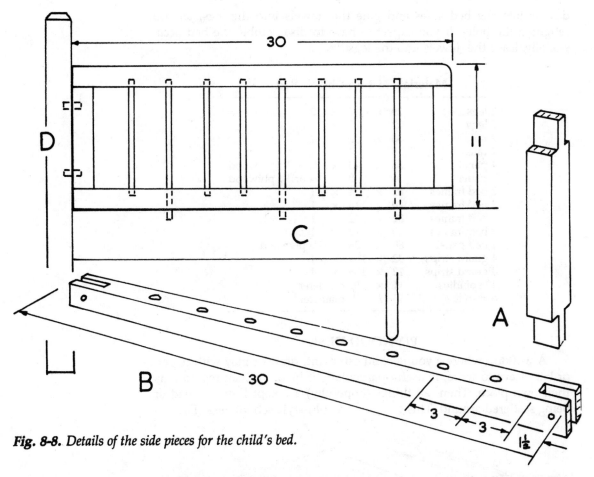

Fig. 8-8. *Details of the side pieces for the child's bed.*

Because of the slim sections, it is stronger to use bridle joints (FIG. 8-8A) than to dowel the corners.

Spindle spacing must be close enough to prevent a child getting its head through and 1/2-inch dowels at 3-inch centers are shown (FIG. 8-8B).

Drill for dowels going about 1/2 inch into each piece; except that three dowels in the bottom edge of a guard go through into the bed side (FIG. 8-8C).

Fit two dowels into each upright that comes against a rear leg (FIG. 8-8D).

Assemble the two guards squarely, with projecting dowels in position. Round the outer corners and exposed edges. Corner joints may be strengthened with dowels across, if you think it necessary. You might paint or apply a clear finish before attaching to the bed. Even if the bed parts are painted, hardwood guards with a clear finish will look good.

Drill holes in the bed sides and rear legs for the guard dowels. Slacken the bolts holding the head to the bed frame; then, first glue the dowels into the bed sides and glue the dowels into the legs, as you retighten the bolts. If you expect to have to disassemble the bed occasionally, leave the dowels into the legs dry.

Materials List for Child's Bed

2 legs	29	×	2	×	2	
2 legs	22	×	2	×	2	
2 rails	38	×	2	×	2	
2 rails	38	×	4	×	2	
1 panel	36	×	13	×	1/4 or 1/2 plywood	
1 panel	36	×	8	×	1/4 or 1/2 plywood	
2 bed frames	82	×	4	×	1	
2 bed frames	40	×	4	×	1	
2 bed frames	82	×	2	×	1	
2 bed frames	40	×	2	×	1	
1 bed panel	80	×	36	×	1/2 plywood	
4 guard strips	32	×	1 1/2	×	1	
4 guard strips	12	×	1 1/2	×	1	
10 spindles	11	×	1/2 diameter			
6 spindles	13	×	1/2 diameter			

PLYWOOD DESK

A worktop where a young child can paint, draw or play with paper, or later learn to write, is useful particularly if he or she can regard it as their own place. Then, all things (hopefully) are kept there instead of being scattered around. This version of an old-style school desk (FIG. 8-9)

Fig. 8-9. *This desk for a small child is made almost completely of plywood.*

should suit a child up to about age 5 in the sizes shown (FIG. 8-10), but it could be made any size. Maybe you should sit the child on a stool and measure what size would suit, allowing for growth.

The desk is intended to be made almost completely of plywood. A fairly stiff 1/2-inch plywood should suit, but it might have to be thicker. It should be a type that will take screws in its edges. There will be mutual support from the assembled parts and the foot rail tenoned through will provide lateral stiffness.

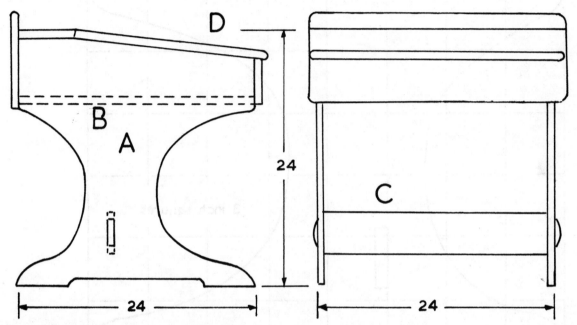

Fig. 8-10. *Suggested sizes for a child's desk.*

The key parts are the two sides (FIGS. 8-10A, 11 and 12A). Draw the outlines within a 24-inch square.

Cut the outlines. Well round the lower shaped parts, but leave the upper boxed parts with square edges.

The important crosswise part is the box bottom (FIGS. 8-10B and 12B). This sets the sizes in that direction. Put 1/2-inch square strips under the ends (FIG. 8-12C) to reinforce the joints to the sides.

The other crosswise parts overlap by 3/4 inch at each side. Make the front (FIG. 8-12D) to this length. Bevel its top edge to match the slope of the sides. Make it deep enough to cover the 1/2-inch strips under the bottom ends. Round its lower corners.

The back (FIG. 8-12E) overlaps in a similar way, but stands above the desk top. Round both outer corners.

Make the top the same length (FIG. 8-12F).

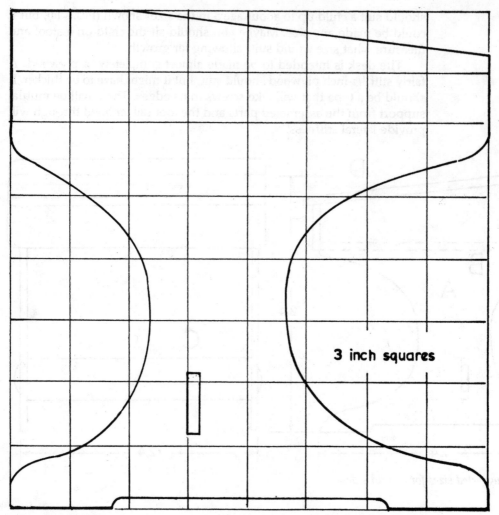

3 inch squares

Fig. 8-11. *Shape of the sides of the child's desk.*

The footrail (FIGS. 8-10C and 12G) has the same length between shoulders as the box bottom, and it extends through the mortises enough to have projecting rounded ends.

Drill the side for screws into the box bottom—#6-gauge × 1¼-inch screws at 3-inch intervals should be satisfactory.

Glue the tenons of the footrail into its mortises and screw and glue the box bottom into place. Check that the assembly stands level and is square.

Screw and glue on front, back and top, with screws at about 3-inch intervals into all crossings.

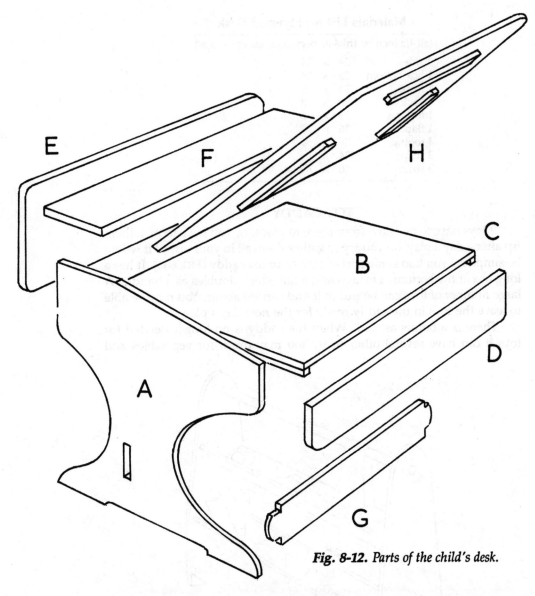

Fig. 8-12. *Parts of the child's desk.*

The flap (FIGS. 8-10D and 12H) overhangs the same amount as the other parts. It could be hinged to the top, but it is shown to lift off. To locate it when in position, put on 1/2-inch square strips to come inside the front and sides. A lift-off flap gives clear access to the interior, and it is less likely to close on small fingers.

A painted finish is advisable; there could be decals on the sides and other parts.

Materials List for Plywood Desk

(all 1/2 inch or thicker plywood, except strips)

2 sides	24 × 24			
1 box bottom	23 × 24			
1 front	26 × 5			
1 back	26 × 8			
1 top	26 × 6			
1 flap	26 × 20			
1 footrail	26 × 4			
2 strips	24 × 1/2 × 1/2			
3 strips	16 × 1/2 × 1/2			

TOY CADDY

If toys have to be taken from place to place, or you have to pick them up after a day's play, do you try to gather them all in your arms? It would be simpler if you had some sort of carrier, or toy caddy (FIG. 8-13). It has a long box at the bottom, a trough and a rail which doubles as a handle. A large number of toys can be put in it and carried about. You may be able to leave the toys in the caddy ready for the next day's play.

There is a bonus as well. When the caddy is no longer needed for toys it can have several other uses. You may use it for vegetables and

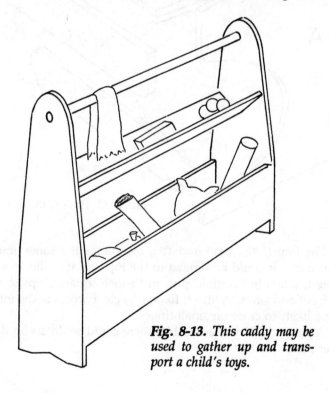

Fig. 8-13. This caddy may be used to gather up and transport a child's toys.

canned goods in the kitchen. It will take small tools and seeds into the garden. It will hold a variety of things in a store or workshop.

Construction could be softwood or hardwood, although you might use plywood of the same thickness. The joints suggested are dowels, which could be ³/8 inch in diameter, spaced not further apart than 3 inches.

Make the two ends first (FIGS. 8-14A and 15A). The edges taper from just above the box to a 3-inch radius curve at the top. The bottom is notched to form feet. Mark on the positions of the other parts. The trough is made at 90 degrees and mounted so the sides are at 45 degrees to the centerline.

Cut the sides and bottom of the box to length. Mark the board ends for dowels to the caddy ends (FIGS. 8-14B and 15B). The bottom may be nailed, or screwed upwards into the box sides.

Cut the piece for the trough (FIGS. 8-14C and 15C) so one is wider than the other by enough to overlap. That joint may be nailed or screwed.

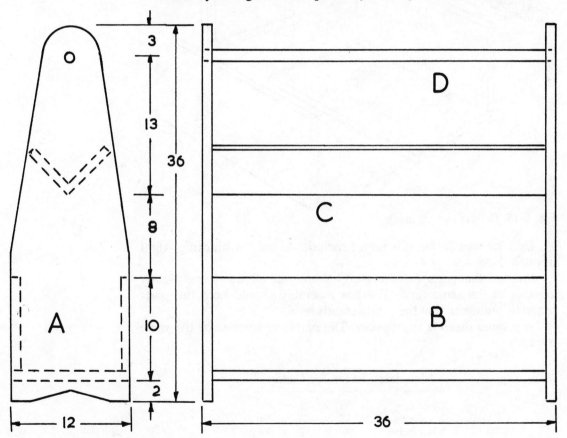

Fig. 8-14. Sizes of the toy caddy.

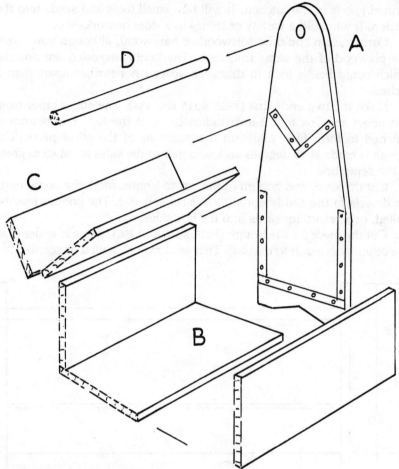

Fig. 8-15. *Parts of the toy caddy.*

Drill the tops of the ends for a 1-inch dowel rod, which can go right through (FIGS. 8-14D and 15D).

Prepare the parts for doweling; then pull all the joints tightly together at the same time. The box assembly should hold the parts squarely, but check that the caddy stands level.

A painted finish is appropriate. The parts need not all be the same color.

Materials List for Toy Caddy

2 ends	38	×	12	× ³/₄
2 box sides	38	×	9¹/₄	× ³/₄
1 box bottom	38	×	12	× ³/₄
1 trough side	38	×	6	× ³/₄
1 trough side	38	×	5¹/₄	× ³/₄
1 handle	38	×	1 diameter	

NURSING CHAIR

It is helpful if a mother dealing with a young child can sit low so as to be within reach of things on the floor. Normal chairs are too high. It is also important that the seat is firm and steady. Upholstery, which would be desirable on another chair intended for longer use, might cause unsteadiness, so a chair with a plain seat and back is acceptable. The user also has a large accumulation of things needed to deal with the baby. This chair (FIG. 8-16) has the necessary low firm seat and a sliding tray or box large enough to contain many of the mother's needs. When no longer needed for nursing, the chair might be used by a child aged 3 years upwards to sit at a low table, and it is sufficiently robust to stand up to rough use during play. Of course, the tray will hold many small toys.

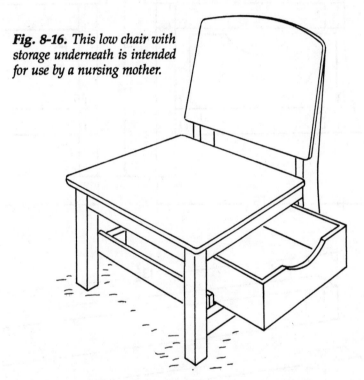

Fig. 8-16. This low chair with storage underneath is intended for use by a nursing mother.

If the chair is to have a long life it should be made of hardwood, but a painted softwood chair might last as long as you need it. Construction is shown with dowels, but you may prefer mortise and tenon joints. Most joints can be made with two, 1/2-inch hardwood dowels. The plywood back and seat brace the chair by being glued and screwed on. The plywood box runs on rails between guides and may be pulled out completely from either side.

Overall sizes are shown (FIG. 8-17A). The side rails are level with the outsides of the legs (FIGS. 8-17B and C and 18A and B). The front seat rail is

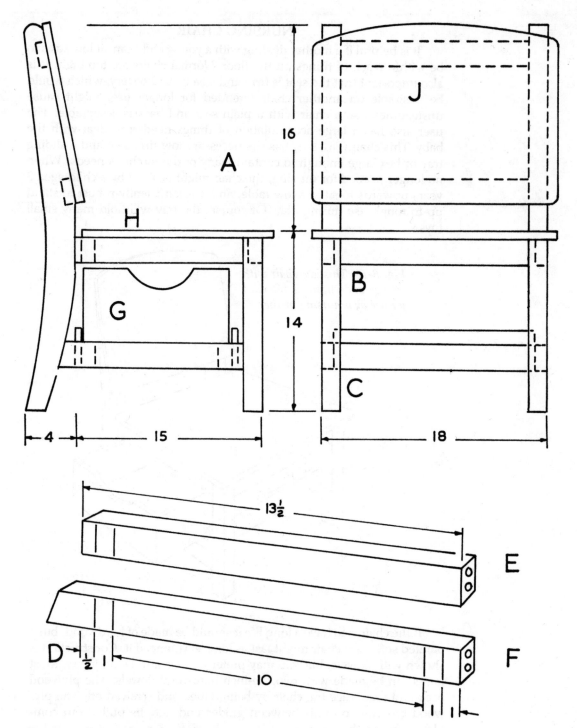

Fig. 8-17. *Sizes and rail details for the nursing chair.*

level with the fronts of the legs, but the other crosswise rails join the side rails and not the legs. This arrangement provides guides for the tray and avoids too many places where dowel holes meet in the legs.

Start with the pair of rear legs. Mark out on a 4-inch width (FIG. 8-18C). The seat rail meets the leg squarely, but the lower rail has to join a sloping part. Before cutting out the leg, note the shape and extra length needed for these two lower rails (FIGS. 8-17D and 18D). Mark the positions of all rails on the shaped legs.

Make the two pairs of side rails (FIGS. 8-17E and F). Mark on them the positions of the crosswise rails.

All of the crosswise rails are 1-inch × 2-inch sections and the same length, except that the front seat rail is shorter to allow for the size of the front legs.

The two lower crosswise rails are bearers for the tray. Provide them with plywood guides to stand 1-inch above them (FIG. 8-18E), glued and pinned on.

Prepare all parts for doweling, allowing two dowels at each place. The holes for the seat rails in the front legs may overlap, but if you stagger them you can avoid cutting much away from the first dowels when drilling the other way. There is no problem at any other position. Holes may be 1-inch deep, or as deep as the thickness will allow.

Assemble the pair of sides with their rails first and see that they match and are without twist.

Join across with all rails in one operation. Check squareness by comparing diagonals, and see that the chair will stand level on a flat surface. It is important that where the tray will slide is square and untwisted.

The tray (FIG. 8-17G) is a simple box. It could be just nailed together with the bottom under the sides, but it is shown (FIG. 8-19) with finger joints at the corners and the bottom enclosed more strongly within the sides.

Make the box to reach the outsides of the side rails and to slide with easy clearance inside the guides. There is no need for a precision fit, which might make it difficult for the parent to get at the contents one-handed.

Make the two sides to size first (FIG. 8-19A); then add the ends to the sizes needed in the openings. Hollow the top edges enough to get a hand in (FIG. 8-19B). Round all top edges.

Cut the finger joints, and glue and pin or nail both ways. Cut the bottom to fit in closely; then glue and nail it (FIG. 8-19C). Round all exposed edges and corners of the tray.

Sand and round the edges before making and fitting the seat and back.

Cut the plywood seat (FIGS. 8-17H and 18F) level with its rear rail and extending 1-inch from the side and front rails. Round all corners and edges.

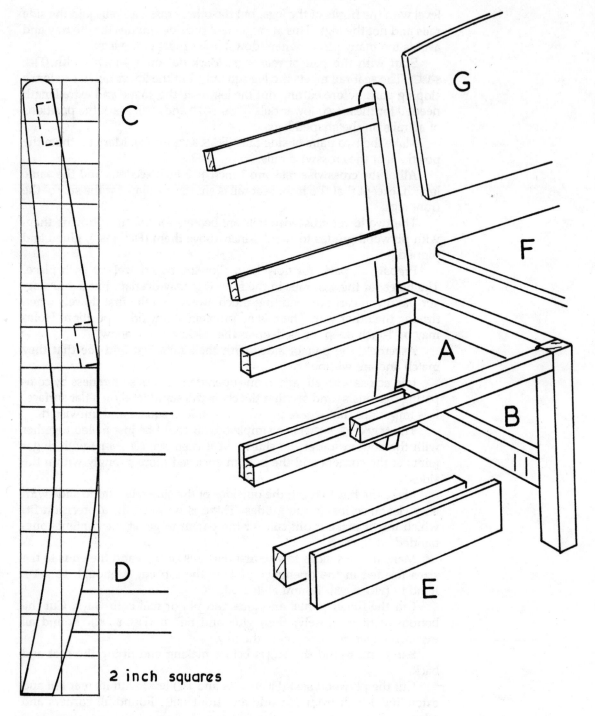

Fig. 8-18. *Leg shape and assembly of the nursing chair.*

2 inch squares

C

D

G

F

A

B

E

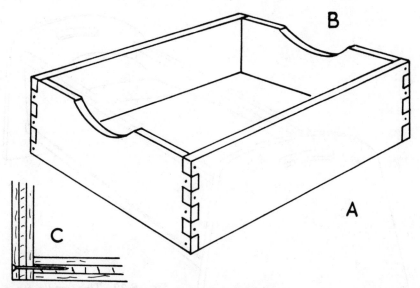

Fig. 8-19. *Details of the drawer of the nursing chair.*

Make the back in the same way, but with a curve to the top (FIGS. 8-17J and 18G). Have its lower edge level with the rail and the sides projecting 1 inch.

Glue and screw on the seat and back to complete assembly.

Finish according to your choice, either clear or painted. A light color inside the tray will make it easier to find things.

Materials List for Nursing Chair

2 rear legs	32	×	4	×	$1^{1}/_{2}$		
2 front legs	15	×	$1^{1}/_{2}$	×	$1^{1}/_{2}$		
2 side rails	15	×	2	×	1		
2 side rails	17	×	2	×	1		
6 rails	18	×	2	×	1		
2 guides	18	×	3	×	$1/_2$ plywood		
1 seat	20	×	16	×	$1/_2$ plywood		
1 back	20	×	16	×	$1/_2$ plywood		
2 tray sides	19	×	6	×	$1/_2$ plywood		
2 tray ends	11	×	6	×	$1/_2$ plywood		
1 tray bottom	18	×	10	×	$1/_2$ plywood		

TAKE-DOWN CRADLE

The need for a cradle for a small baby is not of much duration, so an elaborate or bulky cradle can become a nuisance if it has to be stored after use and will not be needed for some time. A cradle that can be taken apart and packed flat is attractive in these circumstances. This take-down cradle (FIG. 8-20) is rigid in use, but it can be taken apart and

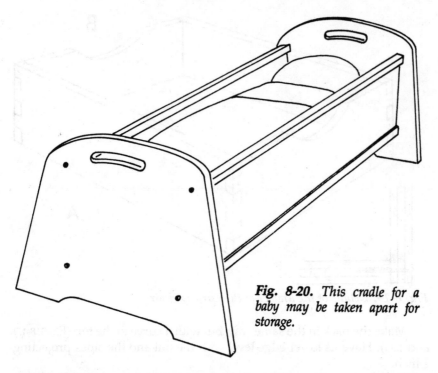

Fig. 8-20. *This cradle for a baby may be taken apart for storage.*

packed flat to a total thickness of no more than 4 inches. If it is not expected to be used as a cradle again, the parts can be separated and the wood used for another purpose. For example, you could make a half size cradle for a doll.

There are two plywood ends supporting two panels made of plywood with strips on the edges. These screw between the ends, and a bottom drops in. The eight screws hold the parts securely together, but they can be withdrawn for disassembly.

Use softwood plywood and strips, or the whole thing could be made of hardwood material, which would look good with a clear finish. Otherwise, finish with paint and possibly add decals on the ends and sides.

Prepare the strips for the tops and bottoms of the sides (FIGS. 8-21A and 22A). Groove 1/2-inch deep to suit the plywood.

Cut the plywood panels and glue them in. The overall width is 12 inches. Squareness of the ends ensures correct assembly.

Round all edges, except those that will come under the loose bottom (FIG. 8-22B). Mark the centers where the screws will come in the ends (FIGS. 8-22C and D).

Cut the two ends (FIGS. 8-21B and 22E). Round the edges of the hand holes and all upper edges. Mark on the positions of the two sides.

If you have used a close-grained hardwood for the tops and bottoms of the sides, it may be sufficient to screw directly into the end grain. For other wood or where you expect to be withdrawing and replacing screws

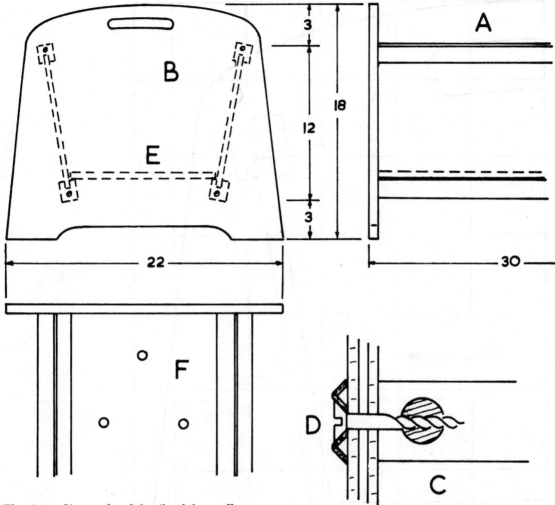

Fig. 8-21. *Sizes and end details of the cradle.*

frequently, it is better to drill across for a 1/2-inch hardwood dowel (FIG. 8-21C), so each screw is able to grip its cross grain. Screws #10-gauge × 1 1/2 inches or 1 3/4 inches should be suitable. Drill the ends and the sides for the screws. Use round head screws and flat washers; also, counter-sunk screws look good with cup or countersink finishing washers (FIG. 8-21D).

Make a temporary assembly so you can get the size of the drop-in bottom (FIG. 8-21E), which need not be a very close fit.

Drill a few 1/2-inch holes in the bottom (FIG. 8-21F) to ventilate the mattress.

Disassemble the cradle and apply your chosen finish.

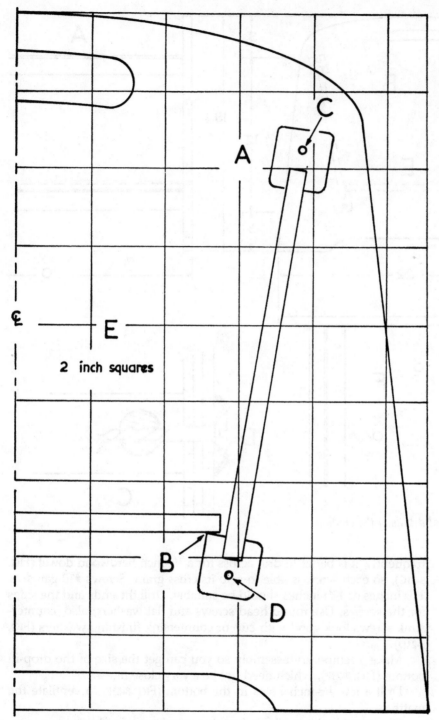

A

℄   E

2 inch squares

C

B

D

Fig. 8-22. *Shape of the end and parts layout for the cradle.*

2 ends	22	×	18	×	1/2 plywood
4 side strips	30	×	1 1/2	×	1/2
2 side panels	30	×	10	×	1/4 or 1/2 plywood
1 bottom	30	×	11	×	1/4 or 1/2 plywood

SMALL CHEST OF DRAWERS

A cabinet containing a block of drawers will encourage a child to put things away. It may be a container for toys in a playroom. It could stand beside the bed and serve as somewhere to keep clothing as well as a stand for a lamp and anything the child wants near him when in bed. This small chest of drawers (FIG. 8-23) is not intended to be a long-lasting piece of furniture that can take its place alongside quality furniture. It is of very simple construction, with plentiful use of plywood with its edges exposed, so a painted finish is advised to hide the edge grain. If the chest of drawers ceases to be needed for a child, it could have uses in a store-room or a workshop.

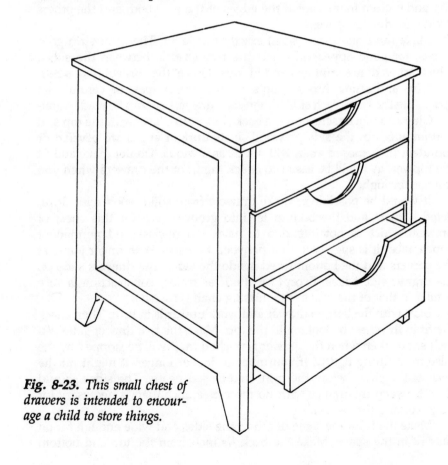

Fig. 8-23. *This small chest of drawers is intended to encourage a child to store things.*

Many of the parts are 1/2-inch plywood and 1-inch × 2-inch strips. Complicated joints are avoided and many parts are simply glued and nailed, or screwed. The design has three drawers of graduated depth, which looks better than having them all the same. The gaps between the legs should allow floor cleaning without moving the cabinet. The drawers have overlapping fronts, which avoids the need for close fitting. They are shown with hand notches instead of handles; this avoids projections, and it will be easy for small hands to grip and pull.

The main parts of the framework consist of a pair of framed sides (FIGS. 8-24A and 25A) and four identical frames (FIG. 8-25B), which act as drawer runners, as well as the top and bottom. The drawers are boxes with false fronts.

The important parts are the pair of sides. Cut the two pieces of plywood 15 inches × 22 inches. Make the legs, which extend 4 inches and may be tapered on the inside edges (FIG. 8-24B).

Use these and two crosspieces to frame the plywood (FIG. 8-25C). Use glue and pins driven at alternate angles (FIG. 8-25D).

Mark on the insides the positions of the frames (FIGS. 8-24C and 25E). Top and bottom frames are at the edges of the plywood, and the others divide the drawer spaces.

Make the frames (FIG. 8-25B) exactly the same. The front strip goes across, for good appearance, but the rear strip is between the sides, which act as drawer runners and kickers. Dowel the corners (FIG. 8-25F).

Glue and screw through the sides into the frames. Be careful that spaces are the same each side; otherwise, drawers cannot be made parallel. Glue and nail or screw on the back (FIG. 8-24D), level with the top and bottom edges of the side plywood. If its upright edges are beveled or rounded, the exposed grain will not be as obvious. Do not make and fit the top yet, as it will be easier to check the fit of the drawers when you can see through.

It would be possible to make drawers from solid wood with dovetailed corners and the bottom let into grooves, but for this chest of drawers which is not intended to have a high-class and permanent appearance, it is suggested that plywood be used. With finger joints at the corners and the bottom fitted inside the sides, the drawers slide on the drawer side edges. Except for the false fronts, construction is very similar to that of the tray in the nursing chair (FIG. 8-19).

Start with the bottom drawer and work upwards in turn. Then check the fit in the chest by looking in the top. Make the two drawer sides 3/4-inch short; then when the drawer is pushed in, it will be stopped by the false front fitting tightly. If you made a drawer longer, it might hit the back of the chest before the front had closed neatly. The sides should slide between the frames with no more clearance than is necessary for easy working (FIG. 8-26A).

Make the front the same depth as the sides and wide enough for an easy fit in the space. Make the back 1/8 inch from the top and bottom

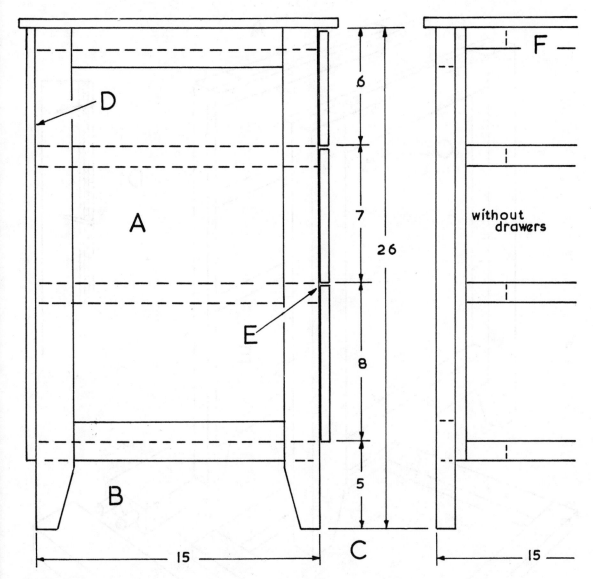

Fig. 8-24. *Sizes of the small chest of drawers.*

edges of the sides (FIG. 8-26B). This makes sure its edges will not touch a frame and impede movement of the drawer.

Cut finger joints at the corners—fingers about 1-inch wide will be satisfactory (FIG. 8-26C).

Assemble the four parts with glue and pins both ways. Try the box in position and make any adjustments necessary.

Fit the bottom inside 1/8-inch up from the edges of the sides, with glue and pins set below the surface of the sides (FIG. 8-26D).

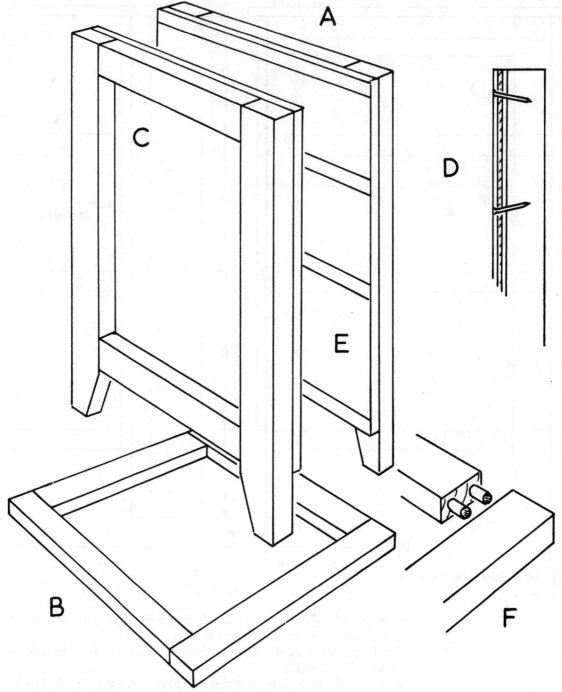

Fig. 8-25. *Assembled sections of the small chest of drawers.*

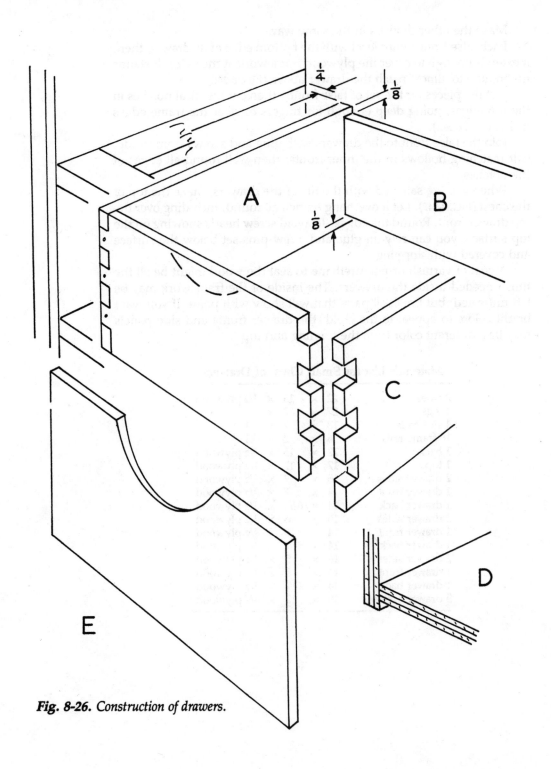

Fig. 8-26. *Construction of drawers.*

Make the other drawers in the same way.

Each false front comes level with the bottom edge of its drawer; then, it extends enough to cover the plywood framework at the sides. It stands up enough to almost reach the drawer above (FIG. 8-24E).

Cut the pieces for the set of false fronts; then cut identical notches in the top edges, going deep enough for fingers to clear the frame edges inside (FIG. 8-26E).

Join the false front to the drawers with glue and screws from inside. Cut matching hollows in the inner fronts; then well round all edges of the notches.

When you are satisfied with the fits of the drawers, make the top of the chest (FIG. 8-24F). Let it overhang 1/2inch all round, including over the top drawer front. Round the edges. To avoid screw heads showing on the top surface, you can rely on glue and a few pins set below the surface and covered with stopping.

A coat of varnish or polyurethane to seal the wood might be all the finish needed inside the drawers. The inside of the framework may be left untreated, but finish all parts that will show with paint. If you want bright colors to appeal to the child, the drawer fronts and side panels may be a different color from the framing and top.

Materials List for Small Chest of Drawers

2 sides	22	×	15	×	1/2	plywood
4 legs	27	×	2	×	1	
4 side rails	13	×	2	×	1	
16 frame rails	16	×	2	×	1	
1 back	22	×	15	×	1/2	plywood
1 top	17	×	17	×	1/2	plywood
2 drawer sides	16	×	7	×	1/2	plywood
1 drawer front	14	×	7	×	1/2	plywood
1 drawer back	14	×	6 3/4	×	1/2	plywood
2 drawer sides	16	×	6	×	1/2	plywood
1 drawer front	14	×	6	×	1/2	plywood
1 drawer back	14	×	5 3/4	×	1/2	plywood
2 drawer sides	16	×	5	×	1/2	plywood
1 drawer front	14	×	5	×	1/2	plywood
1 drawer back	14	×	4 3/4	×	1/2	plywood
3 drawer bottoms	16	×	12	×	1/2	plywood

9
Bathroom
and Laundry

Neither bathroom nor laundry room is regarded by house planners as a main living area, so space allocated to either of them is slight. There is not much space for free-standing furniture; any additions you may make have to be attached to the walls or even the door. If an item can be taken apart and stowed compactly when not needed, that might be the only way of providing a needed service in a confined space. It will be helpful if furniture can be made for a dual purpose.

Furniture in a bathroom or laundry room will have to withstand damper conditions than elsewhere in the house, so the wood should be suitable and be given an appropriate water-resistant finish.

LAUNDRY BASKET

A container for clothing and other items ready to be washed may be plain and utilitarian, or it could be decorative. This laundry basket is a compromise (FIG. 9-1). It has a shaped top edge and a lifting lid. If carefully made and painted, it would look smart enough for a bedroom, bathroom or laundry room. It is given slight taper and a lift-off lid, so the contents could be tipped out.

The main parts are plywood (preferably exterior grade) with 3/4-inch square strip framing. The four sides are identical, with their framing arranged to fit into the next part. Join most parts with glue and fine nails.

Set out and cut the four sides (FIG. 9-2A). Shape the top edges if you wish.

The strips across meet the upright on one edge and at the other edge are cut short to clear the thickness of plywood and strips on the adjoining piece (FIG. 9-2B).

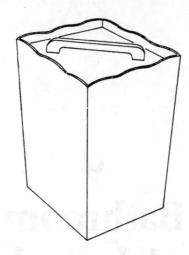

Fig. 9-1. *This laundry basket is tapered and has a lift-off lid.*

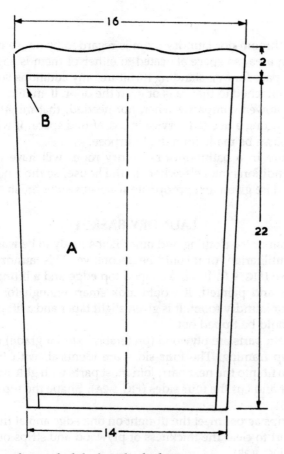

Fig. 9-2. *Sizes of a panel of the laundry basket.*

Bring the parts together and join them (FIG. 9-3A); check that the assembly is square and stands level.

Cut the bottom (FIG. 9-3B) to fit closely inside on top of the bottom strips. Glue and nail it there.

Cut the lid plywood to fit easily inside (FIG. 9-3C). It should be loose enough to put in, even if there are slight variations in the box sizes.

Make the handle to fit diagonally across the lid (FIG. 9-3D). Cut away to about half thickness, and thoroughly round all parts that will be gripped. Fix it with screws upwards through the lid.

Finish with paint. The inside could be a lighter color than the outside. If the box is to spend most of its time in the steamy atmosphere of a laundry room, use exterior grade paint.

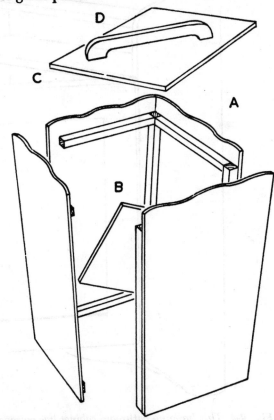

Fig. 9-3. *Parts of the laundry basket.*

Materials List for Laundry Basket

4 sides	25	×	16	×	1/2 plywood
1 bottom	14	×	14	×	1/2 plywood
1 lid	16	×	16	×	1/2 plywood
4 frames	14	×	3/4	×	3/4
4 frames	14	×	3/4	×	3/4
4 frames	16	×	3/4	×	3/4
1 handle	22	×	2	×	1

HANGING BATHROOM CABINET

This cabinet is intended to hang on the bathroom wall and to hold medicines, cosmetic items and many other small things that always seem to accumulate in a bathroom (FIG. 9-4). It has a door which could be wood, transparent, or obscured glass, or mirrored. There is one inside shelf and there is another below, although that arrangement could be replaced by a towel rail.

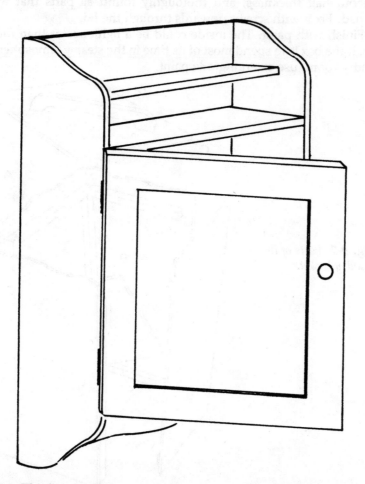

Fig. 9-4. *This hanging bathroom cabinet has storage for medicines and toiletries and a shelf below.*

Sizes are suggested (FIG. 9-5); vary them to make the best use of available wall space. If you use softwood, main parts may be 5/8-inch thick, but hardwood need only be 1/2-inch thick. Cut dado joints between the main parts, but dowels are suggested and they might be 1/4 inch in diameter.

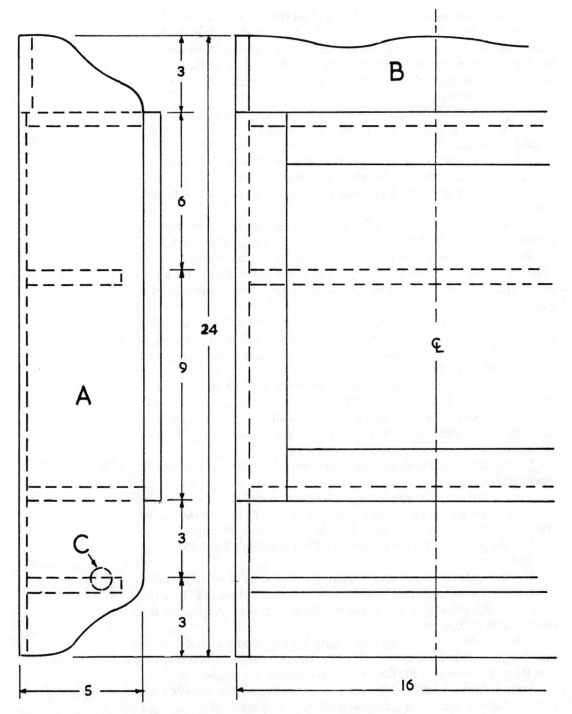

Fig. 9-5. *Sizes for the hanging bathroom cabinet and an alternative towel rail (C).*

Mark out and make the pair of sides first (FIG. 9-5A). Cut rabbets for the plywood back (FIG. 9-6A) for the full length; then widen the parts above the cabinet top to take the thicker back piece (FIGS. 9-6B and 7A). Mark on the positions of the other parts. The shelves are set back. If you want a towel rail instead of the bottom shelf, drill partly through for the end of the 3/4-inch dowel rod (FIG. 9-5C).

Shape their ends (FIG. 9-6C), which are the same, top and bottom.

Make the top and bottom of the cabinet and the shelves, which should finish the same lengths.

Mark their ends and the adjoining sides for dowels (FIG. 9-7B) and drill the holes. Drill the sides as deeply as it is possible to go (FIG. 9-6D) without breaking through. A Forstner bit would be the ideal tool for this task.

Make the solid wood back (FIG. 9-5B) long enough to extend past the cabinet top piece into the rabbets. Shape its upper edge (FIG. 9-6E).

Ready the plywood back; then assemble all the parts made so far. Clamp the doweled joints tightly until the glue has set. Fit the back plywood with glue and fine nails or screws into the side rabbets and the rear edges of the other pieces.

The door fits over the front and not into it. This allows it to swing away to give full access to the interior; it is easier to fit than if it were to go inside the framing. Overall sizes can first be made slightly large and the edges trimmed during fitting.

If you want to fit a plywood panel, there will have to be a groove to take it (FIG. 9-6F). If you want to fit clear, obscured glass, or a mirror, include a rabbet (FIG. 9-6G). This rabbet should allow for the thickness of the glass and a fillet behind it. However, do not prepare the grooves or rabbets yet, as it is easier to drill for dowels first.

Cut the door sides too long; mark on them where the top and bottom pieces will come.

Cut the top and bottom pieces to a length marked to go between the sides and extra allowed to go in the groove (FIG. 9-7C) or into the rabbet (FIG. 9-7D). Drill for dowels into both parts of each joint (FIG. 9-7E).

Cut the grooves or rabbets, which will probably go through part of the dowel holes.

Cut the ends of the top and bottom of the door to fit into the sides.

If there is to be a plywood panel, cut it to size so it does not reach the bottoms of the grooves. If it is made too close a fit, it might prevent the corner joints pulling tight.

Glue and dowel the corner joints, with the plywood panel, if there is one. For glass, check squareness. Try the door against the cabinet, whatever its type. See that it fits flat as well as matches the shape.

Trim off excess lengths of the sides, and trim the outline to match the cabinet shape. If much has to be taken off, do it symmetrically, planing a little from each opposite side.

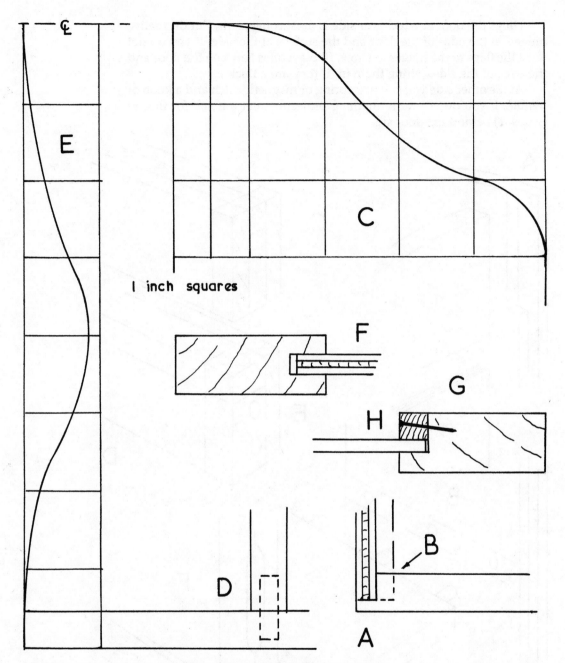

Fig. 9-6. *Shaped parts and sections of the hanging bathroom cabinet.*

Glass should fit reasonably closely, but it does not have to be forced in. Cut fillets to go in the rabbets behind the glass, and fix them with thin pins (FIG. 9-6H), spaced about 3-inches apart. Do not glue the fillets. If you ever have to replace the glass, the fillet strips can be levered out.

Hinge the door at whichever side is most convenient. Put decorative hinges on the edge of the door and the surface of the side. If you do not want the flaps of the hinges to show, fit plain ones between the door and the edge of the side, letting them in, if they are a thick type.

At the other side you can fit a spring or magnetic catch and a knob or handle. If you do not want anything projecting, cut a notch for fingers (FIG. 9-7F) behind the door side.

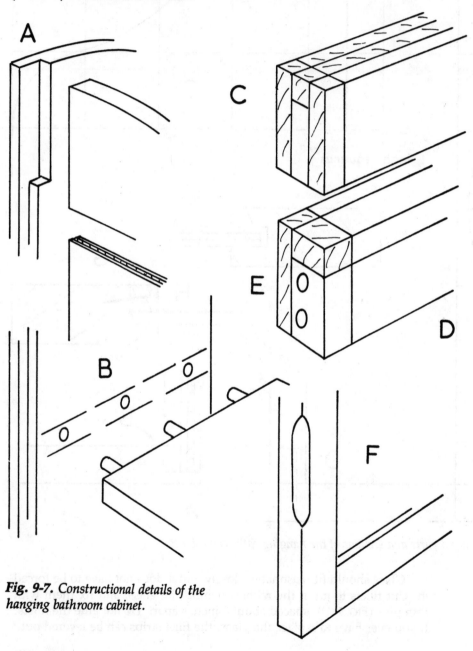

Fig. 9-7. *Constructional details of the hanging bathroom cabinet.*

The best finish will probably be a hard enamel to match the decor of the bathroom, but if you have used a good hardwood, you may prefer a clear finish. The plywood should be well-protected against a damp atmosphere, by painting on edges and back as well as visible parts. In most places, it should be satisfactory to hang the cabinet with two screws wide apart and high inside the upper part of the back.

Materials List for Hanging Bathroom Cabinet

2 sides	26 ×	5 ×	$5/8$ or $1/2$
2 shelves	16 ×	$4^3/4$ ×	$5/8$ or $1/2$
1 or 2 shelves	16 ×	4 ×	$5/8$ or $1/2$
1 rail	16 ×	$3/4$ diameter (optional)	
1 back	17 ×	3 ×	$5/8$ or $1/2$
1 back	22 ×	16 ×	$1/4$ plywood
4 door frames	16 ×	2 ×	$3/4$
1 door panel	14 ×	13 ×	$1/4$ plywood (optional)
4 door fillets	14 ×	$3/8$ ×	$3/8$ (optional)

STANDING BATHROOM CABINET

This cabinet (FIG. 9-8) is related to the hanging cabinet, but it is intended to stand as well as be suitable for hanging. Its size makes it suitable for standing on the tank, but it could also go on a shelf. It could be

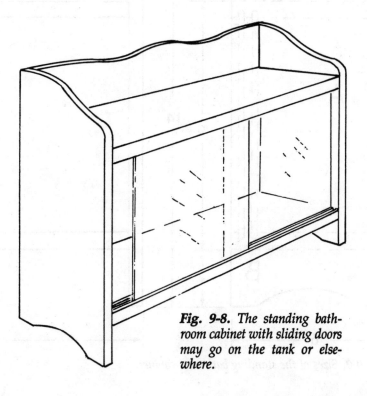

Fig. 9-8. *The standing bathroom cabinet with sliding doors may go on the tank or elsewhere.*

made as a matching set with the hanging cabinet or as an individual project.

Instead of opening doors there are overlapping sliding doors, which might be thin plywood or glass. However, avoid having to get someone else to cut and polish glass by using Plexiglas or similar plastic, which may be clear or in one of the patterned designs.

The suggested sizes (FIG. 9-9) show a design that is very similar to the previous cabinet, although different in size. Most of the joints and shaping can be the same. Whether you use hard or soft wood, top and bottom should be ⅝-inch thick to allow for grooving without weakening the wood. Other main parts are of similar sections to the hanging cabinet.

Mark out and make the pair of sides (FIG. 9-9A).

Rabbet the rear edges for the plywood and widen to take the solid wood top piece (FIG. 9-7A). Shape the top edges (FIG. 9-6C).

Hollow the lower edges to leave feet 1-inch wide (FIG. 9-9B).

Cut the top and bottom pieces to length. Cut the back piece longer to fit into the rabbet. Shape its top edge (FIG. 9-6E).

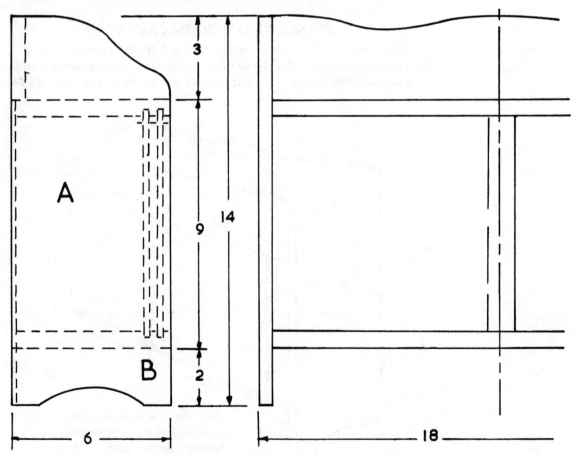

Fig. 9-9. *Sizes of the standing bathroom cabinet.*

The grooves have to be wide enough for the doors to slide easily. If the glass or Plexiglas is less than 3/16-inch thick, the grooves may be 1/4-inch wide in both parts (FIG. 9-10A). Sand the grooves smooth.

Attach strips under the top piece, so the grooves are deepened to 1/2 inch (FIG. 9-10B). The doors will then slide and stay in place by their own weight. To remove them, lift them into the deeper top grooves and pull the bottoms out.

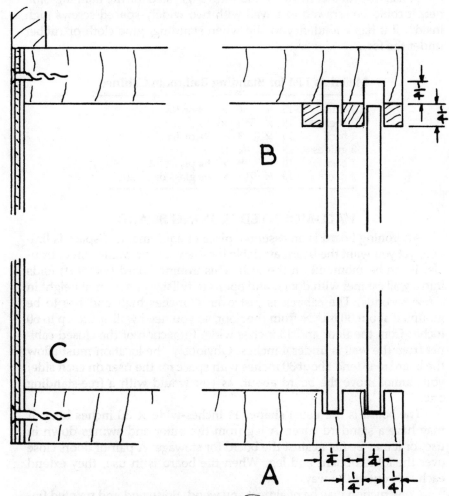

Fig. 9-10. *Sections of the standing bathroom cabinet.*

Prepare the parts for joining with glue and dowels (FIG. 9-7B).

Ready the back plywood. Stop it at the lower shelf (FIG. 9-10C). Join the parts. Tightly clamp the doweled joints. Add the back parts with glue and fine nails, or screws.

Make the doors wide enough to overlap about 1 inch at the center. Make the depths so when the lower edge is in its groove, the top is no higher than the underside of the top shelf; then, lifting into the further top groove allows the bottom to be brought out. Try the sliding action. It should be possible to grip the doors without handles. If the doors do not slide freely, put wax in the grooves. If you wish, you can put a small knob or handle at the central edge of the outer door. When that has been opened, you can reach inside and grip and move the other door. However, finger pressure on the doors may be all you need to slide them.

Finish this cabinet in one of the ways suggested for the hanging cabinet. It could be screwed to a wall with two widely-spaced screws high inside. If it has a tendency to slip when standing, glue cloth or rubber under the feet.

Materials List for Standing Bathroom Cabinet

2 sides	15 ×	6 ×	$5/8$ or $1/2$
2 shelves	18 ×	$53/4$ ×	$5/8$
1 back	19 ×	3 ×	$5/8$ or $1/2$
3 guides	18 ×	$1/4$ ×	$1/4$
1 back	18 ×	9 ×	$1/4$ plywood
2 doors	10 ×	$91/4$ ×	$1/8$ glass or plastic

WALL-MOUNTED IRONING BOARD

An ironing board is an essential piece of equipment. If space is limited, yet you want the board available for use with the minimum of trouble, it can be mounted on the wall. This ironing board (FIG. 9-11) folds into a wall cabinet with doors, and opens to fullsize at a normal height in a few seconds. The cabinet is just over 30-inches high and has to be mounted about 30 inches from the floor, so you need wall space up to 60 inches from the floor and 13-inches wide. Projection of the closed cabinet from the wall is under 4 inches. Obviously, the location must allow the board to extend about 30 inches with space for the user on each side; you cannot move the board about, as you would with a free-standing one.

The board is the usual shape, 11 inches-wide × 30 inches long. It may have a standard cover. A leg from the outer end swings down in use, or it may be flat against the board for stowage. A pair of doors close over the folded board and leg. When the board is in use, they extend each side out of the way.

Construction may be of almost any wood. Softwood and painted finish should suit most situations, but a hardwood cabinet with a clear finish would look attractive. The ironing board might be solid wood or plywood $3/4$ inch or thicker. It is more important with this project than some others to get all your wood together and prepare it to thickness *before* making the parts. You need to know actual thicknesses so you can lay out the folding arrangements, particularly if you want the cabinet to

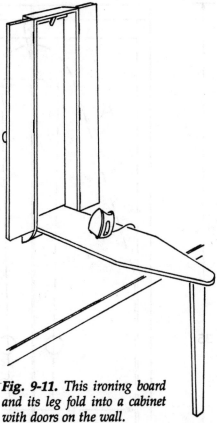

Fig. 9-11. *This ironing board and its leg fold into a cabinet with doors on the wall.*

have the minimum projection from the wall. Slight differences in thickness from those specified may not matter, if you know what they are before starting fabricating.

Overall sizes and general layout are shown (FIG. 9-12). If you decide to alter sizes, remember that the working height has to be between 28 inches and 32 inches. Also, you must arrange the leg length, and the board length against which it folds, to allow for this.

On paper or the wood for one side, draw a section at the top of the cabinet. Against the back (FIG. 9-13A) allow for the ironing board (FIG. 9-13B). If it is to fold with its cover in place, leave space for that between the board and the back. Then comes the leg (FIG. 9-13C), which will be held away from the underside of the board by the thickness of the folded hinge. Allow a little clearance in front of that to get the width of the cabinet side (FIG. 9-13D).

Project downwards from this to get the layout at the bottom of the cabinet (FIG. 9-13E). There is a strip across the end of the board (FIG. 9-13F) to take the pivot rods. The leg folds to just above this (FIG. 9-13G). The doors go over the edges of the sides (FIG. 9-13H).

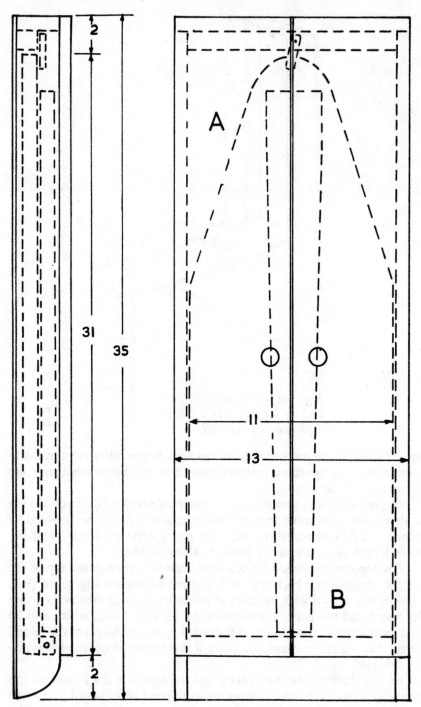

Fig. 9-12. *Main sizes of the wall-mounted ironing board.*

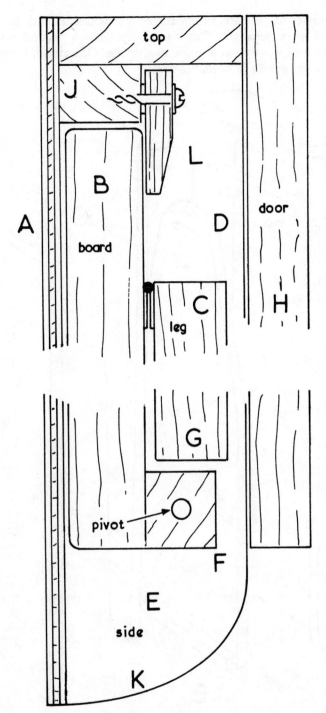

Fig. 9-13. *Sections showing the layout of the wall-mounted ironing board.*

It is easier to get parts fitting correctly if you start with the ironing board and work outwards. Cut it to shape (FIGS. 9-12A and 14A). For a standard cover, use this as a guide to shaping. Otherwise, taper from a curve 3-inches across to 12 inches back.

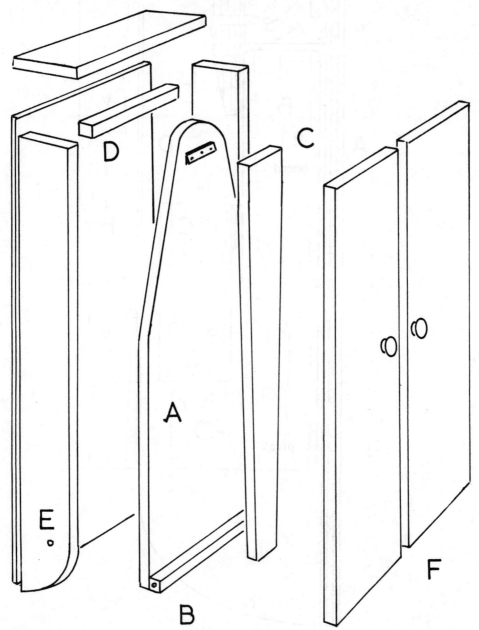

Fig. 9-14. *Parts of the wall-mounted ironing board.*

Drill the ends of the pivot strip (FIG. 9-14B) 2-inches deep to take ¼-inch steel rods. Glue and screw this at the end of the board.

Make the leg (FIG. 9-14C). When folded, its top is 2-inches back from the end of the board and its tapered foot comes above the pivot strip (FIG. 9-12B). Use a 3-inch hinge across the top to join it to the board. When the leg is opened square to the board, its top should rest against the board and not depend just on its hinge and screws for strength, as the downward thrust of ironing may be heavy.

Using the board as a guide, mark the lengths of the pair of sides. There is a strip across at the top (FIGS. 9-13J and 14D) clear of the end of the folded board; then the cabinet top goes above this and the sides. Allow enough for shaped ends at the bottom (FIG. 9-13K).

Cut the back to overlap the sides, so they have a small clearance each side of the ironing board. The top goes over the sides and the back will be behind that.

Check the parts against each other. Fit the board in place against the sides, and from this get the pivot positions (FIG. 9-14E). Drill for the pivots. They might be large screws, but pieces of ¼-inch steel rod are suggested. If they project a short distance with rounded ends, grip them with pliers if you ever need to remove the board from the cabinet. You might have to round the rear edge of the board end a little, so it misses the back as it swings, if you have not allowed much vertical clearance.

Join the top and sides to the back, and fit in the board and its leg. At this stage, you might only partially drive the pivot rods, so they can be removed for convenience in painting the wood.

Make the two doors (FIGS. 9-13H and 14F). They should meet with a little clearance and come level with the sides. Hinge them to the sides. Because they are long and narrow, they will be held in shape better by three hinges than two each side. The hinges could be 2-inches long. Put decorative hinges on the surface, or use plain hinges between the doors and the sides.

Put spring or magnetic catches behind the doors under the top. Position knobs or other handles at a suitable height. They may have to come below the center to be within a comfortable reach of the user.

The board should be level in use, so get the position for screwing to the wall by lowering the board onto its leg and checking that the position chosen leaves the lowered board parallel with the floor.

Make a small wood turnbutton (FIG. 9-13L) to hold the board in its raised position. Use washers on a roundhead screw.

With a stiff hinge, you might find that the leg stays in the down position without further treatment. Put a dowel in the end (and notch the pivot strip to clear it) to go into a hole in the floor. There could be a hook and eye arranged at the top at the side of the leg and diagonally to the board when the two parts are linked in the down position.

When you are satisfied with the operation of the parts, separate them for sanding, rounding the board and leg edges and painting, before finally assembling and mounting in place on the wall.

Materials List for Wall-mounted Ironing Board

1 board	34	×	11	×	3/4 or 1 solid wood or plywood
1 leg	32	×	3	×	1
1 pivot strip	12	×	1	×	1
2 sides	36	×	4	×	3/4
1 top	15	×	4	×	3/4
1 strip	12	×	1¼	×	1
2 doors	35	×	6½	×	3/4
1 back	36	×	13	×	1/4 plywood

DRYING RAILS

Some things have to be air dried after washing, while others need airing after machine drying, so rails which will allow them to be folded over or hung from hangers are useful, but a suitable rack could be too bulky for storage when out of use if it would not fold. This arrangement (FIG. 9-15) has three rails, with one of them high enough for hanging dresses and the lower two suitable for some jackets and children's clothes on hangers and such things as towels folded over. The whole thing will fold flat to less than 6-inches thick, but it opens to stand steadily with a spread of legs 33-inches or 39-inches across.

The top rail is about 5 feet from the floor and the others are about 24 inches. The strut across the rails which holds the rack in shape swings down, so it does not project below the ends of the legs. If you alter sizes, keep the strut short enough to allow this.

The legs may be straight-grained softwood, nominally 1-inch × 3-inch section, but it is likely to be 7/8 inch × 2³/4 inches after planing. If you use hardwood, it could be a slightly smaller section. The rails are hardwood dowels 1 inch in diameter. They are shown 36-inches long (FIG. 9-16A), but you may choose a different length.

Make the four legs (FIG. 9-16B). The tops extend past the dowel rod holes to avoid any weakness of short grain. Drill the holes to fit on the dowel rods. Take the sharpness off all edges.

The two struts (FIG. 9-16C) extend past the holes, and allow two spreads of the legs. Drill them to be a loose fit on the dowel rods. The single hole has to pivot on a rail. Notch the other two to drop over the other rail. For ease of hooking on, slightly taper the notches (FIG. 9-16D).

When you assemble, remember that the struts have to pivot on a lower rail, the inner legs have to pivot on the top rail, and the ends of the dowel rods must be glued into their legs. Cut the lower rails which glue into the inner legs short enough for these legs to be parallel, but an easy fit inside the outer legs.

Try the action of the assembly. Remove any surplus glue. Leave the wood untreated, or seal it with varnish or polyurethane to prevent dirt getting into the grain.

Materials List for Drying Rails

4 legs	66	× 3	× 1	
2 struts	28	× 3	× 1	
3 rails	36	× 1 diameter		

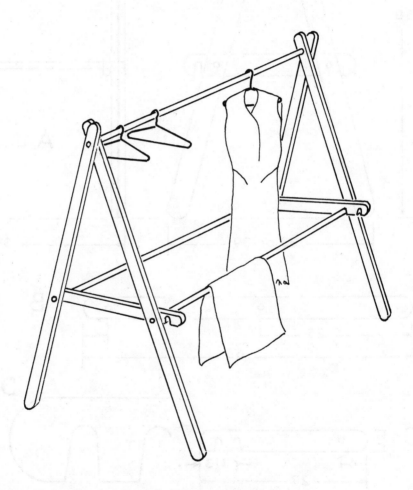

Fig. 9-15. *These clothes-drying rails are designed to fold flat.*

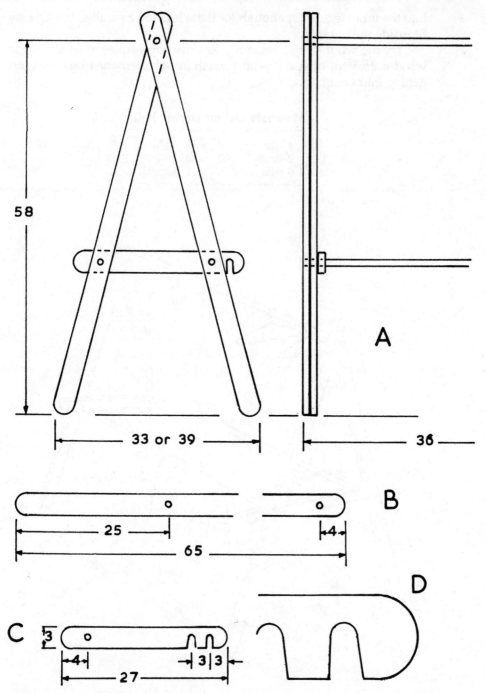

58

33 or 39

36

A

B

25

65

4

C

3

4

27

3 3

D

Fig. 9-16. *Details of the drying rails.*

10
Den and Playroom

Both den and playroom, by their very nature, do not warrant such important or imposing furniture as might be selected for other rooms. The furniture should be functional and may have to withstand rougher treatment. It needs to be strong, but it can also be attractive. There is no reason why it should be crude.

A den might also be a study or office and be equipped accordingly. The playroom should offer comfort, as well as facilities for games and relaxation. There is plenty of scope for making furniture which may not be built in such a traditional way, as may be expected for items which have to take their place alongside more ambitious pieces in other rooms. If you have doubts about your ability to make high-class furniture, something for the playroom or den might be a good beginning.

Several pieces of furniture described for other rooms might find their way into a den or playroom, either as they are or adapted in some way, but the furniture described in this chapter will be built for a purpose.

WALL DESK

If floor space is limited and the need only intermittent, a desk or work surface supported on the wall, and able to fold back has many attractions. This desk (FIG. 10-1) could be used for writing or typing, but it would also serve as a bench for a light hobby. It would not withstand heavy hammering, but for such things as paper modeling and fabric crafts, it makes a work table that can be swung out of the way when not needed.

The design suggested is 28-inches square (FIG. 10-2); when closed, the unit projects 5 inches from the wall and does not reach the floor.

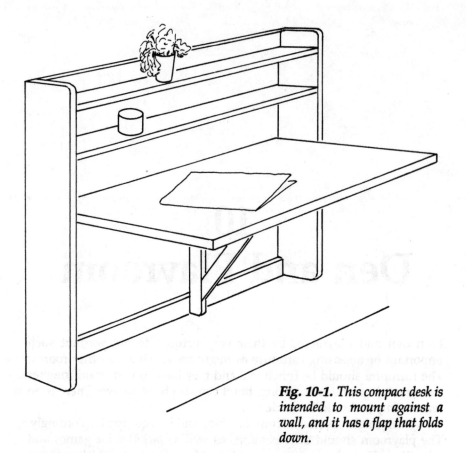

Fig. 10-1. *This compact desk is intended to mount against a wall, and it has a flap that folds down.*

When opened, the working surface is about 26-inches wide, extends 20 inches and is supported by a substantial bracket. There are two shelves shown, but you could alter the unit height and put in more shelves or compartments.

Most parts are solid wood 3/4-inch thick. The working surface is framed plywood. Construction is with 5/16-inch or 3/8-inch dowels.

Mark out the pair of sides (FIG. 10-3A) with the positions of the other parts, including the flap in *up* and *down* positions, so you can see where the pivot holes will come.

Mark and cut the crosswise parts to the same length with square ends. There are two lower braces (FIG. 10-2A), two shelves (FIG. 10-2B) and a top (FIG. 10-2C).

Mark the ends for dowels (FIG. 10-3B). Glue and dowel the top to its shelf.

Round the front corners of the sides. Take sharpness off the exposed edges of all parts and do any necessary sanding.

Join the crosswise parts to the sides with glue and dowels.

Measure diagonals to check squareness.

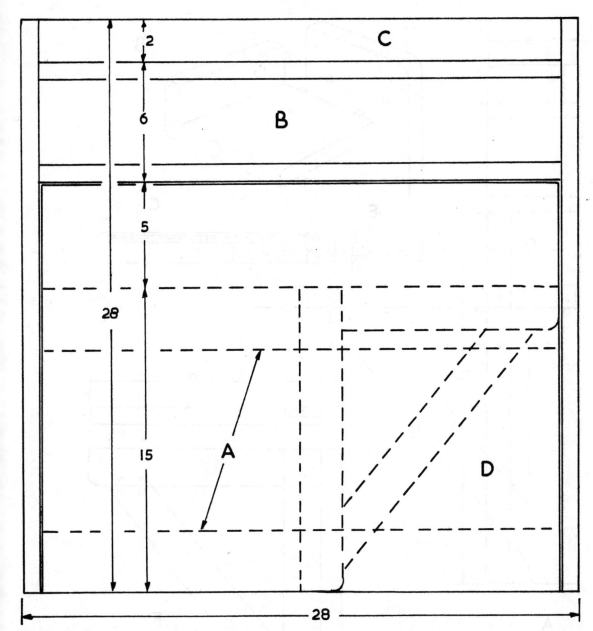

Fig. 10-2. *Sizes of the wall desk.*

The flap could be made to suit the intended use. Veneered particleboard might be suitable. It is shown as 1/2-inch plywood framed with 3/4-inch strips and edged (FIG. 10-3C). Make the overall width to fit easily between the sides. The depth, when folded down, should go under the shelf and reach the bottom of the sides (FIG. 10-3D).

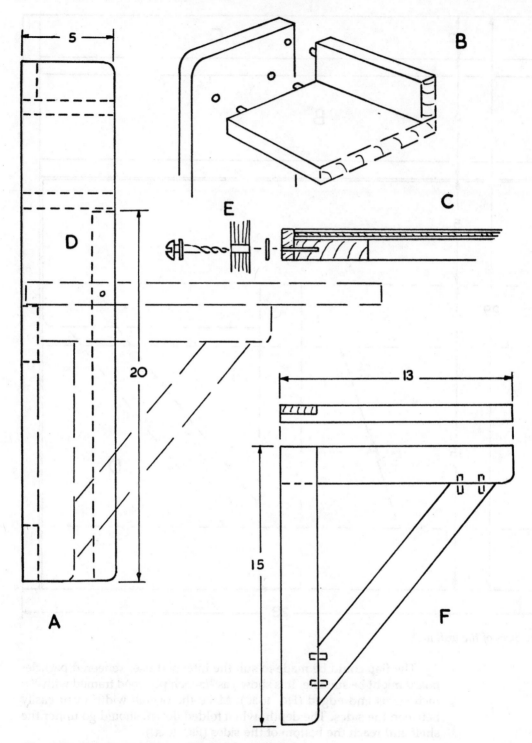

Fig. 10-3. Details of part assemblies of the wall desk.

When the flap is opened horizontally, its rear edge should rest on the brace at the back. Try the flap in this position, and drill the sides in the screw position. However, first drill a 1/8-inch hole each side for nails to be pushed through. When you are satisfied with the action on nails, drill out for the pivot screws, which should be fairly large. Round head screws #12-gauge × 2 1/2 inches would be suitable. Put clearance holes through the sides and drill undersize holes in the flap, to prevent splitting. When you finally assemble, include washers on the screws (FIG. 10-3E).

The bracket (FIG. 10-3F) is built up from strips. Cut a halved joint at the corner. Temporarily assemble this squarely, so you can mark the size and shape of the strut. Dowel the strut joints.

Position the bracket so it will fold inside (FIG. 10-2D). Attach it to the braces with 2-inch or larger hinges. The bracket should stop under the flap when it is about square, but if you think it is necessary, put a stop block under the flap.

Finish the wood in a way to match the surroundings; although, the working surface may be best without a gloss.

Mount the unit on the wall so the working surface will be at a suitable height, probably between 27 inches and 31 inches.

Materials List for Wall Desk

2 ends	29 ×	4 ×	3/4
2 shelves	29 ×	5 ×	3/4
1 top	29 ×	2 ×	3/4
2 braces	29 ×	3 ×	3/4
3 brackets	16 ×	2 ×	1
1 flap	28 ×	20 ×	1/2 plywood
2 flaps	28 ×	3 ×	3/4
2 flaps	21 ×	3 ×	3/4
2 flap edges	28 ×	1 1/4 ×	1/4
2 flap edges	21 ×	1 1/4 ×	1/4

STACKING COFFEE TABLES

A single coffee table is useful, but if several of you want to sit around with coffee mugs within reach you need more tables. A collection of individual tables may take up too much room when they are not in use, but if you can nest or stack them the problem is solved. This set of three stacking coffee tables (FIG. 10-4) fits into the floor space occupied by only one. As shown (FIG. 10-5A), the floor area is 12 inches × 20 inches and the largest table is 18 inches high. The other two tables are smaller in steps of about 1 inch in height and depth and 2 1/2 inches in length. This does not make any appreciable difference in use.

The tops and legs are made from wide boards, which could be solid wood, or you might use veneered particleboard. Stiffness has to come from a rear rail under each top and another rear rail lower down. There

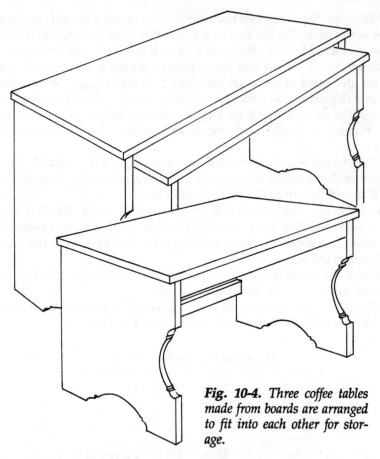

Fig. 10-4. *Three coffee tables made from boards are arranged to fit into each other for storage.*

cannot be any front rails on the two larger tables, or you would not be able to fit one into the other. However, you might have a rail under the top of the smallest table. This may not be essential for strength, but it improves the appearance of the stack.

In height there is 1/4-inch clearance between the table tops (FIG. 10-5B). Each table top overlaps the board, forming an end by 1/4 inch (FIG. 10-5C), to give you something to grip when lifting the table. The tops have 1/4-inch clearance inside the legs of the next larger table, so each table is 2 1/2-inches shorter than the next one. Providing you work accurately and cut ends squarely, 1/4-inch clearance both ways should be enough. However, if you wish to allow more clearance, that is easy to arrange.

Cutouts are shown at the bottoms of the legs to form feet; similar cutouts may be arranged at the front edges. If you only want utilitarian tables without frills for use in a playroom, the decorations may be left off, but you should still cut away the bottoms of the legs to help the tables stand level.

For the sake of appearance in the stack, the lower edges of all top rails are level, which means that the rails are different depths. All lower

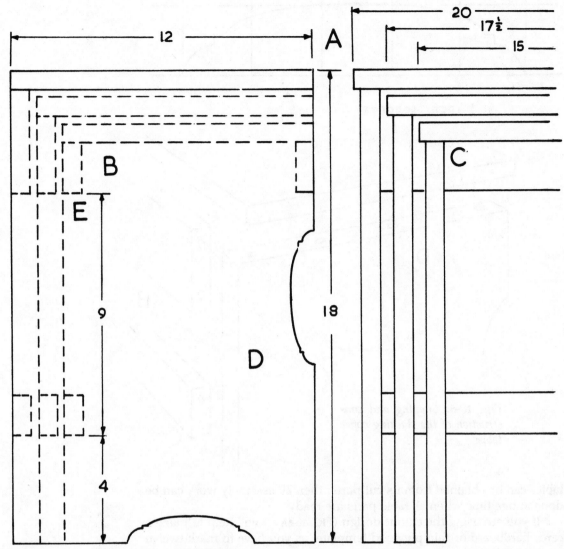

Fig. 10-5. *Sizes of the stacking coffee tables.*

rails are level, although their legs are different lengths; this also applies to the cutouts. The bottom cutout is central in the smallest legs and the same distance from the front edge in the others, so each foot behind is wider. Similarly, the cutout on the front edge is the same height from the floor on each leg. The effect is for the appearance of the three tables fitted together to be the same throughout, which looks neater than if rails and cutouts are different on each table.

It would be possible to start with the large table and make the others to fit into it; an easier way is to start with the smallest table and get the other sizes from it. You need not completely assemble, but sizes of other

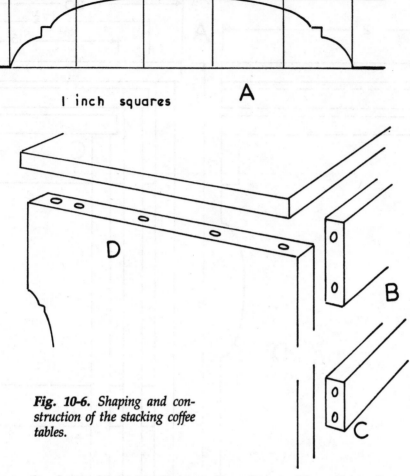

I inch squares   A

D   B

C

Fig. 10-6. *Shaping and construction of the stacking coffee tables.*

tables can be obtained from its cut parts; then all assembly work can be done at one time when all table parts are ready.

If you are using the cutout design (FIG. 10-6A) it will help to make a card, hardboard or thin plywood template, as you have to mark twelve matching shapes.

For the smallest table, mark a pair of legs (FIG. 10-5D). If the largest table is to be 18-inches high, these legs will be 16 inches less the thickness of the top.

Mark the rail positions on the rear edges. Cut out the shaped parts.

Cut the top to size. Mark the leg and rail positions, with the legs 1/4 inch in from the ends. Note the positions of the lower edge of the top rail (FIG. 10-5E), which will have to be at the same height as on the other legs.

Make the rails (FIG. 10-6B). For the small table there may be a front rail the same depth as the rear one.

Mark the dowel hole positions. With the 3/4-inch wood, the dowels may be 3/8 inch in diameter. Put two dowels in each rail end (FIG. 10-6C).

In this table, you can space the dowels between the legs and top evenly, but in the other tables there will not be a front rail to share the load at the front. Therefore, those dowels are best arranged with two close together near the front edge and others more widely spaced (FIG. 10-6D).

Drill the dowel holes; then sand and assemble this table now, if you wish. However, in overall timing it would be better to wait until the parts of all the tables are ready. If you are keeping the table in parts, mark them so they will not be confused with those for the other two tables.

Make the middle-size table in the same way, but without a front rail. Allow 1/4-inch clearance in height over the smallest table, and space the legs under the top so there is 1/4-inch spare at each end.

Make the rails to match the first table, and have the cutouts the same distance from the floor and front edge.

Make the large table with the same clearance over the second table, with rails and cutouts matching.

Check sizes by comparing relevant parts. When you are satisfied, drill dowel holes and sand all parts. Assemble with glue and dowels. The parts should pull each other square, but start with the small table and check squareness in all directions. As you progress to the other tables, use the small table as a guide to appearance by fitting the others over it.

Finish with stain and polish, or apply whatever treatment suits the wood and your wishes.

Materials List for Stacking Coffee Tables

1 top	21	×	12	×	3/4	
1 top	19	×	11	×	3/4	
1 top	17	×	10	×	3/4	
2 legs	18	×	12	×	3/4	
2 legs	17	×	11	×	3/4	
2 legs	16	×	10	×	3/4	
3 rails	20	×	1 1/2	×	3/4	
1 rail	20	×	4 1/4	×	3/4	
1 rail	18	×	3 1/4	×	3/4	
2 rails	16	×	2 1/4	×	3/4	

ANGLED BOOKCASE

Do you get frustrated when trying to read the title, or pull out a book from the bottom shelf of the usual upright bookcase? The only way to identify some books is to crawl on the floor. This problem can be solved by making the racks at angles, which bring the backs of the books into positions where the titles are more easily read; then you can remove the one you want with no difficulty.

This bookcase (FIG. 10-7) has its bottom rack tilted at 30 degrees, the middle rack at 15 degrees and the top rack at level. The bottom shelf is intended for books up to 8 inches × 10 inches; the middle rack will take

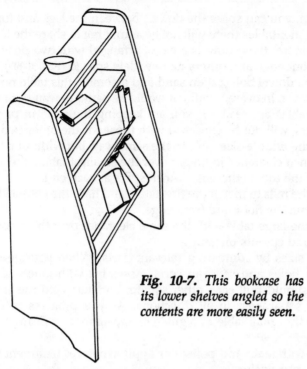

Fig. 10-7. *This bookcase has its lower shelves angled so the contents are more easily seen.*

them almost as big; and the top rack will suit page sizes of 6 inches × 8 inches. Above that, is a shelf to take all the things that most people want to put on a bookcase.

To accommodate books of these sizes and at the specified angles, the ends have to be fairly wide. If your books are smaller or different angles would suit your need, you can lay out the pattern to use narrower ends. This design is intended for solid wood. Construction is with dowels.

The key part that controls the layout is an end (FIG. 10-8A). Work from the rear edge and have a square line at the bottom. Draw a line 2 inches from the rear edge and mark on it the distances shown (FIG. 10-8B). Imagine the shapes of books and work from them. At the inner corners of a book, the rack parts are cut 1 inch from it (FIGS. 10-8C and 9A).

The top shelf and the rack below it are marked square (FIG. 10-8D). Draw in the full outlines of the ends of the pieces to avoid confusion when locating dowel holes.

For the other two racks, start by drawing lines at 30 degrees and 15 degrees from the marked points. Use these angled lines and the imaginary square-cornered book to draw in the outlines of the rack part (FIGS. 10-8E and F).

Mark the rack positions on both ends, then mark and cut the outlines. Round all edges, except those that touch the floor.

Make the lengthwise pieces, matching their widths to the marked positions on the ends. Keep all lengths exactly the same, if joints are to pull tight and assembly is to be square.

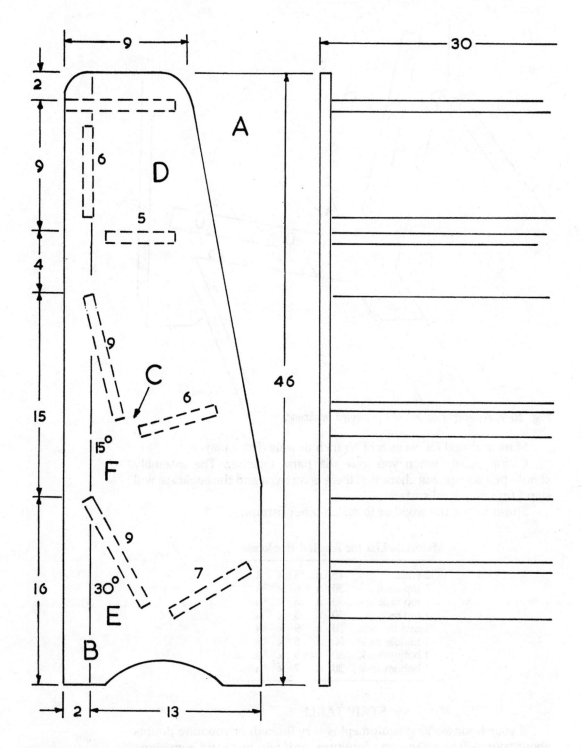

Fig. 10-8. *Sizes of the angled bookcase.*

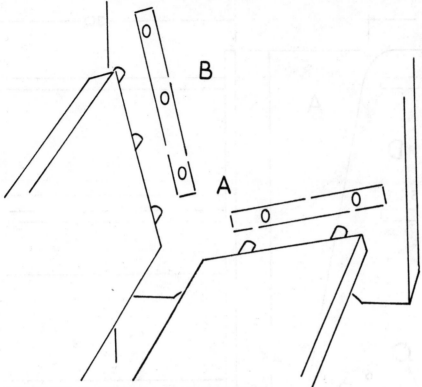

Fig. 10-9. *Assembly details of the angled bookcase.*

Mark and drill for ³/₈ inch of ¹/₂ inch dowels (FIG. 10-9B).

Clamp tightly when you glue the parts together. The assembly should pull square, but check that there is no twist and the bookcase will stand firm on a level surface.

Finish to suit the wood or to match other furniture.

Materials List for Angled Bookcase

2 ends	48	×	15	×		1
1 top shelf	30	×	8	×	³/₄
1 top rack	30	×	6	×	³/₄
1 top rack	30	×	5	×	³/₄
1 middle rack	30	×	9	×	³/₄
1 middle rack	30	×	6	×	³/₄
1 bottom rack	30	×	9	×	³/₄
1 bottom rack	30	×	7	×	³/₄

STRIP TABLE

If your woodworking equipment is very limited, or you have doubts about your skill to make some furniture, or if you just want something

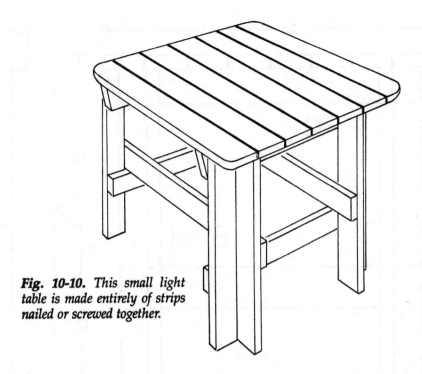

Fig. 10-10. *This small light table is made entirely of strips nailed or screwed together.*

easy to make, there is an attraction about a project where all you do for most of the construction is to lay one piece of wood on top of another and nail or screw it there. This table (FIG. 10-10) is built that way. Another attraction is that all the wood is of the same section—1 inch × 3 inch.

The lower structure is made of overlapping pieces. Make the top with strips, allowing narrow gaps between, or fill these gaps with wood of a contrasting color. This would be the better treatment for a table to be used in the den or elsewhere indoors. For use outside where the table may occasionally be rained on, leave gaps for drainage.

The sizes suggested (FIG. 10-11) fit the table into a 24-inch cube, which is between coffee table dimensions and a fullsize table. This makes the table a compromise in size, so it might be used for a variety of purposes, but alter the design to suit particular needs. Build the table of softwood and finish with paint, but consider using hardwood for the top, with a clear finish, while the lower parts are painted.

Prepare all the wood to the same section. Check that pieces are straight. A few knots will not matter, providing that they are not loose. Planed size will probably be about 1/8-inch undersize, but that will not matter.

Cut the eight pieces for the legs. Join them so the overlapping pieces will be lengthwise under the table (FIG. 10-11A). In these and most other joints, use glue and #8-gauge × 1 1/2 inch-screws. A 4-inch spacing should be sufficient in the legs.

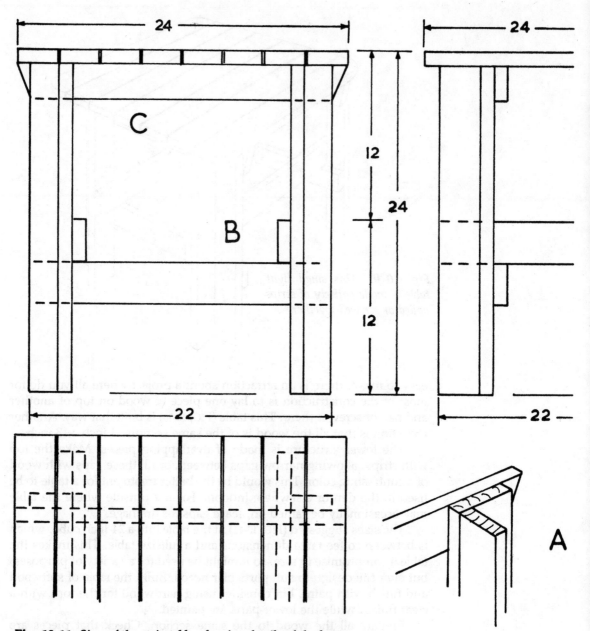

Fig. 10-11. *Sizes of the strip table, showing details of the legs.*

Mark on the legs the positions of the rails. The lengthwise lower rails come above those across the legs (FIGS. 10-11B and 12A).

Make the top rails (FIGS. 10-11C and 12B) 24-inches long, to extend over the legs 1 inch with beveled ends. The lower rails finish level with the leg edges.

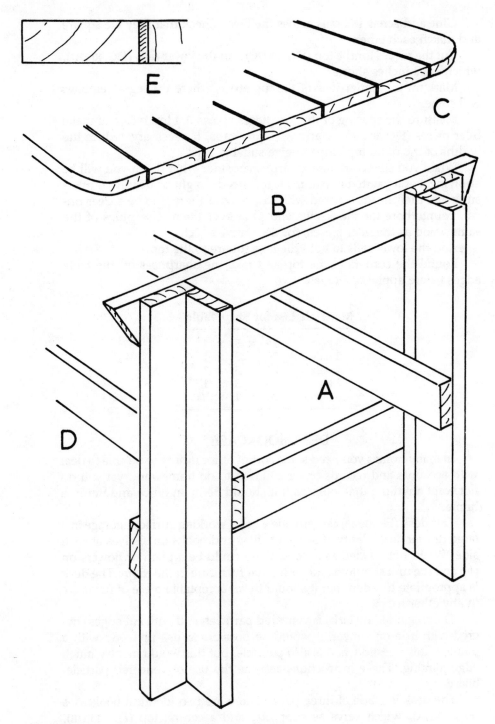

Fig. 10-12. *How the strip table parts are assembled.*

Glue and screw the rails across the legs. Check that they are square and match each other.

Cut the pieces for the top (FIG. 10-12C) and the lower rails (FIG. 10-12D), which are 2-inches shorter.

Mark on the undersides of the top strips where the leg assemblies will come.

Measure the spacing of the top pieces across the top rails and make filler pieces (FIG. 10-12E), or arrange equal gaps. If necessary, reduce the widths of the outer top strips to give suitable gaps.

When you screw on the top strips, consider what finish you will be applying. For a painted finish, the screw heads might be deeply countersunk and their heads covered with stopping. If there is to be a clear finish, counterbore for the screws and plug over them. Use plugs of the same wood as the filler pieces, for decorative effect.

Add the lower rails to hold the legs square to the top.

Round the corners of the top and take the sharpness off the table edges before applying a finish.

Materials List for Strip Table

8 legs	24	×	3	×	1	
2 rails	26	×	3	×	1	
4 rails	24	×	3	×	1	
7 tops	26	×	3	×	1	
6 fillers	26	×	1	×	1/4	

DESK/BOOKCASE

In many homes you need some sort of office facility to be able to deal with accounts and records or for children to do homework, yet you do not want anything that looks as if it should be in an office and not in a home.

This desk (FIG. 10-13) can provide a good working surface, storage in a large drawer, and plenty of space for files and books on shelves at each side. When not needed as a desk, there could be a plant or flowers on top and the unit should blend with other furniture in the room. The desk is appropriate to a den, but it should be an acceptable piece of furniture in any other room.

The suggested material is veneered particleboard with cut edges covered with iron-on veneer. It would be possible to use plywood with a painted finish. Solid wood is also possible, but this would involve much edge jointing. These instructions assume the use of veneered particleboard.

The desk is made of three parts. There are two identical bookcases (FIG. 10-14A), which serve as supports, and a central top (FIG. 10-14B), which contains a drawer and fits between the bookcases. The working

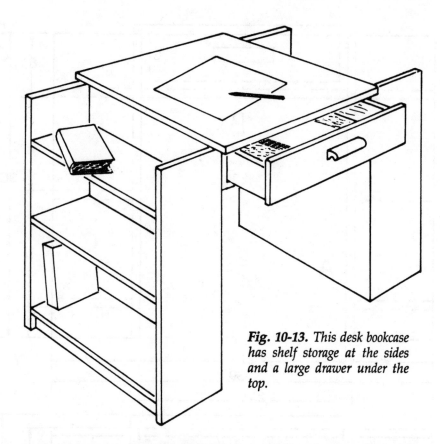

Fig. 10-13. *This desk bookcase has shelf storage at the sides and a large drawer under the top.*

surface overhangs a little all round. The suggested sizes provide knee room when using a normal chair, a working surface at a comfortable height, and a drawer about 4¹/₂-inches deep inside. Alter the arrangement of shelves in one or both bookcases if you want to store files or books of a particular size. To alter overall sizes, check that there will be space for comfortable and convenient movement.

Make the two bookcases completely first. They serve as a guide to sizes of parts of the central unit, which is made up as a box; then the drawer is fitted to it. The parts are finally screwed together.

Most joints may be glued and doweled, using ³/₈-inch dowels at about a 3-inch spacing. Where they enter the thickness of the material, take them as deeply as possible.

Mark out and cut the two pairs of desk sides (FIGS. 10-14C and 15A). Allow for the back fitting between the sides, and the base being set back 1-inch below the bottom shelf.

Make the back to fit between the sides (FIG. 10-15B). Because all edges will be covered, there is no need to veneer them.

Make the shelves (FIG. 10-15C) to fit in front of their backs, with lengths to match the width of the backs.

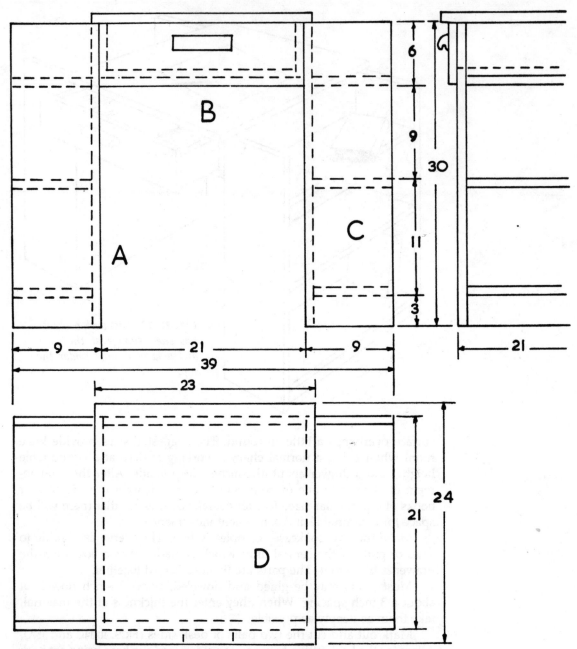

Fig. 10-14. *Sizes for the desk/bookcase.*

Cut the bases (FIG. 10-15D) to the same lengths.

Mark and drill all these parts for dowels. Arrange dowels fairly near the fronts of the shelves, for strength. Dowels between the shelves and the backs may be more widely spaced. The tops of the sides should be veneered, but this is unnecessary for the backs, which will be covered.

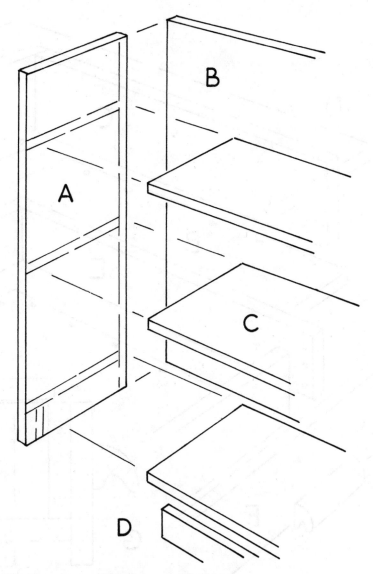

Fig. 10-15. *Details of the bookcase parts of the desk.*

However, it is important that all these parts are level at the top and bottom.

There should be no difficulty in squaring the bookcases when you assemble them, as the parts will pull each other into shape, but check that all joints are tight and the two units match.

Cut the back of the central unit first (FIG. 10-16A). This is the full width and depth of the unit, and it will serve as a guide to the sizes of other parts.

Cut the bottom to go in front of the back; it comes level with the fronts of the bookcases (FIG. 10-16B).

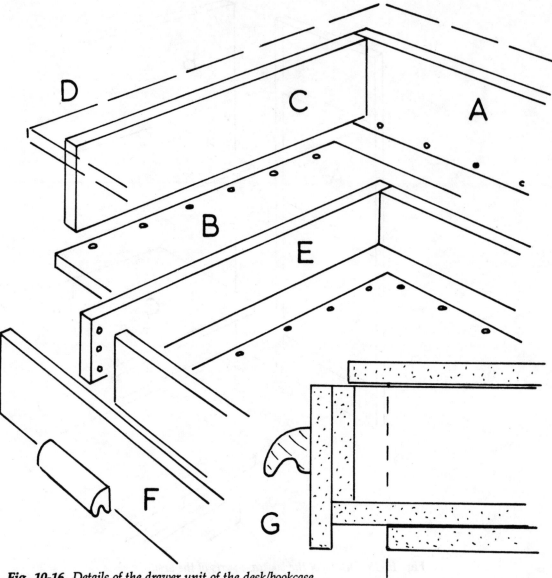

Fig. 10-16. *Details of the drawer unit of the desk/bookcase.*

Make the sides (FIG. 10-16C) to fit above the bottom.

Make the top (FIGS. 10-14D and 16D) to overlap the bookcase sides and extend 1¹/₂ inches at the back and front.

Mark and drill all these parts for dowels. Assemble the bottom to the back and sides. Do not glue the top on yet, but try it in place, with a few dry dowels. Check that the front edges of the sides and bottom are level and will match the bookcases.

Make the two sides of the drawer (FIG. 10-16E) to slide in easily, but without excessive play, allowing for the thickness of the drawer bottom.

Make the back and front of the drawer to fit between the sides.

Glue and dowel these parts together and join on the bottom. This makes a box which should slide easily into the unit. At this stage, the front should come level with the front edges of the casing around it. If it sets back a little that is preferable to projecting, as the addition of the false front will pull it level.

Make the false drawer front (FIG. 10-16F). It is level with the top of the drawer, but extends enough at the sides and bottom to cover its casing (FIG. 10-16G).

Fit a handle to the front. A wood handle glued and screwed from inside would be a good choice. Screw on the false front from inside the drawer.

Try the assembly of the drawer and its casing. If this is satisfactory, glue and dowel the top to the casing.

Drill through the tops of the bookcase backs for screws into the sides of the drawer unit. Apply a finish before finally screwing the parts together.

Materials List for Desk/Bookcase

(all 3/4 inch veneered particleboard)

4 bookcase sides	31 ×	9
6 bookcase shelves	20 ×	8¼
2 bookcase backs	31 ×	19½
1 top	24 ×	24
1 case back	22 ×	6
1 case bottom	22 ×	20¼
2 case sides	21 ×	5¼
2 drawer sides	21 ×	4½
1 drawer back	21 ×	4½
1 drawer front	21 ×	4½
1 drawer bottom	21 ×	21
1 false drawer front	22 ×	6

PLYWOOD TAKE-DOWN TABLE AND STOOLS

A playroom may be used for many purposes that do not all require the same furniture. If you have too many permanent tables, chairs, cabinets and boxes there might not be much space left for activities. Yet, there are occasions when you want to gather with your friends and you need plenty of things to sit on and tables for refreshments. It is useful then to have some take-down furniture that can be used.

This design is for a table and matching stool (FIG. 10-17), which will take apart and pack flat, each to a total thickness of less than 2½ inches. There are no nuts and bolts or other fastenings to deal with. If you make three or four stools for every table, you can offer your guests seating for refreshments in moderate comfort. Obviously, these items are not

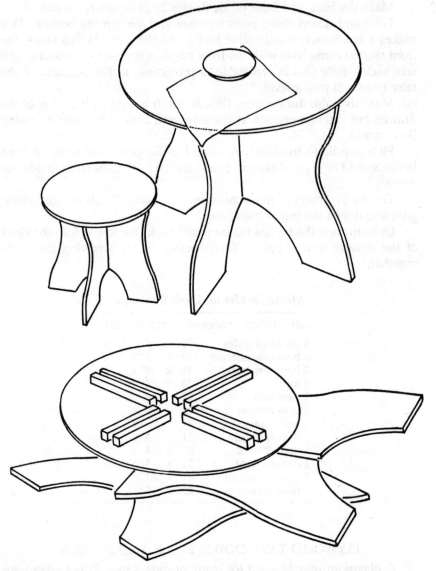

Fig. 10-17. *This table and stool are made of plywood; they can be taken down for flat storage.*

intended for rough treatment, but for normal use they should have a reasonable life. All of the main parts are plywood. This could be 1/2-inch softwood or hardwood. Also, you could increase the thickness to 3/4 inch or you might use 3/4-inch plywood for the legs, and 1/2-inch plywood for the tops. Other parts are 3/4-inch square strips.

The drawing (FIG. 10-18) shows a table 24 inches in diameter and height. Sizes in brackets are for the stool, which is made in the same way. Vary sizes, but if you decide on anything much bigger, use thicker

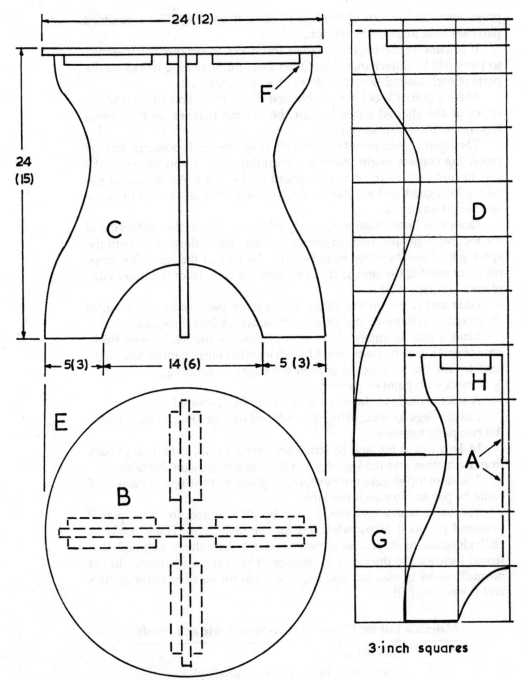

Fig. 10-18. *Sizes of the table with stool sizes in brackets.*

plywood. The legs are notched to fit into each other, meeting halfway, with one notch upwards and one downwards (FIG. 10-18A). Except for this, a pair of legs is the same. The top has strips of wood attached to press down on the tops of the legs (FIGS. 10-17 and 18B). The assembled parts are held together by friction.

If you intend making many tables and stools, make them all together, so parts will be interchangeable. Otherwise, put matching marks on the parts of each assembly so you do not become confused.

Make a pair of legs for the table first (FIGS. 10-18C and D). Round the edges of the shaped outlines. Cut the mating notches so they press together without excessive play.

The top is shown round (FIG. 10-18E). A square top is possible, but the projecting corners might make for instability, unless you arranged the legs to come under the corners instead of the sides. An octagonal top would look good and not have stability problems. Cut the top to shape and round its edges.

Draw two lines crossing squarely and centrally on the underside of the top. Mark the positions of the strips each side of these lines with the spacing to allow the strips to press onto the tops of the legs. The strips need not meet at the center; they can stop 1 inch in from the outer edge of each leg (FIG. 10-18F).

Glue and screw on the strips. Use a scrap piece of leg plywood to check spacing. Remove any glue which squeezes into the spaces.

Make a trial assembly of the table. Allow for the slight extra thickness of paint, but the parts should push together fairly tightly. You might have to ease the leg notches or their top edges by sanding.

Finish with paint or varnish.

A stool is made in the same way, using the bracketed sizes.

Cut the legs to size, using the reduced outline (FIG. 10-18G). Notch the two parts together.

Make a round top and fit strips underneath (FIG. 10-18H), kept back from each other and the leg edges in the same way as on the table.

The stool top should not have a high gloss, but the rest of each stool could be painted to match the table.

The basic tables and stools may be all you require. Use plastic veneered plywood or particleboard for the table tops. There could be cloth glued on the stool tops, or you could upholster them, although that would increase the thickness for storage. The strips underneath do not normally show in use, but you might wish to round their outer corners and the exposed edges.

Materials List for Plywood Take-down Table and Stools

(one of each)

1 table top	24	×	24	×	1/2 plywood
2 table legs	24	×	24	×	1/2 plywood
8 strips	10	×	3/4	×	3/4
1 stool top	12	×	12	×	1/2 plywood
2 stool legs	15	×	12	×	1/2 plywood
8 strips	5	×	3/4	×	3/4

11
Storeroom

You may have a room exclusively for storage. You may have to use part of
the garage or another room. Too often, the things that have to be stored
are arranged haphazardly. As they accumulate, you begin to lose track of
them and some are forgotten. It will help to keep the place tidy and get
more in it if you provide storage furniture.

Some storage might only be temporary or seasonal. This applies to
gardening requirements, such as seeds and fertilizers, or harvested produce. There may be a case for take-down storage arrangements or for
racks, shelves, and bins that can have other uses.

Furniture for storage usually need not be highly finished, but some
of it may also have uses in other parts of the house, so it should be presentable. In any case, as a craftsman you will not want people to see your
products as crude and inferior.

Some furniture intended for use elsewhere may find its way into the
storeroom. You might adapt it for storage, but remember that it may one
day have to go back to its original use. This may apply if another child
arrives or if you decide to move. It could apply the other way when what
you make for the storeroom may be needed elsewhere. In short, make it
attractive and functional, even if it is not exactly fine cabinetmaking.

LIGHT SHELVING

Shelving for storage items does not have to be heavy. Maybe you
have to spread harvested apples or other fruit. There could be piles of
magazines kept for reference, or stocks of wool kept for knitting or weaving. Instead of long shelves, it may be better to have units, which can be
arranged in different ways. These may be freestanding and built lighter
than one large block of shelves.

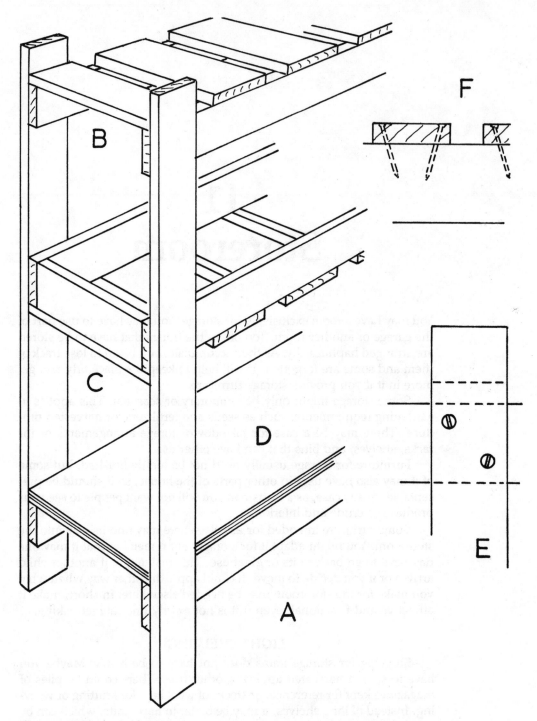

Fig. 11-1. *Three shelf arrangements for a light storage unit are shown, with parts nailed and screwed together.*

The suggested shelving unit is intended to be built all of wood of one section. For the lightest assembly this could be 1/2 inch × 2 inches. With wood of that section, a unit could be made with five shelves 8-inches apart, about 36-inches high × 24-inches long. Several units might be put together.

This unit consists of shelf assemblies held between uprights (FIG. 11-1A). Each shelf may be made of strips across lengthwise pieces (FIG. 11-1B). This will suit many needs, and it is particularly appropriate where ventilation is wanted.

If the storage item might roll off, a shelf can be arranged the other way (FIG. 11-1C).

For a solid top to a shelf, use plywood (FIG. 11-1D) instead of strips across.

The uprights extend to form feet and may go above the top shelf, or be cut off level.

If you expect to have to disassemble temporary shelving, join the legs to the shelves without glue. For permanent shelves, glue in the joints will aid stiffness. It should be sufficient to arrange two screws diagonally in each joint (FIG. 11-1E). Use screws that will go almost through the joint to get a good grip on the wood.

Simple nailing may be all that is needed to hold the crosspieces in place on a shelf. However, the joints will be stronger, particularly with inverted shelves, if you drive the nails at alternate angles in a dovetail fashion (FIG. 11-1F).

GRAIN BIN

If you want to store such things as grain or any produce up to the size of beans and potatoes in a manner that allows you to scoop or lift out small quantities as you need them, you may use bags. However, for many of these things, it is better to use compartmented boxes or bins. A rectangular box has a good capacity for its size, but it is not easy to remove the last of its contents. If you use a V-shaped trough, it is easier to scoop or scrape out everything. However, a trough does not have as good a capacity as a box. Another advantage of a trough is that it does not obscure anything below, so it may be arranged fairly close to a lower container with access still reasonable.

Arrange bins according to your needs, but as an example this one (FIG. 11-2) has a trough above and a rectangular bin below, with each divided into three. All of the main parts are made of 1/2-inch plywood, with strips of solid wood 1/2-inch × 3/4-inch section to stiffen the joints.

Mark out the pair of ends (FIGS. 11-3A and 4A). The trough sides are at 45 degrees to the edges, so they meet at 90 degrees. Take off the top corners of the ends, and notch the bottom edges to make feet.

Obtain the widths of the trough sides from the layout on an end. If the plywood is suitable for taking screws in its edges, allow a simple overlap. If you have doubt about such a joint being strong enough, let

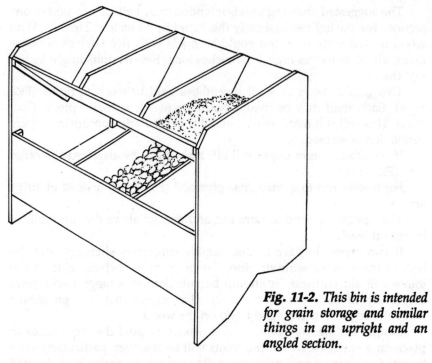

Fig. 11-2. *This bin is intended for grain storage and similar things in an upright and an angled section.*

one side of the trough overlap the other enough for a strip to be included outside to make the joint.

Cut the box sides (FIG. 11-4B) and the bottom, (FIG. 11-4C) as well as the trough sides, (FIG. 11-4D) all the same length and mark on them the positions of the divisions.

Arrange strips on the ends to join to the trough sides (FIGS. 11-3B and 4E). Put more strips across (FIGS. 11-3C and 4F) for the bottom of the box.

Put strips at the ends of the box sides (FIG. 11-4G). All the strip joints should be glued and nailed, or screwed.

Join the bottom edges of the trough together.

The box sides overlap the bottom (FIG. 11-3D). Join these parts with strips underneath to fit against the supporting strips on the ends.

Make the divisions for the trough. They are shown extending up in the same way as the ends (FIG. 11-4H). Fit them by screwing through the trough. Include strips in the joints, if necessary.

Make and fit the divisions in the box (FIG. 11-4J) in the same way. Check sizes and angles against the ends to see that the joints there will be correct.

Join the trough and box to the ends. The parts should pull each other square, but check that the bin will stand firm on a level surface.

Remove sharpness from edges. There will probably be no need to apply a finish, but you may seal the wood with varnish or polyurethane to prevent it absorbing dirt.

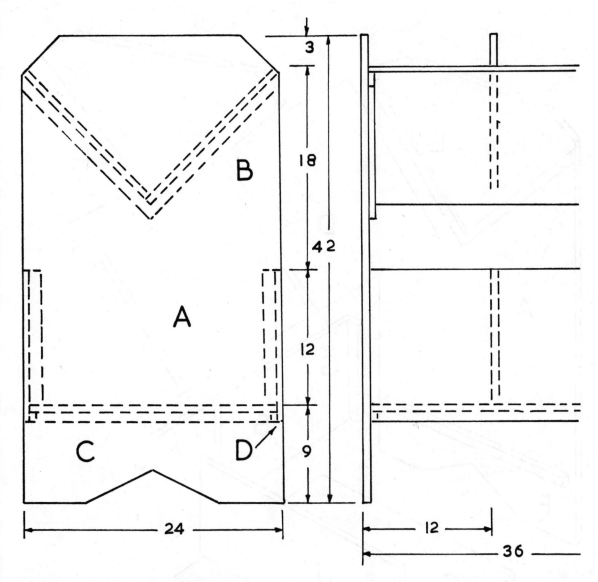

Fig. 11-3. *Suggested sizes of the grain bin.*

Materials List for Grain Bin

2 ends	33 × 24 ×	½ plywood
2 trough sides	36 × 18 ×	½ plywood
2 box sides	36 × 14 ×	½ plywood
1 box bottom	36 × 24 ×	½ plywood
strips from 4 pieces	72 × 1 ×	½

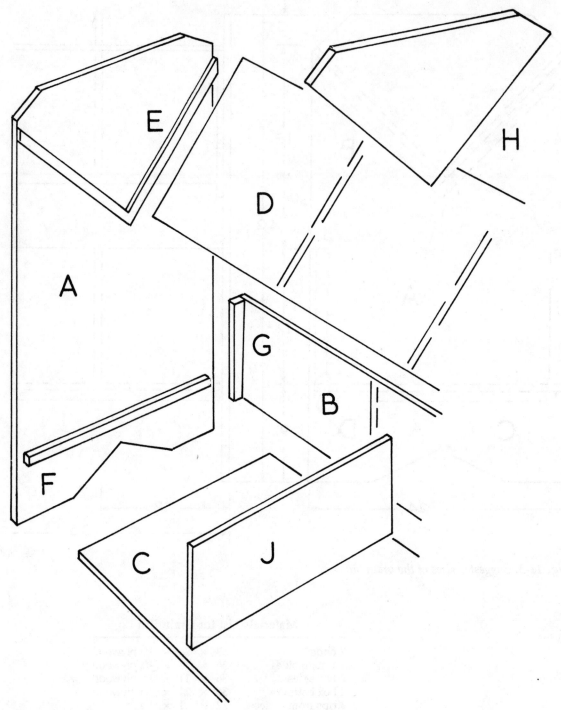

Fig. 11-4. *Parts of the grain bin.*

HANGING RACKS

The Shakers had the idea of hanging furniture when not needed on the wall. The name has continued for their pegs to this day, and you can buy or make Shaker pegs. You might not want to hang furniture, but the idea of using the wall for storage is a good one. There are a great many things that will hang. If you suspend them from a wall, you free floor space for other things.

There are two main choices. Put the hooks, pegs and special hanging arrangements directly on the wall, or attach them to strips of wood or sheets of plywood; then attach *that* to the wall. You might have to compromise and use both methods. The Shakers put their pegs at intervals on strips mounted fairly high on the wall. If you have a great many things that would hang and they do not require special fittings, it might be worthwhile buying or turning some Shaker pegs and mounting them on a backing strip at about 9-inch intervals (FIG. 11-5A). With the strips mounted at head height or above, you will be surprised at how much you can hang out of the way. If you drill holes through the ends of long handles, cord may be looped through for hanging brooms and many garden tools.

Instead of turned pegs, you can use pieces of dowel rod. Slope these upwards to prevent anything falling off (FIG. 11-5B). If you have the use of a lathe, turn other supports than the standard Shaker pegs. Similar pegs of the same diameters need only project an inch or so if all they have to do is take cords through handles. There is nothing wrong with a nail or screw, if it will take what you want to hang except that they may not satisfy your sense of craftsmanship!

For anything with a T handle, such as some garden tools, you can bring pegs closer together (FIG. 11-5C). This arrangement might be better than single pegs for coils of rope or hosepipe, because the loops will not be allowed to close tightly and become kinked.

If you want to hang such things as brooms, rakes and hoes with their heads upwards, something better than pegs may be required. You could make shaped pieces to fit the head (FIG. 11-5D). There might be tenons through the back (FIG. 11-5E), or use screws (FIG. 11-5F) or dowels.

If you have anything to hang which needs to extend along the wall, two or more blocks with plywood fronts will form hooks to take the length (FIG. 11-5G). With these and many other major supports, include hooks, dowels or buttons below (FIG. 11-5H) for small items. With a little ingenuity, you can arrange to hang many things in front of others, but be careful of getting too ingenious if things are too complicated you may find yourself not bothering to use these facilities.

There are many smaller items that will fit through holes. Some small garden tools will go through round or slotted holes (FIG. 11-6A). You may make a narrow shelf with a row of holes of several sizes without particular uses in mind. They will be waiting when you bring in more small

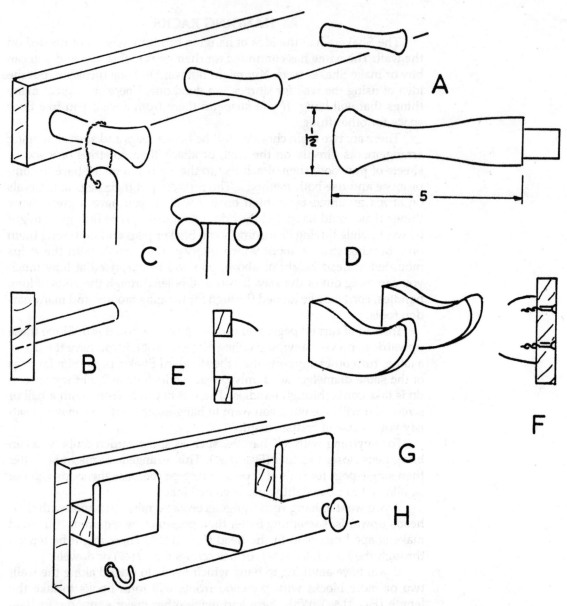

Fig. 11-5. *Suggestions for several types of racks for hanging tools and other items in a storeroom.*

items to store. Not all small tools can just hang through holes; they may need to rest on something, so you can make a double shelf (FIG. 11-6B). Household screwdrivers (which you may keep away from your shop) will fit in this rack.

Holes provide another way of holding long-handled garden tools. A handle can go through a hole in a shelf to a block on the floor with another hole (FIG. 11-6C). To avoid the need to lift the handle a long way,

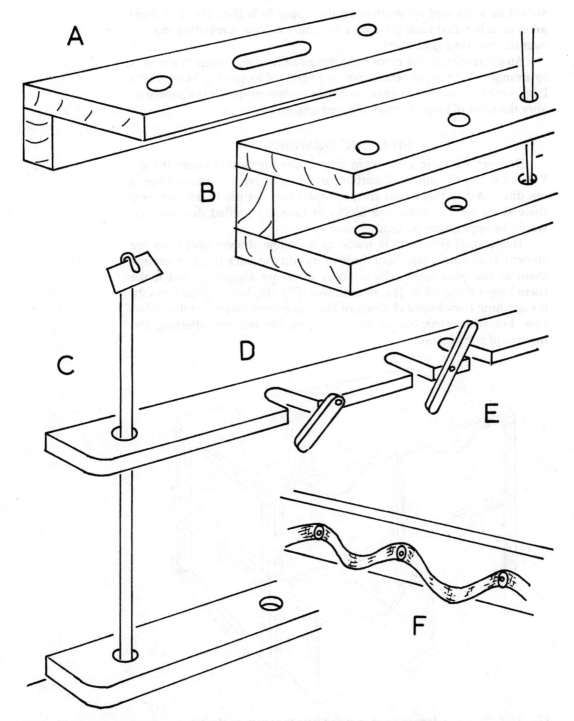

Fig. 11-6. *Drilled and slotted storage arrangements for tools and equipment.*

substitute a slot and turnbutton for the upper hole (FIG. 11-6D). If there are several handled tools to be stored in this way, one turnbutton may go over the two slots (FIG. 11-6E).

An alternative to the more rigid means of holding things to a wall is to arrange a webbing or other strap in a series of loops (FIG. 11-6F). Put a large washer under the head of each fixing screw to spread the pressure. Vary the sizes of loops to take different articles.

STACKING DRAWERS

Drawers are more convenient than boxes for storing many things. Pull out a drawer without disturbing anything above it. A drawer keeps out dirt and dust that might enter an open box. For use in a storeroom, there is no need to make the blocks of carefully jointed drawers that would be appropriate in another room.

This project (FIG. 11-7) is made as a double drawer unit (two are shown). If you make several of these units you can stack them or arrange them to suit your needs. Two-drawer units are suggested, but make them longer if you wish. The sizes shown (FIG. 11-8) have a good capacity for anything from folded clothing or linen to accumulations of discarded toys, but wide variations of sizes are possible without affecting the method of construction.

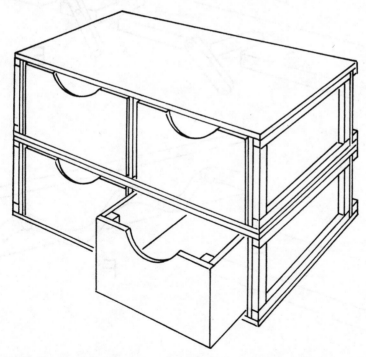

Fig. 11-7. *Two, two-drawer units showing how they may be stacked.*

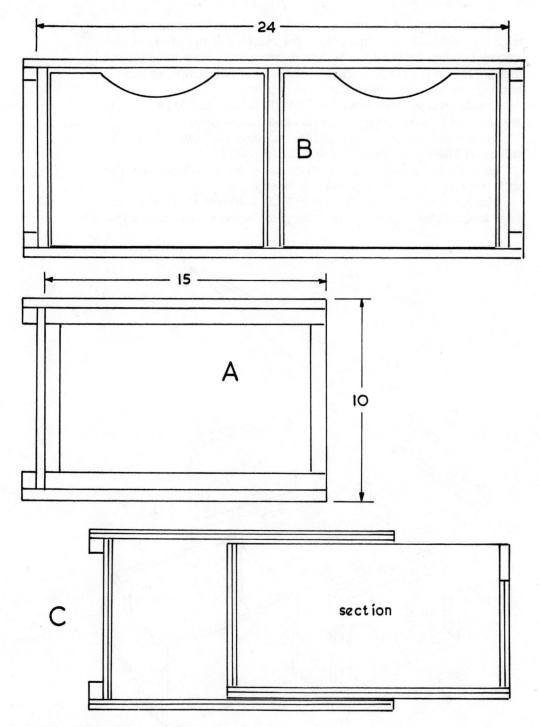

Fig. 11-8. *Sizes and section of a two-drawer unit.*

A unit is made of 1/2-inch plywood with 3/4-inch square strips to reinforce joints. All the strips are on the outsides of the cases, to give smooth interiors for the drawers. The drawers could have handles, but they are shown with hollows cut away to provide hand grips, so there is nothing projecting in front of the drawers.

Decide on sizes; then make two ends (FIGS. 11-8A and 9A) first. They are pieces of plywood edges all round outside with strips.

Make a division (FIGS. 11-8B and 9B) the same size, but without any stiffening. These parts should be square and match.

Make the back (FIGS. 11-8C and 9C) the same depth as these parts. Put stiffening strips along the top and bottom edges.

The top and bottom are the same (FIGS. 11-9D and E). They are the same length as the back, but wide enough to overlap its stiffening strips.

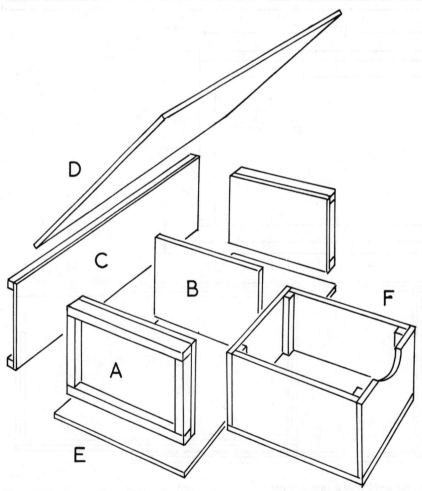

Fig. 11-9. *Parts of a stacking drawer unit.*

Assemble the parts of the case. If all parts are glued, it should be strong enough to just use pins or fine nails. Add screws towards the ends of joints for additional strength. The back should keep the assembly square, but check that the front is true, or you might have difficulty fitting the drawers.

Each drawer (FIG. 11-9F) is a box with its ends overlapping the sides and the bottom added below. If the plywood is suitable for edge screwing, you might be able to assemble with glue and plenty of fine screws, but otherwise use framing strips inside.

There is no need for the close fitting that would be arranged in drawers of a cabinet intended for another room. Instead, you can allow about 1/4-inch clearance all round, so a drawer is very easy to move in and out.

Cut a hollow in the top edge of each drawer front. It should be large enough to take your fingers easily. Round its edges.

Assemble each drawer with glue and nails or screws.

If you intend making several units, it will save time and ensure matching if you make parts for all units at the same time. The loosely-fitting drawers should be interchangeable.

Materials List for Stacking Drawers (one two-drawer unit)

2 ends	15	×	9	×	1/2	plywood
1 division	15	×	9	×	1/2	plywood
1 back	27	×	9	×	1/2	plywood
1 top	27	×	17	×	1/2	plywood
1 bottom	27	×	17	×	1/2	plywood
4 frames	16	×	3/4	×	3/4	
4 frames	10	×	3/4	×	3/4	
2 frames	27	×	3/4	×	3/4	
4 drawer sides	15	×	9	×	1/2	plywood
4 drawer ends	12	×	9	×	1/2	plywood
2 drawer bottoms	15	×	12	×	1/2	plywood
drawer frames from	70	×	3/4	×	3/4	

PORTABLE BOX

If you want to store sand, gravel, powders of all sorts, peas, and seeds, or anything that would spread around if not enclosed, you need a box with handles that will hold as much as you can conveniently lift with two hands. This is such a box (FIG. 11-10). The two gripped ends are at a distance to suit the spread of your hands, and there is a lid to protect the contents.

This is a box to make from any available wood and is shown made from solid wood finished 5/8-inch thick. Use stout plywood for all or part of the construction. Sizes may be varied to suit your needs or the available storage space, but do not increase the length much if you want to be able to lift the box single-handedly. The bottom fits inside the sides,

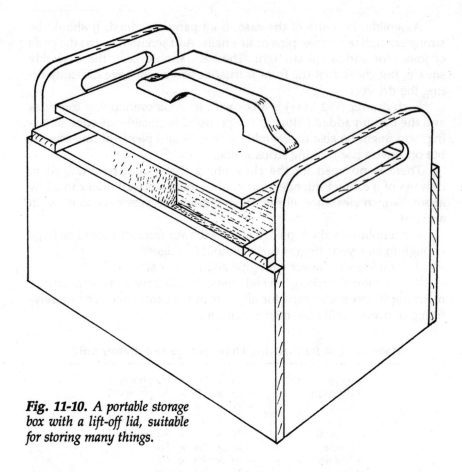

Fig. 11-10. *A portable storage box with a lift-off lid, suitable for storing many things.*

which are nailed or screwed to the ends, so most loads come across the fastenings.

Make the two ends first (FIGS. 11-11A and 12A). The hand holes are 1¹/₂-inches down from the top edges, and made by drilling two, 1¹/₄-inch holes at 4-inch centers, then cutting away the waste. Round the edges of each hole and the top as far down as the sides will come.

Make the bottom the same width as the ends, to fit between them and the sides (FIG. 11-12B).

Cut the sides to overhang the bottom and ends. Nail the bottom between the ends and the sides on to both parts (FIG. 11-12C). Screw all joints, or a compromise should be satisfactory, with nails for most of the length of a joint and screws at ends or corners.

Fit the two strips across inside the ends (FIGS. 11-11B and 12D).

The lid is intended to lift off, but you could hinge it at one side or to an end cross strip. Make it to overhang the width and to fit easily between the end strips.

Put strips under the lid (FIG. 11-12E) to locate it when it is dropped into position. Allow a reasonable clearance, so putting the lid on is easy.

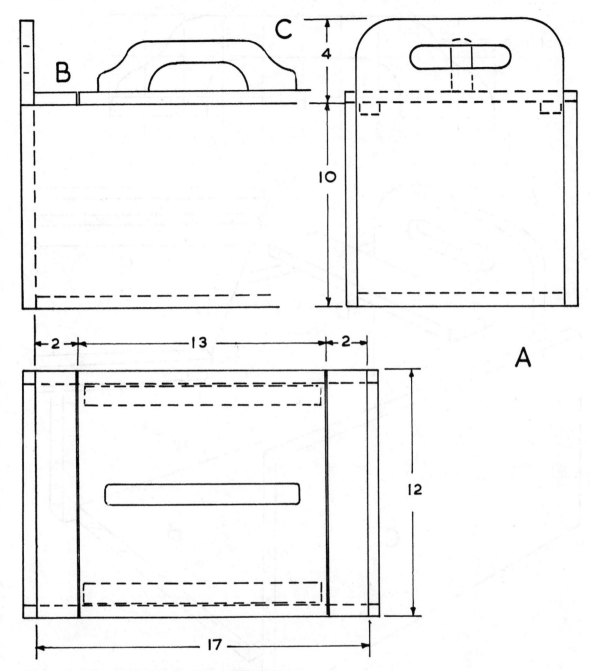

Fig. 11-11. *Suggested sizes for the portable storage box.*

You could fit a bought metal handle to the center of the lid, but a wood one is shown (FIG. 11-11C). Cut it from solid wood (FIG. 11-12F). Round the parts that will be gripped, and take the sharpness off all other upward edges.

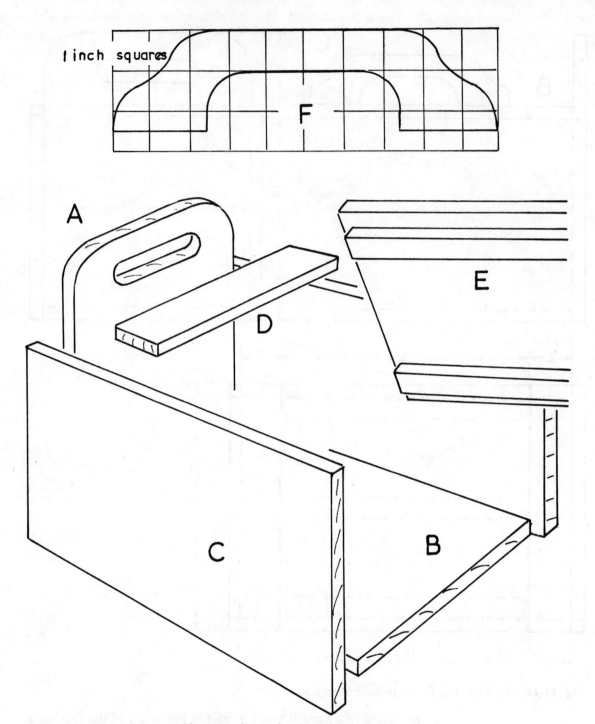

Fig. 11-12. *Parts of the portable storage box and a shape for the handle.*

1 inch squares

A B C D E F

Attach it with two screws driven upwards through the lid.

For many purposes, you might leave the wood untreated, but it could be painted or just sealed with a coat of varnish or polyurethane.

Materials List for Portable Box

2 ends	16	×	$10^{3}/_{4}$	×	$^{5}/_{8}$	
1 bottom	18	×	$10^{3}/_{4}$	×	$^{5}/_{8}$	
2 sides	19	×	10	×	$^{5}/_{8}$	
2 strips	13	×	2	×	$^{5}/_{8}$	
1 lid	14	×	13	×	$^{5}/_{8}$	
1 handle	11	×	$2^{1}/_{2}$	×	1	

12
Workshop

You may not regard much of the equipment in your shop as furniture, but you do need benches, stands, racks, etc. which may be considered furniture when compared with machines and hand tools, or other equipment supported by them.

When compared with **furniture** in other parts of your home, these things are usually substantial; and you might not be so concerned with appearance. Fitness for purpose is your main aim, but that does not mean what you make is necessarily crude. A properly proportioned assembly with the correct joints will not offend your craftsman's eye, and it will encourage you to do good work when using this aid to production.

Many pieces of shop furniture, particularly if built in, will have to be fashioned to suit the situation and surroundings, but in this chapter there are suggestions for items that will be made in the shop and will stay there.

TRESTLE/SEAT

There is a need in a woodworking shop for a strong stable support at not much more than half the bench height for such things as hand sawing, the use of some portable power tools, assembly, and getting at the tops of projects too high for convenient handling on a bench. You may also want to sit, possibly just to rest or because it is better than standing for some tool operations.

Any trestle for low work should be almost as strong as the bench, and there should be little risk of tipping it. This means strong, durable construction and a spread of feet greater than the area of the top. The same thing can then become a safe seat, even when you have to move about and lever whatever you are manipulating on the bench top.

Space is not usually very plentiful in the shop, so a combined trestle and stool can have its dual purpose and take up minimum space. When you want to work outside, it can double as a temporary bench, possibly with a portable vise clamped to its end.

This trestle/seat (FIG. 12-1) has a top 8 inches × 16 inches, with the corners of the feet extending 1-inch outside that. The height is 18 inches, which should be convenient for working and sitting. You could use softwood throughout. Making the whole project of hardwood might give too heavy a result, but you could compromise by using a tough hardwood for the worktop and softwood for its supports. If you regularly deal with long parts or whole sheets of plywood, consider making two of these trestle/seats at the same time, or you could supplement the one with the light trestle described as the next project.

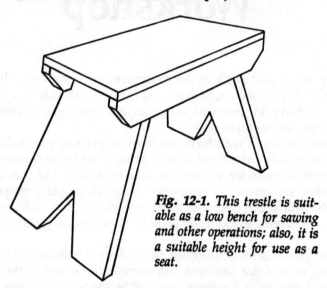

Fig. 12-1. This trestle is suitable as a low bench for sawing and other operations; also, it is a suitable height for use as a seat.

The key information you need is the angle of the legs (FIG. 12-2A). To obtain this angle, set out the slope (FIG. 12-3A). Set an adjustable bevel to this and use it for marking angles on the legs and sides.

Make the two sides (FIG. 12-2B) with the positions and angles of the legs marked.

Set out the two legs about a centerline (FIG. 12-3B). The parts that fit to the sides are parallel; then the legs flare to the full width. Mark the cuts on the legs for the sides, using the adjustable bevel and the actual sides when marking the notches.

Cut the legs to shape, and try the assembly with the sides. Drill the sides for screws into the legs (FIG. 12-2C) #12-gauge × 2¹/₂ inches would be suitable.

Join the legs to the sides with glue as well as screws.

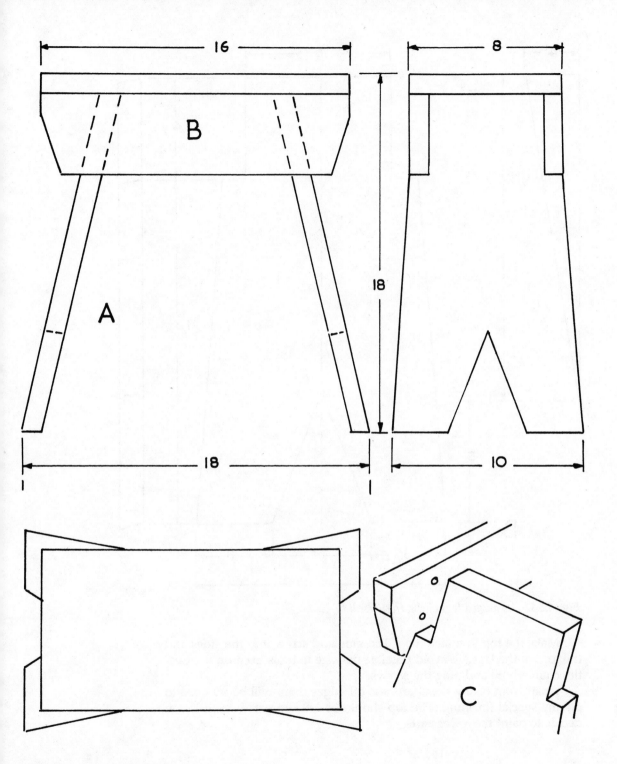

Fig. 12-2. *Sizes of the trestle/seat.*

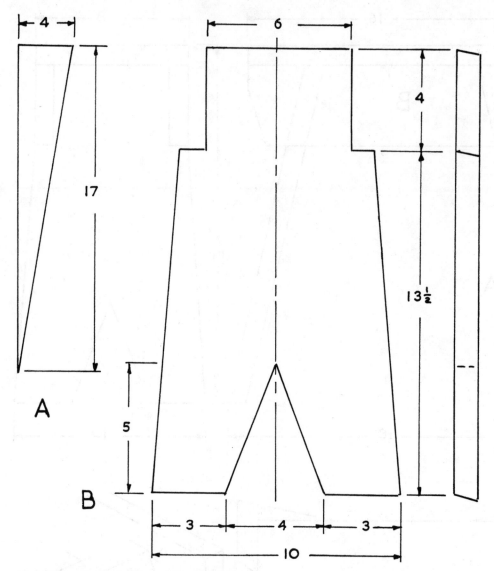

Fig. 12-3. *The angled legs of the trestle/seat.*

Make the top to match the sides; glue and screw it to the sides and the tops of the legs. To avoid possible damage to tools used on the trestle, counterbore and plug the screws.

Apart from taking the sharpness off edges there will be no need to do any special finishing. The top should be left untreated, even if you decide to paint the lower parts.

Materials List for Trestle/Seat

2 legs	19	×	10	×	1
2 sides	17	×	4	×	1
1 top	17	×	8	×	1

LIGHT TRESTLE

Supports at about knee height have frequent uses in a woodworking shop. The last project is a combined trestle and seat, but when you have to support long or large pieces, it is a help to have at least two supports all at the same height. You probably only want one seat, but there are occasions when you need additional trestle support, and a second trestle seat would not be the answer.

This project is a light trestle (FIG. 12-4). You could make two of them, if you do not need the seat, or you might prefer the one seat/trestle, with its broader working surface, and one of these when it is necessary to spread supports. The top is the same length as the trestle/seat, and it is the same height.

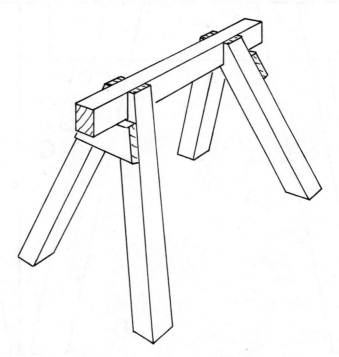

Fig. 12-4. *A light shop trestle to match the trestle/seat.*

The top is 2 inches × 3 inches and the legs are 2-inch square. The floor area covered is the same as the first project. Parts are glued and screwed.

Cut the wood for the top, and mark where the tops of the legs come 3 inches from the ends (FIG. 12-5A).

The angles of the lefts have to be set out: one for bevels across the trestle (FIG. 12-6A) and for those in the direction of its length (FIG. 12-6B). Set two adjustable bevels to these angles.

Each pair of legs meets under the top (FIG. 12-5B). Mark the bevels across and the notches that will come under the top (FIG. 12-6C) on the faces that will be towards the ends.

Using the lengthwise bevels, project these lines in the other direction (FIG. 12-6D). Work in pairs.

Cut the ends and notches. Leave a little extra at the tops for leveling after assembly.

Mark bevels on the sides of the top, and check the fit of the legs to these lines.

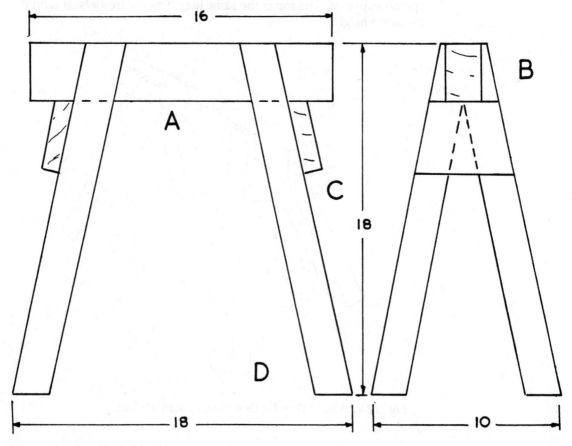

Fig. 12-5. *Sizes of the light trestle.*

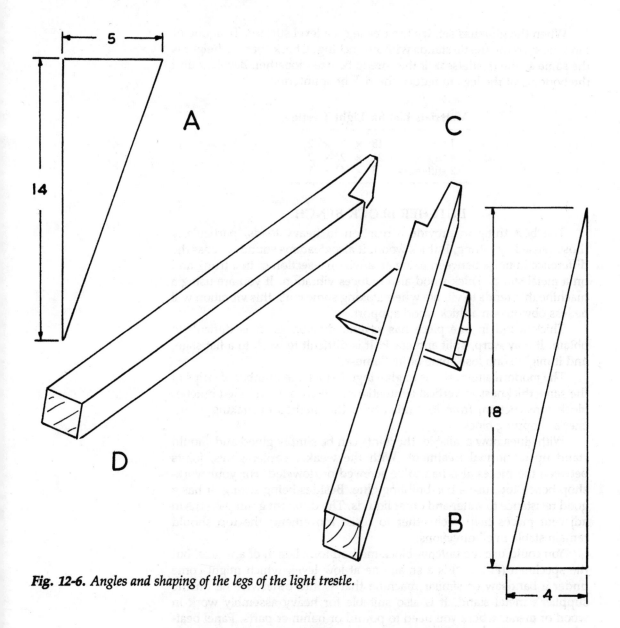

Fig. 12-6. *Angles and shaping of the legs of the light trestle.*

Make the two stiffeners (FIG. 12-5C), beveled at the top and long enough to go over the outer surfaces of the legs.

Drill the tops of the legs for screws into the trestle top. Three, #10-gauge screws on each side should be adequate if they are long enough to go almost to the center of the top. Drill the stiffeners for screwing to the legs.

Assemble with glue and screws. Check the spread of the legs (FIG. 12-5D) and that the angles are the same each end.

When the glue has set, try the trestle on a level surface. Trim one or more legs, so the trestle stands without rocking. Check that the height is the same as the trestle/seat, if they are to be used together. Bevel around the bottoms of the legs to reduce the risk of splintering.

Materials List for Light Trestle

1 top	18	× 3	× 2
4 legs	21	× 2	× 2
2 stiffeners	8	× 4	× 1

BUTCHER BLOCK BENCH

The best thing to provide a reaction to heavy loads, particularly those caused by hitting, is thick wood. It also deadens sound witness the difference in noise between using an anvil on a section of tree trunk and on a metal stand. Thick wood also reduces vibration. If you are using a machine that tends to vibrate when making some cuts, this vibration will be less obvious on a thick wood support.

Thick wood in one piece has several drawbacks. It is difficult to obtain. It may warp, split and crack. It is difficult to work to a flat state, and it might soon lose some of its flatness.

The modern alternative is to glue together a large number of strips of the same thickness in vertical laminations, which is often called butcher block construction, from its similarity to the method of making a butcher's chopping block.

With glues now available, the joints can be simply glued and should stand up to normal treatment. With the weaker earlier glues, joints between the pieces also had to be screwed or doweled. For your workshop bench top, use a boatbuilding glue. Besides being strong, it has a good resistance to water and other liquids. The different grain patterns in adjacent pieces help each other to resist movement; the top should remain stable in all directions.

You could use the butcher block method for a bench of any size, but the specimen (FIG. 12-7) is a small one at low level, which might come under a bandsaw or similar machine that would otherwise be on the supplier's metal stand. It is also suitable for heavy assembly work in wood or metal, where you need to pound or hammer parts. Panel beating or making sheet metal bowls are other activities where the solid surface and deadening effect of the thick wood reaction would be an advantage.

This bench may be made throughout of 2-inch × 3-inch softwood, which is about 1/4-inch less each way when planed. For a more substantial bench, use 2-inch × 4-inch wood. The underframing could be mortise and tenon (FIG. 12-9A), some of the joints could be halved (FIG. 12-9B), or it would be satisfactory to use 1-inch hardwood dowels (FIG. 12-9C).

Fig. 12-7. *A strong bench with a butcher block top.*

The top provides plenty of rigidity, but the lower parts must be joined so they resist wracking or twisting loads, as well as any downward thrust.

Instructions apply to a bench of the size suggested (FIG. 12-8A), but the same method can be used for any other size. Avoid an excessive overhang, and check that joints are tight to give mutual support.

Make the top first. If this does not work out exactly to the intended size, this does not matter, as you can make the underframing to match the actual sizes. Cut the pieces a little too long. See that they are straight on the broad surfaces. The other surfaces can be planed level with each other later.

Make the top up in stages, to avoid uneven joints and possible twists. Join pairs of strips, clamping while the glue sets; then, join these pairs in groups of four (FIG. 12-8B) and so on, until you have made up the full width.

Treat the made-up top as a single board. Cut the ends level; check that edges are square across. Level the top and bottom surfaces.

The supports should be 1 inch in from the edges of the top. Mark their positions.

Cut the four legs (FIGS. 12-8C and 10A) to size, with a little extra left at the tops to be trimmed level during assembly. Mark on the positions of the rails.

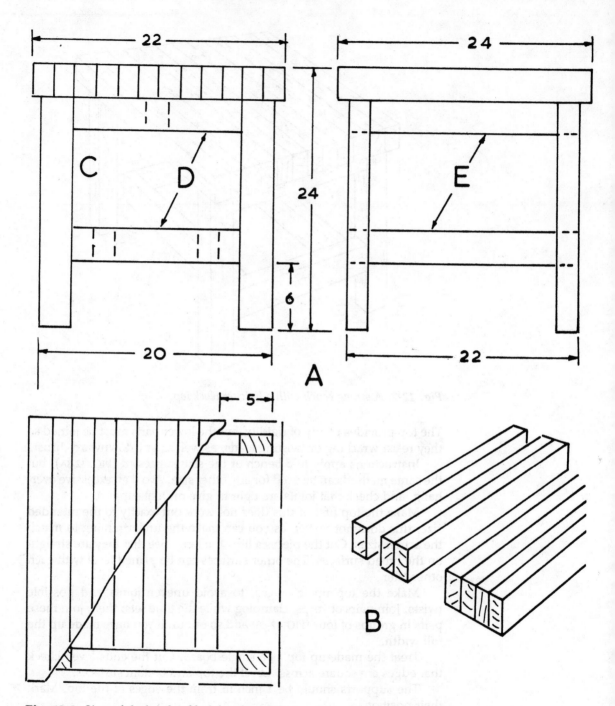

Fig. 12-8. Sizes of the butcher block bench and the sequence of assembly of the top.

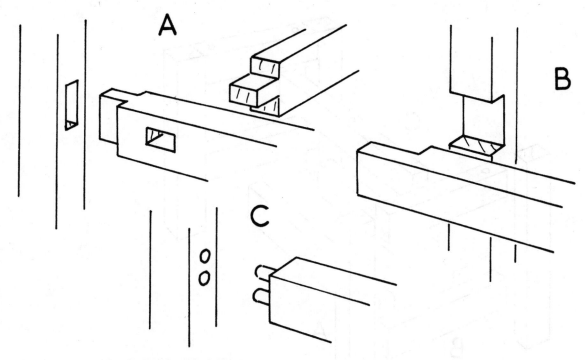

***Fig. 12-9.** Joints for the butcher block bench.*

Make the four end rails (FIGS. 12-8D and 10B). Allow extra length for tenons or halved joints, but cut ends squarely if you will be using dowels.

Cut the lengthwise rails (FIGS. 12-8E and 10C) to suit the spacing of the ends, with allowance for joints. The top one is central and the others meet the end rails 2-inches in from the legs.

Drill the top rails for dowels into the underside of the top. These will reinforce glue and it should be sufficient to use hardwood dowels, one at the center of the middle rail and one near each of the end frame rails, but you could use more.

Assemble the two end frames squarely and see that they match.

Add the lengthwise rails and use the top to check accuracy by assembling it inverted on the underside of the top.

Drill the top for dowels about 1-inch deep; then glue the top to the underframing.

What finish you apply depends on the intended use. You might paint to match a machine that will be mounted on the bench. If the top is liable to become oily, a good varnish can be used to seal the wood. For general woodworking, you may prefer to leave the top untreated and paint the other parts.

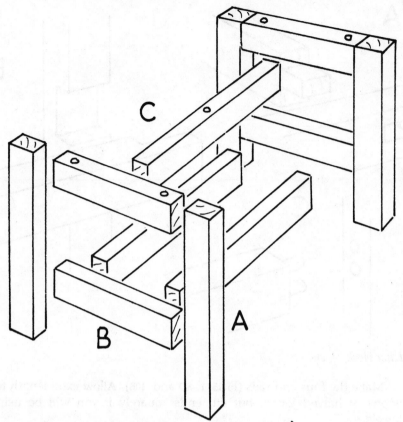

Fig. 12-10. *Parts of the framework of the butcher block bench.*

The space below is shown open, and this will allow strip materials to be stored across the rails. However, you could put a shelf on the rails if that would suit your needs.

Materials List for Butcher Block Bench

12 tops	25	× 3	× 2
4 legs	23	× 3	× 2
2 rails	20	× 3	× 2
3 rails	22	× 3	× 2

WORK SUPPORT

The supporting surfaces on machines are necessarily small. You may push 10 feet of wood through a jointer, but its table length may be under 3 feet. You may have to cut shapes on a bandsaw when its table is not much over 12-inches square, yet your plywood is 4-feet across. In a large shop, you might be able to rig benches or other surface to support the excess area, but in the usual small home shop there is no room for permanent extensions to machines when they are only required intermittently.

In some cases, you can improvise, but to do good work there has to be adequate support for excess length or area while you machine a particular part. Fortunately, the support does not have to do much more than keep the wood in position, because there is no real working load on it. This means that for many operations the supporting arrangement can be light and folding.

This work support (FIG. 12-11) provides an area 24 inches × 48 inches at machine height, but when not needed, it folds to 24 inches × 56 inches and about 6-inches thick. It can be made adjustable in height, so it may be used for more than one machine. The example (FIG. 12-12) is shown able to be at 30-inches or 40-inches above the floor, which may suit the table saw or jointer, then the usually higher table of a bandsaw. Make it to set at any required height and at more than two heights, if you wish. Besides its use in the shop, the work support can be taken elsewhere for use as a spare table indoors or outdoors.

If you design your own table there are some points to watch. To keep the top level at any height, the lengths of the legs above the pivot point should be the same, and those below should also match each other. It makes the arrangement simpler if all four of these sizes are the same (FIG. 12-13A). It would be possible to make the legs short enough to fold inside the top, but then the unit, particularly in the high position, could be rather unstable due to the feet being closer together.

The suggested top is a piece cut across a standard sheet of plywood and framed round (FIG. 12-13B). The legs pivot inside one end; then there are notched pieces at the other end to provide adjustment. Stiffness in the legs is provided by plywood braces.

Hardwood is advisable for the legs, but the top framing could be softwood. Pivot bolts are $1/4$ inch, or $5/16$ inch with countersunk heads, washers and some form of locking nuts.

Cut the top plywood to size and frame it round like a box (FIGS. 12-12A and 12B). The corners could be merely screwed or you could use finger joints or dovetails. Drill the sides for the pivot screws (FIG. 12-12B).

Make the two outer legs (FIG. 12-13C). Drill for pivot screws at the upper ends, and countersink the holes on the inner surface to clear the other legs when folded.

The inner legs are almost the same (FIG. 12-13D), but at their upper end they have a crossbar with a rounded edge (FIGS. 12-12C and D). This crossbar may be joined to the legs with dowels (FIG. 12-13E). Its length must allow the folded legs to fit easily inside the outer ones. So the work support will keep its top parallel to the floor at any height adjustment, the center of the curve on the crossbar should be at the same distance from the pivot as the hole at the top of the other leg. Slight errors are unlikely to make enough difference to matter.

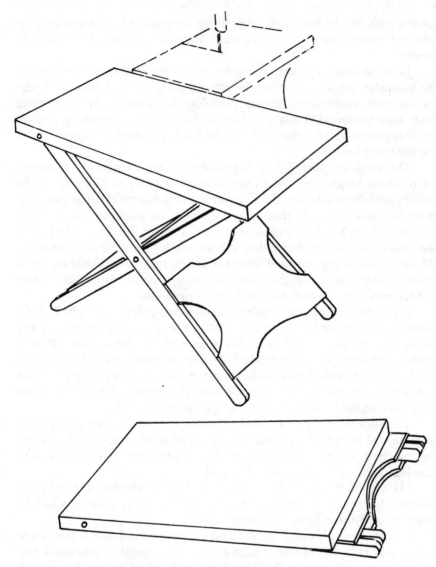

Fig. 12-11. *A folding work support for use with shop machines.*

Stiffen both pairs of legs below the central pivot with plywood braces (FIG. 12-12E). These come on what will be the upper surfaces of the legs (FIGS. 12-12F and G), where they will not interfere with folding. The plywood could be cut with straight edges, but it is shown with cutout edges for the sake of appearance.

For the adjustments suggested, there are two notched blocks at the end of the top (FIG. 12-13F), positioned so they come inside the inner legs and engage with the crossbar. They do not have to come tightly against the legs, but do not leave excessive clearance.

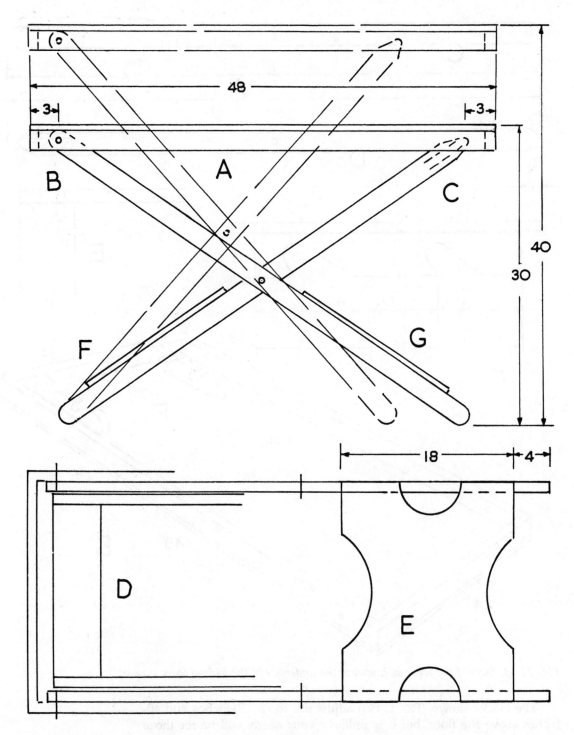

Fig. 12-12. *Sizes for the folding work support, with adjustment for two heights.*

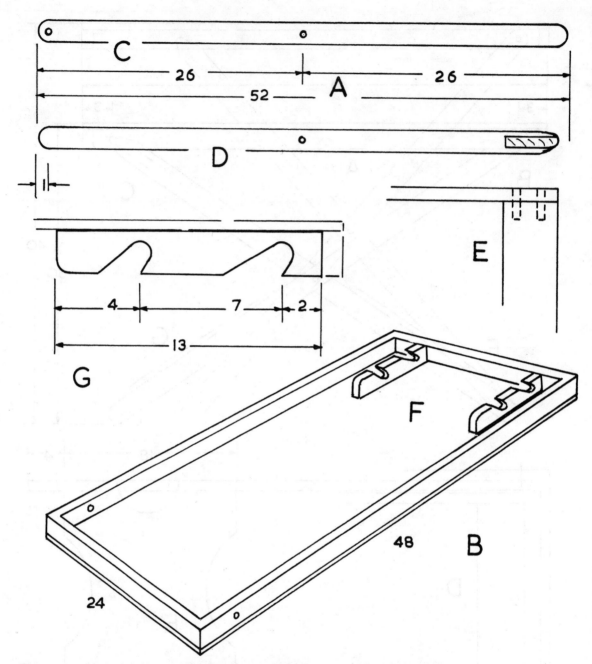

Fig. 12-13. *Sizes of the legs and layout of the underside of the folding work support.*

The blocks shown (FIG. 12-13G) adjust the top to 30-inches and 40-inches above the floor, but it is unlikely your needs will be for those heights exactly. For other heights, pivot the legs together and to the top on temporary bolts, and experiment with positions of the crossbar that will give the heights you want. Notch the blocks to suit. Screw and glue the blocks in place.

Make a trial assembly, and try the folding and erecting the action. You may have to ease the tops of the legs to give clearance.

Separate the parts as far as possible. Take the sharpness off edges. You may choose to leave the work support untreated, but paint or varnish will prevent dirt absorption. It will help foster smooth operation if you put thin washers between moving parts, as well as under nuts.

Materials List for Work Support

1 top	48	× 24	×	$1/4$ or $1/2$ plywood
2 top sides	50	× 2	×	1
2 top ends	26	× 2	×	1
4 legs	54	× 2	×	1
2 blocks	15	× 2	×	1
1 crossbar	20	× 5	×	1
2 leg braces	24	× 18	×	$1/4$ or $1/2$ plywood

13
Outdoor Furniture

If you have the space and the weather is good, you will want to live outside on the deck, patio, yard, or garden. Some indoor furniture might also be used outside, but if you are going to make much use of it, it is better to have furniture specially for use outdoors. It may be suitable for leaving outside in any weather, or you may keep it under cover and only take it out when needed.

There are a great many designs for outdoor furniture, and complete books on the subject, but a few ideas given here might be expanded and modified to suit your needs.

In general, outdoor furniture does not have to be given the cabinet-making finish of most interior furniture, so much of it is easier to make, particularly if your skill and equipment are limited. For anyone doubtful of their ability to make more ambitious projects, some simple outdoor furniture may be a good choice before embarking on what may seem a much more complex piece of indoor furniture.

PLANT POT CONTAINER

You will probably grow plants in pots of many sizes, which you want to display in the yard or on a deck. You may want to bring them indoors. The usual plant pot is not a thing of beauty, but you can disguise it in a more attractive container.

This container (FIG. 13-1) is all wood and may be given a quality finish for use indoors, or it may be made to an outdoor finish with paint. The sizes suggested (FIG. 13-2) will suit a pot about 9 inches in diameter and height. The same method might be used to make a container of almost any size. Any wood could be used.

Fig. 13-1. *A plant pot container for use on the patio or indoors.*

There are four slotted posts, into which the sectional sides are fitted. Pieces on the top and bottom close the slotted posts. Strips on bearers inside support the pot. Of course, the container is not intended to be watertight. For indoor use, there would have to be a bowl or tray inside under the pot. Outdoors, any surplus water can drain away between the bottom strips.

Make four identical posts and cut grooves in them (FIG. 13-2A) to suit the wood which will be used for the sides.

There are three sections in each side, so you have to make twelve pieces. Cut them all to the same length and hollow their lower edges (FIG. 13-2B).

Put bearers on two bottom side pieces (FIG. 13-2C) to come between the posts and support the bottom strips (FIG. 13-2D).

Use waterproof glue to fix the side sections into the slots. You can avoid the complications of clamping if you drive a nail through each joint from inside, to hold the parts while the glue sets. Assemble two opposite

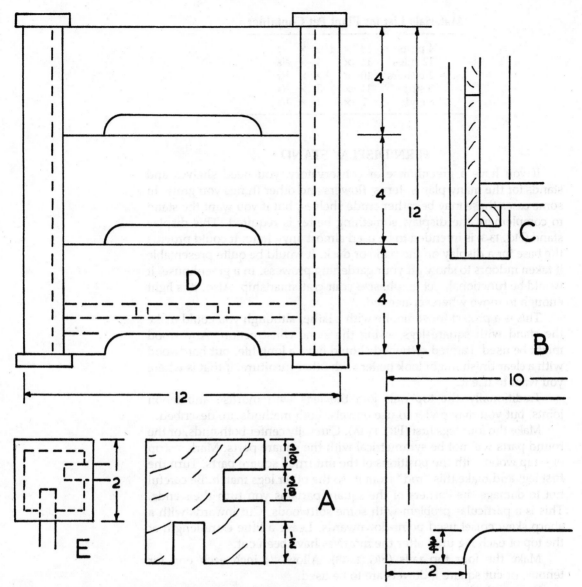

Fig. 13-2. *Sizes and sections for the plant pot container.*

sides first; then bring them together with the other sections. Check squareness as viewed from above.

Fit bottom strips on the bearers inside. Exact widths do not matter, but leave drainage gaps.

Make 2-inch square pieces for the top and bottom (FIG. 13-2E), and nail or screw them on.

Finish to suit your requirements.

Materials List for Plant Pot Container

4 posts	13	×	1 1/2	×	1/2
12 sides	11	×	4	×	3/8
2 bearers	10	×	1/2	×	1/2
3 strips	11	×	3	×	1/4
8 ends	2	×	2	×	1/2

FERN DISPLAY STAND

If you have a greenhouse or conservatory, you need shelves and stands for the many plants, ferns, flowers and other things you grow. In some cases these may be rather crude shelves, but if you want the stand to complement the display, something better is required. This display stand (FIG. 13-3) is intended to be used almost anywhere. It could provide the base for a display on the patio or deck. It would be quite presentable if taken indoors to show off your gardening prowess. In a greenhouse, it would be functional, yet emphasize your craftsmanship. Also, it is light enough to move wherever needed.

This is a project for someone with a lathe, although you could make the stand with square legs, using the same construction. Any wood might be used. Painted softwood should have a long life, but hardwood with a clear finish might look better with other furniture, if that is where you want to use it.

Traditionally, the top rails join the legs with mortise and tenon joints, but you may prefer to use dowels. Both methods are described.

Make the four legs first (FIG. 13-4A). Carefully center both ends, or the round parts will not be symmetrical with the square parts. Mark a strip of scrap wood with the positions of the unturned square parts. Turn the first leg, and make this "rod" from it, so the other legs match. Be careful not to damage the corners of the square parts as you turn their ends. This is a particular problem with some softwoods. Cut inwards with a sharp skew chisel used point-downwards. Leave a little extra length at the top of each leg until after the mortises have been cut.

Make the four top rails (FIG. 13-4B). Allow 3/4 inch each end for tenons, or cut square if dowels are to be used.

Prepare the inner surfaces for attaching the top. Cut grooves for buttons or pockets for screws (FIG. 1-3). One fastening each end and two each side should be sufficient.

If tenons are chosen, they could be barefaced (FIG. 13-4C). Mark and cut mortises to suit (FIG. 13-4D).

If you choose dowels, they could be 1/2 inch, arranged two at each joint (FIG. 13-4E). Take them into the legs far enough to meet (FIG. 13-4F).

The shelf joints are cut diagonally in the legs (FIG. 13-4G). Make them a close fit, and take the cuts to about half the width of each leg face.

Fig. 13-3. *This fern stand may be used indoors, in a greenhouse or outdoors.*

Make the two shelves of suitable length and width to fit closely into the legs while keeping them upright and parallel.

Assemble the opposite long sides first. Check that they match and are square; then join them with the shelves and rails across. It should be sufficient to rely on glue only, but if any rail joints are slack, pins may be driven across them from inside. Shelf joints might be strengthened by thin nails or screws driven diagonally upwards from below. Level the tops of the legs and rails.

Make the top to overhang the legs about 1¹/₂-inches all round. The edges could be left square, be rounded or molded (FIG. 13-4H).

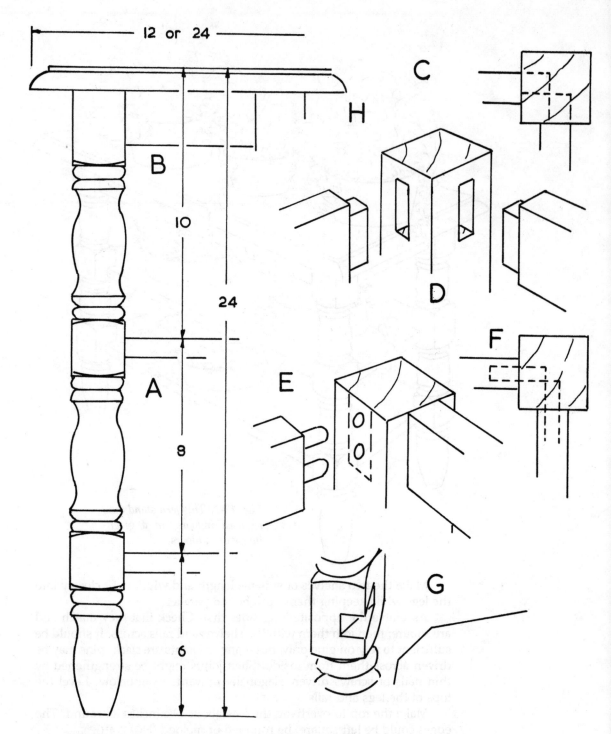

Fig. 13-4. *Sizes and constructional details of the fern stand.*

Invert the stand, and attach the framework to the top with screws or buttons. Do not glue the top, as it might expand and contract slightly in use.

Finish with paint or a clear finish. As the stand may get wet, boat varnish makes a suitable clear finish.

Materials List for Fern Display Stand

4 legs	25	× 1³/₄	×	1³/₄
2 rails	20	× 2	×	1
2 rails	9	× 2	×	1
2 shelves	20	× 9	×	7/8
1 top	25	× 12	×	7/8

YARD CHAIR

This is a strong chair (FIG. 13-5) that should be suitable for leaving outdoors for at least part of the year. It could be used on a lawn, beside a path, on the patio, or on a deck.

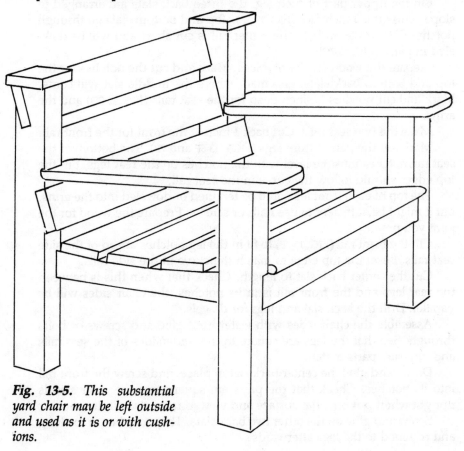

Fig. 13-5. *This substantial yard chair may be left outside and used as it is or with cushions.*

It is large enough to take cushions, although its shaping offers reasonable comfort unpadded. The slatted seat is curved and the back slopes. There is nowhere for rain to be trapped and the wood is easy to wash and dry. The finest chair would be made of hardwood that is durable and resistant to exposure, but you could use softwood treated with preservative. If finished with paint and any subsequent bare patches touched up, a softwood chair should have a long life.

Most parts are either 2 inches × 3 inches or 1-inch × 4-inch section. Waterproof glue should be used in the joints as well as screws. Steel screws should be zinc-plated or galvanized but it might be better to use bronze or brass screws. Use bolts instead of screws through the main joints.

The chair stands on a square with 21-inch sides and is 28-inches high (FIG. 13-6A). It will be a help if you set out the side view of the seat rail (FIG. 13-6B) and the back (FIG. 13-6C) fullsize.

The curve of the seat rail should drop about 1 inch at the center. Continue the curve over the front rail (FIG. 13-6D), and mark on the spacing of the seat slats.

On the upper part of each leg, the three back slats are arranged to slope across the 3-inch face (FIG. 13-6E). Top and bottom slats go through notches (FIGS. 13-7A and B). The center rail is cut short and will be doweled in place (FIG. 13-7C).

Prepare the wood for the rear legs. Mark and cut the notches for the top and bottom back slats, and mark where the middle slat will come. Mark and cut notches 1/2-inch deep for the seat rails (FIG. 13-7D) and the arms.

Make the two seat rails. Cut back 1 inch at the front for the front rail.

Mark out the pair of front legs (FIGS. 13-6F and 7E). The bottom of the seat rail notches must be level with the notches on the rear legs, but the top edges should follow the curve in the seat rail.

The top of each front leg could be tenoned or doweled into the arms, but it might be sufficient to use nails or screws. Prepare the wood for the joint you prefer.

Cut the front rail (FIG. 13-7F) to fit in the leg notches ahead of the side seat rails. Bevel the top edge to match the curve in the side rails.

Cut the center back slat to length. Check that when this is between the rear legs and the front rail is in its notches, the chair sides will be parallel. Drill the back slat and legs for dowels.

Assemble the chair sides with waterproof glue and screws or bolts through. See that the legs are square to the undersides of the seat rails and opposite parts match.

Dowel and glue the center back slat in place, and screw the front rail into its notches. Check that the parts are square and the chair stands upright when put on a flat surface and viewed from several directions.

Screw and glue on the other two back slats. They may be cut too long and trimmed to the legs afterwards.

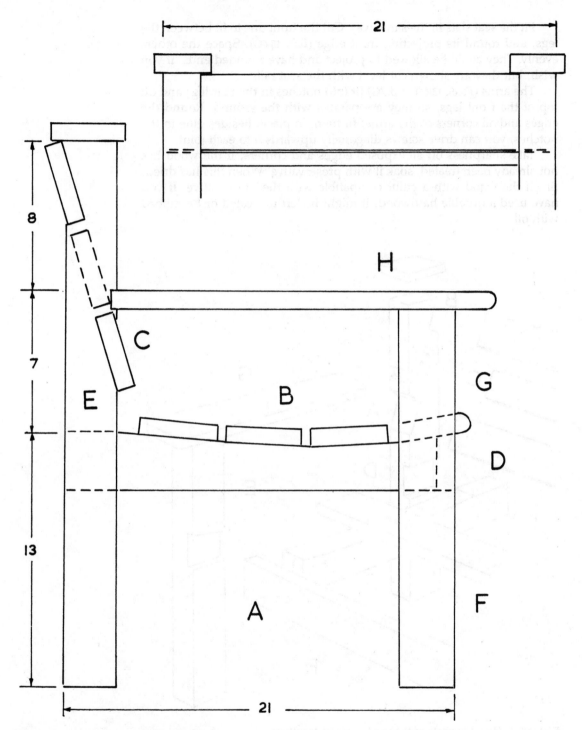

Fig. 13-6. *Main sizes of the yard chair.*

Fit the seat slats in the same way. Cut the front one to fit between the legs, and round its projecting front edge (FIG. 13-6G). Space the others evenly. They could be allowed to project and have rounded ends, if you wish, but they are shown cut level with the seat rails.

The arms (FIGS. 13-6H and 7G) fit into notches in the rear legs and on top of the front legs, so they are parallel with the ground. Round the edges and all corners of the arms; fit them in place. Besides glue in the notches, you can drive screws diagonally upwards into each joint.

Take sharpness off all exposed edges and corners. If the wood has not already been treated, soak it with preservative. When this has dried, finish the wood with a paint compatible with the preservative. If you have used a durable hardwood, it might be left untreated or be rubbed with oil.

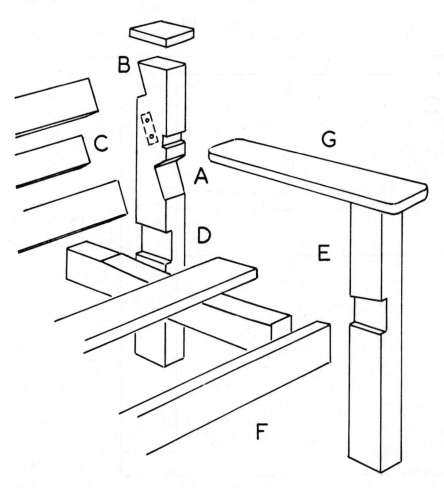

Fig. 13-7. *How the parts of the yard chair fit together.*

Materials List for Yard Chair

2 rear legs	30 × 3 × 2
2 front legs	22 × 3 × 2
2 seat rails	22 × 3 × 2
1 front rail	22 × 3 × 1
2 back slats	22 × 4 × 1
1 back slat	18 × 4 × 1
3 seat slats	22 × 4 × 1
1 seat slat	19 × 4 × 1
2 arms	22 × 4 × 1

YARD TABLE

This is a strong octagonal table (FIG. 13-8) of a suitable size and height for at least four people to use for a meal, or it may become the general-purpose table on a deck, patio or elsewhere outdoors. It should be sufficiently durable to be left outside for much of the year.

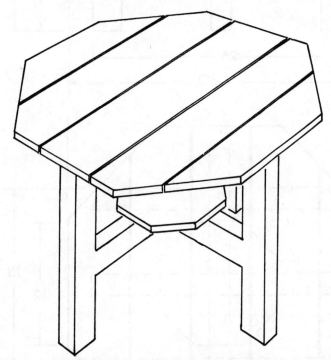

Fig. 13-8. *This yard table has an octagonal top on four legs, with a shelf underneath.*

The main parts are 2-inch × 3-inch softwood. The top could also be softwood, although you may choose a weather-resistant hardwood. The suggested joints are half laps, joined with waterproof glue and screws. You could use mortise and tenon joints, but dowels are not advised.

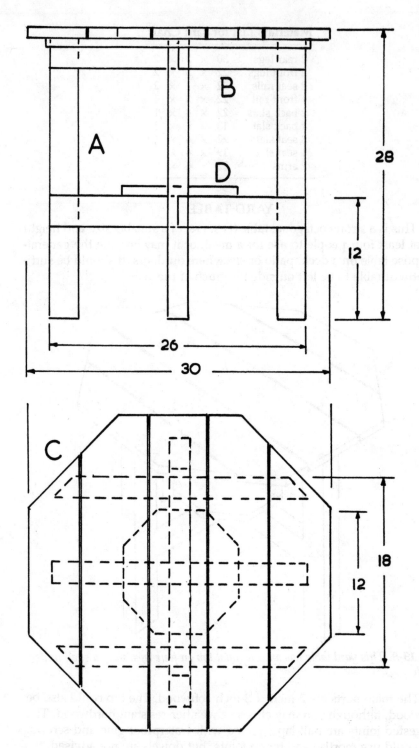

Fig. 13-9. *Sizes of the octagonal table.*

As shown (FIG. 13-9), the table is arranged as a 30-inch octagon supported 28-inches from the ground. Tables of different sizes could be made in the same way.

Make the four legs (FIGS. 13-9A and 10A). Mark the lengths and the positions of the joints. Mark the widths of the halving joints from the actual wood which will be used for the rails.

The top rails (FIGS. 13-9B and 10B) and the lower rails are the same sizes. Mark their lengths and joints, using the legs to obtain the widths of the end halving joints and arranging the central crossing to suit the thickness of the wood. Mark halfway through at all places. There will be two strips crossing under the top (FIG. 13-10C), and one top rail will have to be notched to take them, but leave marking and cutting the notches until later.

Join the legs to their rails, and then join the frames across. Use waterproof glue in each joint. At the leg joints, it will probably be sufficient to drive four screws across each place, with two from each side diagonally #10-gauge × 1³/₄-inch screws would be suitable (FIG. 13-10D).

Be careful to get each frame square; then, make sure they cross squarely. See that top surfaces are level.

Set out the top as a regular octagon. Make up the top with an odd number of boards, which reduces the number of sharp corners exposed (FIG. 13-9C). Allow for a gap of about ¹/₄-inch between boards, so rainwater can drain through. Lightly bevel all edges and where the boards meet.

Assemble the top upside-down. Screws through the rails will provide most support, but fit the two strips of 1-inch × 2-inch section across, to hold the extending boards (FIG. 13-10C). Arrange the space between them so they will cross a supporting rail 1-inch in from the halving joints. Notch the rail to suit (FIG. 13-10E).

Join the top boards to the strips and to the rails in both directions with waterproof glue and screws.

Check that the table will stand level. If not, take a little off the bottoms of one or more legs.

Put a shelf over the crossing of the lower rails, if you wish (FIG. 13-9D).

Softwood might be treated with preservative followed by several coats of paint. Hardwood may be varnished or oiled.

Materials List for Yard Table

4 legs	28	×	3	×	2
4 rails	28	×	3	×	2
3 tops	32	×	6	×	1
2 tops	24	×	6	×	1
2 strips	28	×	2	×	1
1 shelf	12	×	12	×	1

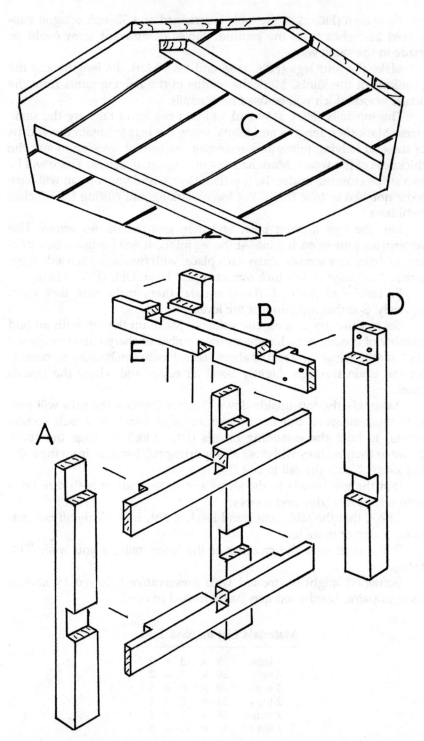

Fig. 13-10. *How the parts of the octagonal table are assembled.*

SERVING TROLLEY

If you eat outside, particularly if you use a barbecue, there are many items of food, crockery, cutlery and equipment to bring from indoors. Therefore, you need a working surface to prepare food and serve from.

This serving trolley (FIG. 13-11) has two large trays, with an extension at the top for a rod which serves as a handle for pushing or pulling as well as a towel rail. One pair of legs finishes with wheels, while the other pair reaches the ground and steadies the trolley when it is not required to move.

Fig. 13-11. *This serving trolley is intended for moving food for a barbecue or outdoor meal, and it is a suitable height for serving.*

The suggested sizes are for a lightweight trolley built of 1-inch × 2-inch strips and 1/4-inch plywood (FIG. 13-12). Assembly is with dowels and screws. This is not intended to be a piece of furniture to leave outside, but if you use waterproof plywood and waterproof glue, then paint well, the trolley should be able to stand up to an occasional wetting.

The sides are grooved for plywood (FIG. 13-13A) and they follow through 1-inch past the tray ends, which are above the plywood (FIG. 13-13B), with screws driven from below. At both tray levels, the legs have shallow notches (FIG. 13-13C), which provide support and location during assembly.

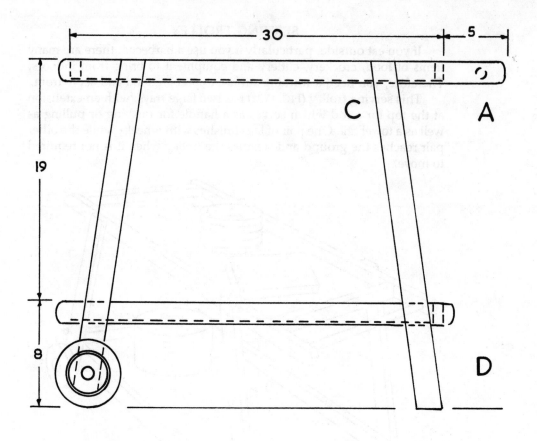

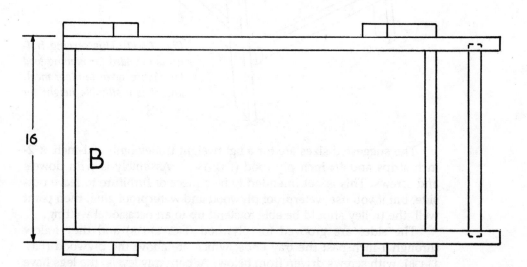

Fig. 13-12. *Sizes for the serving trolley. The leg end must be arranged to match the wheeled end so the top is level.*

Make the two trays at the same time. Their sizes are the same, except the sides of the top tray extend to take the rod handle/towel rail (FIG. 13-12A).

Cut grooves to suit the plywood 1/4-inch from the bottom edges of the sides (FIG. 13-13D).

Cut the tray ends (FIGS. 13-12B and 13E) to the same depth as the sides above the grooves.

Round the outer ends of the sides; drill the handle end of the top sides halfway through for the 1 inch in diameter rod.

Prepare the joints for 3/8-inch dowels (FIG. 13-13F), and cut the pieces of plywood.

Glue the parts of the trays together. Also, glue at the ends. Drive screws upwards at about 3-inch intervals.

Set out one end of the trolley to obtain the angle and length of the legs. The bottom of a leg is under the line of the ends of the trays, and starts from 3-inches in at the top (FIG. 13-12C).

The legs to the ground and the legs with wheels have to be arranged so the trays stand level, so obtain the wheels and axle before making the legs. Wheels about 5 inches in diameter would be suitable. They will probably have a steel axle 3/8 inch or 1/2 inch in diameter.

Using your setting out angle, make the pair of legs that are at the handle end and reach the ground (FIG. 13-12D). The notches at tray level should not be more than 1/4-inch deep (FIG. 13-13G).

Using this pair as a guide, make the other two legs, drilled for the axle at a suitable height and shaped at the bottom to clear the ground.

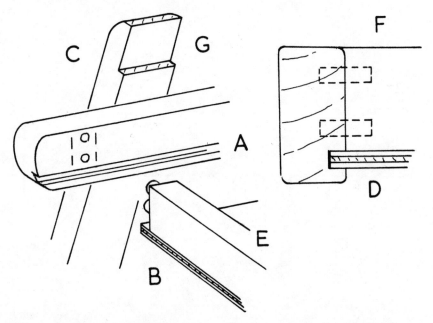

Fig. 13-13. *Assembly details of the legs and trays of the serving trolley.*

Round the outer parts of the tops of the legs. Take the sharpness off exposed edges of all parts of the trolley.

Join the legs to the trays with glue and screws at each crossing. Check that each pair of legs is parallel when sighted across and the trolley stands level on its legs and wheels.

Finish the trolley with paint, including the parts which are not normally visible, to protect from the damp. The trays might be a different color from the legs. Line the trays with Formica, either laid first and taken into the grooves with the plywood, or cut to fit inside the tray sides.

Materials List for Serving Trolley

2 tray sides	33	× 2	× 1	
2 tray sides	38	× 2	× 1	
4 tray ends	16	× 2	× 1	
2 tray bottoms	31	× 16	× ¼ plywood	
1 handle	16	× 1 diameter		
4 legs	30	× 2	× 1	

Glossary

The making of furniture forms only part of the craft of woodworking. There are hundreds of woodworking terms, but the selection that follows are appropriate to the subject of this book and include some alternatives which may be met elsewhere.

apron A rail below a drawer, which may be straight or can have its lower edge decorated by shaping, molding or carving.

arris The sharp edge between two flat surfaces.

backboard The piece of wood closing the back of a cabinet or other piece of furniture.

bail A swinging loop handle.

barefaced tenon A tenon shouldered on one face only.

base The foundation of anything. The main bottom portion of a piece of furniture; it is also called a plinth.

batten Any narrow strip of wood. Any board fitted across other boards to join them (also then called a cleat).

blind Not all the way through, as with a mortise for a short tenon or a hole for a short dowel.

blockboard A form of thick plywood in which the core is made with solid wood strips; it is also called lumber-core plywood.

butt hinge The commonest form of hinge, which is usually let into edges of doors.

carcass, carcase The main assembled parts that compose the skeleton of a piece of furniture, such as the framework of a cabinet or chest.

cast Twisting of a surface that should be flat.

chamfer An angle or bevel cut on an edge.

check Split in wood in direction of grain.

clamp Any device for drawing parts together. It may be a tool or a part built into an assembly.

cleat A strip of wood holding other parts together and to prevent them warping.

counter The working top of a cabinet.

counterbore To drill a large hole over a small one, so a screw head can be driven below the surface and then be covered with a plug.

countersink To bevel the top of a hole, so a flathead screw can be driven level with the surface.

dado joint A groove cut across the surface of a piece of wood to take the end of a shelf or other part. It is also called a housing joint.

dovetail The fan-shaped piece that projects between pins in the other part of a dovetail joint; it is made that way to resist pulling out.

dovetail nailing Driving a row of nails alternately at opposite angles to give an increased resistance to parts being pulled apart.

dowel A cylindrical piece of wood used as a peg when making joints. Dowel rods, bought in long lengths, may be cut into pieces to make dowels, but they have other uses where spindles are required.

drawer kicker A piece of wood above a drawer edge to prevent the drawer tilting when pulled out.

drawer runner A piece of wood under a drawer side, on which the drawer runs. A runner for one drawer may be the kicker for the one below.

face marks Marks put on the first planed side and edge to indicate that further measuring should be from them.

fastenings (fasteners) A collective name for nails, screws and bolts.

feather edge A wide smooth bevel, taking the edge of a board to a very thin line.

fielded panel A panel with a raised center.

fillet A narrow strip of wood, such as is used to keep a mirror in its frame.

gateleg table A table with drop leaves, which are held up by swinging legs outwards like gates.

gauge A marking tool, also a measure of thickness, such as the diameters of screws.

half-lap joint Two crossing pieces notched into each other, usually to bring their surfaces level.

handed Something made as a pair.

hardboard Thin manufactured board with one smooth side.

hardwood Wood from deciduous trees, which is usually, but not always, harder than softwoods.

heartwood The mature wood near the center of a tree.

housing joint Another name for a dado joint.

jointing The making of any joint. It also means planing an edge straight.

kerf The slot made by a saw.

knot A flaw in the wood caused where a branch projected from the trunk of a tree.

knuckle, hinge The pivot point of a hinge.

laminate Building up with several layers of wood glued together.

laying out Setting out details of design and construction.

lineal Length only. It is sometimes used in pricing wood.

lumber-core plywood An alternative name for blockboard.

matched boarding Boards joined edge-to-edge with matching tongues and grooves.

miter A joint where the meeting angle of the surfaces is divided or bisected, as in the corner of a picture frame.

molding Decorative strip edging or border.

mortise and tenon joint One of the most common joints (with many variations) characterized by the projecting tenon on the end of one piece fitting into a mortise cut in the other.

mullion A vertical division of a window.

nosing A curved molded edge.

particleboard Board manufactured with wood chips or particles and resin. It is also called chipboard.

patina Surface texture that is due to old age.

pedestal In furniture, a supporting post.

planted Applied instead of cut in the solid. Molding attached to a surface is planted. If it is cut in the solid wood, it is stuck.

plastic laminate (laminated plastic) A hard-surface decorative thin plastic sheeting used as a veneer on surfaces, particularly counter tops. Its best-known trade name is "Formica."

plinth The base of a piece of furniture. Its front edge may be called a toe board.

rabbet (rebate) An angular cutout section at an edge, as in the back of a picture frame.

rail Any horizontal framing member.

rod A strip of wood marked with construction details and used for comparing parts instead of measuring with a rule.

run In a long length. Lumber quantities may be quoted as so many feet run.

sapwood The wood nearer the outside of a tree. It is not usually as strong or durable as the heartwood.

seasoning Dry wood to a controlled moisture content.

set To punch a nail below the surface. The bending of saw teeth alternately in opposite directions to cut a kerf wider than the thickness of the saw steel.

setting out An alternative term for laying out.

shake A defect or crack in the growing tree that might not be apparent until it has been cut into boards.

slat Narrow thin wood.

softwood The wood from a coniferous needle-leaf tree.

stile A vertical member in a door frame.

stretcher A lengthwise rail in the lower parts of a table or chair.

stub tenon A short tenon engaging with a mortise that is not cut right through.

tote A handle, particularly on a plane.

treenail (trunnel) A peg or dowel through a joint.

tusk tenon A tenon which goes through and projects on the far side of its mortise.

underbracing (underframing) An arrangement of rails and stretchers providing stiffness in the lower parts of an assembly.

veneer A thin piece of wood, usually decorative, intended to be glued to a thicker base piece.

warping Distortion of wood because of unequal shrinkage.

winding A board twisted in its length when sighted from one end.

Index